Mariela Nuñez-Janes, Aaron Thornburg, Angela Booker (Eds.)
Deep Stories Practicing, Teaching, and Learning Anthropology with Digital Storytelling

Mariela Nuñez-Janes, Aaron Thornburg,
Angela Booker (Eds.)

Deep Stories

Practicing, Teaching, and Learning Anthropology
with Digital Storytelling

Managing Editor: Izabella Penier

Associate Editor: Sam Pack

Language Editor: Adam Leverton

DE GRUYTER
OPEN

ISBN: 978-3-11-053932-5
e-ISBN: 978-3-11-053935-6
ISBN EPUB: 978-3-11-053936-3

Library of Congress Cataloging-in-Publication Data
A CIP catalog record for this book has been applied for at the Library of Congress.

© 2017 Mariela Nuñez-Janes, Aaron Thornburg, and Angela Booker and Chapters' Contributors
Published by De Gruyter Open Ltd, Warsaw/Berlin
Part of Walter de Gruyter GmbH, Berlin/Boston
The book is published with open access at www.degruyter.com.

Managing Editor: Izabella Penier
Associate Editor: Sam Pack
Language Editor: Adam Leverton

www.degruyteropen.com
Cover illustration: © thumb / iStock.com

Contents

Ernesto Colín and Philip Molebash

Edward González-Tennant

Nina Shapiro-Perl

Aaron Thornburg

Acknowledgments

We are thankful for the guidance and insight provided by Sam Pack, Associate Professor of Anthropology at Kenyon College, who facilitated the creation of this volume. We also appreciate the feedback and encouragement provided by Lalitha Vasudevan in her role as AAA session discussant. We also thank Izabella Penier, Kathryn Lichti-Harriman, and others on the staff of De Gruyter Open/Versita who have contributed to this collection. Our contributors were extremely responsive and patient as we moved through the journey of publication. And, of course, we thank our families, who support us every step of the way.

Bios

Darcy Alexandra is an assistant researcher and lecturer at the Institute for Social Anthropology, University of Bern, Switzerland. She specializes in co-creative documentary storytelling, visual anthropology, and the politics of voice and listening. Since 2007, she has designed and facilitated participatory media research centering audiovisual production as a means of inquiry and public engagement. She teaches digital storytelling in university, non-governmental and governmental contexts, and develops audiovisual research in the Americas and Europe.

Angela Booker is an Assistant Professor in the Department of Communication at UC San Diego. She studies the ways youth, families, and schools make use of media and technology for participation, learning, and community development. She uses ethnographic and participatory design-based research methods in collaborative ways that involve youth, community partners, educators, undergraduates, and scholars.

Ernesto Colín is an Associate Professor of Urban Education at Loyola Marymount University in Los Angeles, CA. A former public school teacher, he is a visual artist and anthropologist of education interested in community-based education, indigenous education, culturally responsive pedagogy, and instructional technology.

Christine Fairless is the Director of Sixth grade and Middle School at St. Paul's Episcopal School in Oakland, CA. She has over twenty years experience as a teacher and administrator in a variety of schools, both public and private. Christine is dedicated to validating and empowering young people in their transition from middle to high school. She has a special interest in the use of digital media to this end.

Shelley Goldman is an educational anthropologist studying learning in and out of school. Her current work includes bringing broadening participation in STEM via design thinking and new technologies. She is a professor at the Stanford Graduate School of Education and affiliated faculty with the Mechanical Engineering-Design Program.

Edward González-Tennant is a Visiting Lecturer in the Department of Anthropology at the University of Central Florida and Senior Principal Investigator with Digital Heritage Interactive, LLC. He has published widely on the archaeology of the African Diaspora and emerging digital technologies as they relate to archaeology and heritage.

Jason E. Miller is a faculty member in the anthropology program at Seattle University. His research and teaching focuses on applied visual anthropology. In particular, he is interested in immigrant families, media, and health.

Philip Molebash is Associate Professor of Urban Education for the Loyola Marymount University School of Education. His research and teaching is focused on ways in which technology can be applied to promote inquiry learning and storytelling in PK-12 and teacher education.

Kindra F. Montgomery-Block is a Program Officer with the Sierra Health Foundation Center for Health Program Management and the lead staff member to the Steering Committee on Reduction of African American Child Deaths. She has an extensive history as a trainer and organizer that has worked with communities of color and schools across the country. Kindra holds a B.A. in Political Science and a Master's in Public Administration.

Mong Thi T. Nguyen received her Ph.D. from the University of California, Davis in Education with emphases in Language, Literacy, and Culture and Second Language Acquisition. Her research interest involves documenting the complexities of bilingual and bicultural development in the home, school, and community environment.

Mariela Nuñez-Janes is an Associate Professor of Anthropology at the University of North Texas in Denton, TX. She has published in journals such as *Anthropology & Education Quarterly, Chicana/Latina Studies, Diaspora, Indigenous, and Minority Education* about her research with immigrant youth, participatory methodologies, and feminist pedagogies.

David Oliveira Franco, Jr.'s extensive professional experience in education, educational research, and program evaluation echoes his broader interests in equity and social justice. David holds degrees from Universidade Paulista, North Lake College, and the University of North Texas.

Adabel Reyes is the Executive Director of Innovation Bridge in Sacramento, CA whose goal is to deliver high quality technical assistance aimed at bridging innovative practices and collaborative partnership for more just and equitable communities and schools. She has over a decade of experience working with various community and youth-adult partnerships. She is pursuing a doctorate in Education from the University of Southern California.

Nina Shapiro-Perl is a Filmmaker in Residence at American University where she teaches documentary filmmaking to anthropology and film students as part of a community storytelling initiative (http://cmsimpact.org/community-voice-project/) A filmmaker for 30 years, her films include the award-winning, *Through the Eye of the Needle: The Art of Esther Nisenthal Krinitz, and Landscape of Power: Freedom and Slavery in the Great Dismal Swam*p.

Aaron Thornburg is an Assistant Professor of Anthropology at Eastern Oregon University in La Grande, OR. His academic interests include the use of digital media technologies in the teaching of anthropology and anthropological research, having undertaken participant-generated visual research projects in both the United States and Ireland.

Molly Bullock Zielenzinski is a doctoral candidate at the Stanford Graduate School of Education with dual specialization in Learning Sciences & Technology Design and Curriculum & Teacher Education. In research and practice is deeply committed to identifying and interrogating innovative practices that support the development of critical thinking, collaboration, and content knowledge in K-12 classrooms.

Aaron Thornburg, Angela Booker, and Mariela Nuñez-Janes

1 Deep Stories: Introduction

1.1 Introduction: Project Genealogy

Digital storytelling is a promising subject for forging theoretical knowledge about reciprocal processes that bring people together. This book examines the opportunities afforded by digital storytelling to think, do, and/or create jointly. "Everyone has many stories to tell" and what's more, the StoryCenter (formerly known as the Center for Digital Storytelling), also claims that "[s]haring stories can lead to positive change" (n.d.a). The StoryCenter is a leading organization in the art and practice of digital storytelling whose tradition is an inspiration behind many of the collective projects discussed in this book. The contributors to this volume all share this belief in the importance and power of stories. We contend that stories can be significant vehicles for social change, that digital storytelling in particular facilitates multiple kinds of border crossings, and that digital stories are indeed *Deep Stories*. We are interested in speaking across U.S. anthropology's sub fields of visual anthropology, anthropology and education, and student anthropology; the chapters in this volume do so through a research-practice approach that emphasizes collaborative processes for reflection, production, and circulation with community partners and anthropology students.

A commitment to storytelling is evident in the ways in which the contributors to this volume harness spaces for school age youth, college students, refugees, and immigrant parents to tell their stories. This commitment is a common thread that runs through the eleven chapters of this book. Another thread among the chapters is their emphasis on the ways in which digital storytelling facilitates the crossing of borders. Each chapter illustrates how anthropologists' and education practitioners' commitment to stories leads them to cross multiple borders and/or help those with whom they work to cross different kinds of borders, between groups of people, between different places, and more. In this regard, stories can be more than mere entertainment and media can aid in deep border crossings. In addition, the chapters facilitate methodological border crossings illustrating anthropological methodologies for empirical study of/with digital storytelling.

This book has a story of its own, and one that relates to its own kind of border crossing in anthropology. This collection began to take shape through formal and informal conversations about media, action, education, and anthropology during the Annual Meetings of the American Anthropological Association (AAA). These meetings are an important venue for anthropologists to come together to share ideas and discover the connections and shared themes that highlight the significance of topics like ours. Our conversations started in 2010 and continued through 2012 in the form of five AAA sessions and one workshop organized by the editors of this volume. The sessions and workshops were sponsored by multiple groups within the AAA: the Society for Visual Anthropology (SVA), the National Association of Student Anthropologists (NASA), and the Council for Anthropology and Education (CAE). We began to cross disciplinary borders by having groups within the AAA collaborate. For example, the 2010 session *Circulating New Media/Circulating New Stories: Lessons for Participation, Action and Anthropology Through Digital Storytelling* was co-sponsored by both SVA and NASA.

We continued inner-disciplinary border crossings by emphasizing new arenas of research. For example, Jason Miller, Mariela Nuñez-Janes, and Nina Shapiro-Perl among others broke new ground by shifting discussions of media in visual anthropology and in student-centered pedagogies from artifacts to processes. Similarly, Aaron Thornburg, Nina Shapiro-Perl, Edward Gonzalez-Tennant, Shelley Goldman and Molly Bullock Zielezinski, Mong Thi Nguyen, Christine Fairless, Angela Booker, and Ernesto Colín and Philip Molebash emphasized the roles digital storytelling plays in teaching and inquiry. Finally, our sessions crossed the boundaries of research and practice. The sessions involved practitioner research and researchers as practitioners. Aaron Thornburg invited Joe Lambert, Executive Director of CDS, to participate as a session discussant and lead an 'Innovent', *Media in Motion in the Mission: Mobile Digital Storytelling*, a mini-workshop on how to create mobile digital stories with iOS devices. Aaron Thornburg's chapter discusses this 'Innovent' in more detail.

All of the chapters in this volume began as contributions to the sessions and workshop organized at the AAA. As our conversations continued we realized that our research provided examples of innovative engagements of media, extended discussions of visual anthropological work into the realms of pedagogy and participatory/action oriented methodologies, addressed issues of agency, and raised critical questions about the ethics of media-centered collaborative practice. Our decision to organize this volume developed as we realized the contributions of our work to understanding digital storytelling as a subject and tool of anthropology. More importantly as we crossed borders within our discipline and situated our discussions of digital storytelling in multiple arenas of inquiry and practice, particularly through the act of putting together this volume, we further realized the possibilities for reciprocity signaled by our work.

Before going into more detail about these themes, it would perhaps be useful to some readers to have more detail about what digital storytelling is and where it came from, to know the story of digital storytelling. This will allow those unfamiliar with digital storytelling to get an idea of what's involved and how the practice itself results from and engages in the crossing of borders.

1.2 The Story of Digital Storytelling

The story of digital storytelling is related to its products, digital stories, and to a history of border crossings across theater, film and media, and education. As products digital stories are video projects that are produced through the use of computers and digital media production software. The projects can be comprised of a wide range of assets, including images, narrative voiceovers, background music, video clips, and/or text written by the producer. While digital stories are often short, averaging two to ten minutes in length, there is no time limit set on digital stories as a genre. The topics covered in digital stories can be extremely diverse. As suggested on the University of Houston's "What is Digital Storytelling" webpage, "[t]he topics used in digital storytelling range from personal tales to the recounting of historical events, from exploring life in one's own community to the search for life in other corners of the universe, and literally, everything in between" (n.d.). Yet, there is very often a decidedly personal orientation to digital stories in that they either focus on personal subjects or look at a topic from a decidedly personal point of view. Individuals are both authors and producers of digital stories controlling the entire process from beginning to end.

In relation to the history of digital storytelling, Bryan Alexander (2011) provides a thoroughgoing history of how multiple traditions of digital storytelling developed. A digital storytelling tradition that is perhaps particularly influential in educational contexts, and one that is influential among many of the contributors to this volume, is that associated with the StoryCenter in Berkeley, California.

The StoryCenter has its origins in the Life On The Water Theater founded in San Francisco in 1986. Influenced by the work of performance artists who were utilizing multimedia as an element of their work, Life On The Water developed digital storytelling workshops hosted by the American Film Institute and began to emphasize digital storytelling training. In 1994, Life On The Water changed its name to the San Francisco Digital Media Center (SFDMC), which was renamed the Center for Digital Storytelling (CDS) in the summer of 1998 when it moved to Berkeley (Lambert, 2013, p. 28–35; see also StoryCenter, n.d.b). The name was then changed to the StoryCenter in 2015 (n.d.b).

From the very early stages of the digital storytelling tradition of what eventually became the StoryCenter a connection to education was developed. The CDS designed an Educator Workshop, which taught K-12 teachers how to facilitate digital storytelling projects in the classroom. The center also developed connections with higher education early on in its development. In a February 2012 interview with staff and faculty from a number of third-level-education institutions, Executive Director Joe Lambert suggested that the SFDMC was approached by someone affiliated with a university just six months after the center's founding in 1994. He goes on to say that by 1997 the center was busy trying to figure out how the methods it was working to spread fit into the things universities were trying to do with new technologies (Lambert, 2013, p. 175).

It was in fact an affiliation with the University of California Berkeley that facilitated the center's relocation to Berkeley and within two years of the move the center began "receiving an increasing number of invitations to assist other universities in the US and abroad in establishing Digital Storytelling projects on campus and in campus community partnerships" (Lambert, 2013, p. 35). As exemplified by the range of work presented in this volume, the use of digital storytelling continues to grow at colleges and universities in the United States and abroad.

From theater to film and digital media to education, the StoryCenter bridged many disciplinary boundaries in its history. We argue that digital storytelling facilitates such crossovers. With this in mind we look in more detail at borders and boundaries, their place in anthropology, and their convergence with digital storytelling.

1.3 Borders and Digital Storytelling: Crossings and Convergences

The 2012 AAA Annual Meeting, with its theme of "Borders & Crossings," was perhaps a particularly appropriate venue to host the number of sessions and other events featuring digital storytelling organized by the authors of this volume. Even before this conference, academic treatments of digital storytelling acknowledged the medium's potential to facilitate border crossings and the blending of spheres often taken to be separate. Both contributors to this volume and non-contributors have called attention to the ability of digital storytelling practices to upset accepted boundaries. As early as 2008, for example, Shelley Goldman, Angela Booker, and Meghan McDermott demonstrated ways that learners engaged in work that integrated digital, cultural, and social practices crafted identities with digital storytelling and similar digital technologies. Outside of contributors to this volume, Ola Erstad and Kenneth Silseth (2008) argued that digital storytelling, in particular, has the effect of bypassing widely accepted divisions between formal and informal learning contexts as a result of requiring students to use digital production skills they more commonly engage in outside of the classroom. The ability of digital storytelling to bring into question commonly-held spheres has been prominent in academic writing.

It is perhaps fitting that we, as anthropologists, should pick up on the theme of borders and boundaries in our approach to thinking about and practicing anthropological methodologies for empirical study of/with digital storytelling. As Hastings Donnan and Thomas Wilson (1999) have observed, borders and boundaries have long been a topic of interest in the discipline of anthropology. From the earliest days of modern anthropology, when societies and cultures were envisioned as coherent groupings of peoples, the boundaries of these perceived totalities were sought "chiefly as a device to define and delimit the 'edges' of their subject matter" (Donnan & Wilson, 1999, p. 20). Attention to borders and boundaries have seen a more recent (re)emergence in anthropology, though in a much different form than that of the early days of the field. As such, it seems appropriate that this volume was crystallized in part during an Annual Meeting of the AAA in which "Borders & Crossings" was a theme.

Donnan and Wilson (1999) suggest that there has been shift from an interest in what a boundary encompasses to an interest in the boundary itself (p. 21), and they elaborate at least three distinct and current anthropological approaches to borders. One of these is attention to geopolitical and state boundaries. These types of boundaries are political "realities" marking the area of dominion of internationally recognized bodies politic, states, countries, and the like, that are often defended by military and police forces.

> State boundaries obviously entail a mapping in geographic space and recognition in international law. They mark the limits of sovereignty and of state control over citizens and subjects, limits which may be upheld by force or by threat of force. Because of this, they have a tangible and visible quality.... They are 'objective,' or at least have an objective dimension to them. (Donnan & Wilson, 1999, p. 26)

While Donnan and Wilson's own work employs this emphasis on recognized geopolitical borders, they are perhaps among a minority of anthropologists who give particular focus to this kind of border, which has traditionally been the purview of those in political science and other disciplines. However, even those anthropologists who do not directly discuss borders of this type in their academic writings are often very acutely aware of these types of boundaries. As Donnan and Wilson point out, "[m]ost anthropologists cross international, regional and provincial borders to reach their field research sites, and are thus made aware of the political, economic, legal and cultural difficulties which such barriers present both to travellers and residents" (1999, p. 14). Likewise, these types of borders have very real effects on the lives of people around the world as they regulate the movement of people across nation-states.

Another anthropological approach to borders and boundaries has been to focus on social and symbolic boundaries. Fredrik Barth's edited collection *Ethnic Groups and Boundaries: The Social Organization of Culture Difference* (1969) is taken to be the foundational work in this genre. The innovation of the contributions to this seminal collection was to shift emphasis from analysis of the culture (behaviors, beliefs, and symbols) of supposedly cohesive groups mentioned above to the boundaries between groups that are maintained at the same time as they are negotiated and crossed. Thus, "groups are not simply the automatic by-product of pre-existing cultural differences, but are the consequences of organizational work undertaken by their members who, for whatever reason, are marked off and mark themselves off from other collectivities" (Donnan & Wilson, 1999, pp. 21-22). Analytical attention should be given, it is therefore argued, to the recognized boundaries that define groups rather than just to the "cultural stuff" of those inside the boundaries.

The final approach to borders and boundaries discussed by Donnan and Wilson (1999) is the most recently developed and the one that is, perhaps, most pursued by anthropologists who address borders in their work today. Donnan and Wilson suggest that this approach developed beginning in the 1980s out of the work of those who were dissatisfied with previous approaches in anthropology that saw culture as patterns of meaning that were consensually shared. Their dissatisfaction often sprung from the inadequacy of this earlier anthropological perspective to "do justice" to these researchers' own life experience(s)[1]. The influential work of Renato Rosaldo (1989) is described as particularly illustrative.

> The American Anthropologist Renato Rosaldo grew up as a Chicano in the United States. Speaking Spanish to his father and English to his mother, Rosaldo was acutely aware of the 'mundane disturbances that so often erupt during border crossings' (Rosaldo 1989:29). Yet the cultural perplexities of his everyday life were not easily accommodated by the conventional anthropological concept of culture, an inadequacy which propelled him and the many others who similarly sought to understand cultural disjuncture to devise new strategies for studying both the interstices between cultures and the difference within them. (Donnan & Wilson, 1999, pp. 35-36)

What came out of the work of this group of researchers was a "border metaphor" that is capable of characterizing different spheres of life (ethnic, gendered, class-based, age-based, and more) as varying borderlands between which individuals moved.

These multiple borderlands intersect when different spheres of life collide in daily struggles over power. Alvarez (1995) argues that anthropological studies of borders, particularly those emphasizing the U.S.-Mexico border, illustrate how power differentials and divergent histories of colonizer and colonized are negotiated and reflected in the behavior of people who inhabit the borderlands. This approach to borders emphasizes the paradoxes, contradictions, and conflicts that result when physical and metaphorical boundaries converge. In particular, the emphasis in both literature and anthropology on the voices of insiders privileges a borderlands ideology and situates peoples' experiences within multiple intersecting boundaries. Gloria Anzaldúa (1987) refers to this ideology as a *mestiza* consciousness–a hybrid consciousness that rejects rigid boundaries. Alvarez explains the implications that hybridity and multiplicity have for understanding border and borderlands in anthropology.

---

1 Donnan and Wilson further note that parallel approaches to borders and borderlands arose in a number of fields (literature, political science, and others).

The coming together and recognition of the voices from the border region sparked a reevaluation of the anthropological canon and spurred a creative debate focusing on local behavior, lives, and situations in the global context. The role of capital and its attendant ideologies and hegemonies are no longer contested as major factors in the social construction of the border region. Our continuing object of study is to identify the particular expressions and accommodations of the human in these borderlands. (1995, p. 461)

One of those human expressions is the struggle of ordinary people to make sense of this hybrid world. Anzaldúa (1990) claims the human quest for knowledge as a form of theorizing and critiques the academy's colonization and encroachment of theory. This critique is also prevalent in the work of feminist anthropologists and action researchers who envision the academy as exerting its power over knowledge production through practices that legitimate certain forms of knowledge over others. For example, Black feminist anthropologist Irma McClaurin (2001) theorizes Black feminism as a standpoint theory situated in the experiences of Black women. Action researchers Greenwood and Levin (2007), challenge the primacy of academic knowledge envisioning the relation between local and professional knowledge as dialectic. In their views, borders that separate domains of knowledge production are bridged (Greenwood and Levin 2007) or transcended (McClaurin 2001) and theory is "de-academized" (Anzaldúa 1990).

This "Cultural and Postmodern Borderlands" approach to boundaries is arguably the one that is most present in the contributions that comprise this volume. The practice of digital storytelling provides an entry point to people's theorizing processes as they attempt to make sense of their multiple and sometimes contradictory lives. In this sense, digital storytelling can identify borderlands and challenge or blur instantiations of state and institutional power that demarcate borders and invalidate the hybrid experiences of those who inhabit them. The implications for projects that seek to address inequalities produced by the imposition of borders and the exertion of dominant forms of power are important because by valorizing subordinate forms of knowledge (Rosaldo 1993) digital storytelling can contribute to democratizing research methodologies and educational spaces.

In almost all of the works contained in this volume borders are noted. Whether it is the borderlands of teachers and students that are highlighted in the work of Mong Thi T. Nguyen as she notes the ways that students crossed over into being teachers through collaborative work on digital projects, or the crossing of socio-economic borderlands facilitated by the digital stories produced by Nina Shapiro-Perl's students, or the borderlands among high school youth highlighted in the work of Mariela Nuñez-Janes and David Oliveira Franco, Jr., or the borderlands of science, technology, engineering, and math crossed by middle schoolers in the work by Shelley Goldman and Molly Bullock Zielezinski, the appearance of borderlands is abundant in this volume's chapters.

However, we must recognize that these 'definitions' of borders proposed by Donnan and Wilson are not mutually exclusive. As Donnan and Wilson themselves recognize:

> [W]e have suggested that three reasonably distinct but mutually interacting streams characterise the anthropological study of borders and boundaries. In such an account there is perhaps a tendency to over-systematise, and to succumb to the temptation to reconstruct rival intellectual genealogies with the possibly misleading benefit of hindsight. Differences may have been stressed at the expense of similarities, edges emphasised rather than overlap. (1999, p. 40)

We cannot agree enough with this sentiment.[2] In line with this assertion, the contributions to this volume show how correlation and connection occur between these types of borders. For example, the borderlands of legal and illegal/documented and undocumented immigrants that are highlighted in Jason Miller's contribution is entirely dependent on the geopolitical borders that those Miller worked with had crossed. And, while the work of Ernesto Colín and Philip Molebash highlight the ways distinctions between teacher candidate and teacher as well as between teachers and students might be reduced as a result of the digital projects that were produced by teacher candidates, those distinctions are still maintained by social structures and the real spaces those involved are permitted to inhabit. Regardless of how boundaries are conceived, the contributions to this collection provide copious examples of the ways border crossings are facilitated through digital storytelling and related digital media processes.

Not only are borders crossed, but they are complicated, problematized, even undone. In this sense, crossing may not be what is in question, but perhaps something slightly different, something akin to convergence. Convergence is a concept that has been applied to media in elaborations on how digital technologies are facilitating new ways of seeing "the audience" as they are increasingly able to contribute to the range of media, as they (we?) are all becoming "produsers" (Bird, 2011; Jenkins & Carpentier, 2013). With the contributions to this volume as case studies, we question whether digital technologies might foster more than just short-lived crossings between borderlands, but convergences of the people who are supposed to inhabit different spheres separated by accepted boundaries. Darcy Alexandra's discussion in this volume of "co-creative documentary

---

2 Donnan and Wilson go on to suggest that anthropologists must be self-aware of which of these approaches to borders their writing predominantly belongs. They note that when any one of them is utilized certain elements and aspects of the world described are underemphasized; the emphasis on cultural or postmodern borderlands, for example, is often accompanied by a lack of emphasis on the role of the state, geopolitical borders, and/or the particularities of social institutions. The editors of this volume also agree that attention must be paid to the unintended consequences of the research focus and writing genre employed by social researchers.

practice," extends notions of digital storytelling as a method of inquiry and also as an opportunity to accompany the storyteller. Similarly, Edward González-Tennant's discussion of digital storytelling as a pedagogical device addresses the opportunities offered by digital storytelling to decolonize college classrooms. And, Christine Fairless provides a practical example of how media can facilitate access to information about social issues that are relevant to young students facing the transition into high school.

We should be conservative, however, regarding the claims we make about the degree to which digital storytelling, in and of itself, is able to facilitate awareness and crossing of borders, as well as the convergence of groups and practices traditionally seen as being on different sides of borders. In the contribution by Angela Booker, Kindra F. Montgomery-Block, and Adabel Reyes, for example, the authors claim "Digital stories did not appear any more effective in crossing that border than did other types of projects." Thus, Booker, Montgomery-Block, and Reyes are realistic about the particular potential of digital storytelling in facilitating convergences. "However," the authors continue, "the production of digital stories opened a door that other projects and practices did not. Digital stories revealed choices about whose practices to privilege, whose voices to privilege, and whose agenda to follow" (this volume, p. 33).

1.4 Advancing a Socially Situated Understanding of Digital Media

Attending to convergence is both conceptually and practically important. It is conceptually important because it helps anthropologists advance a theoretical position about digital media and social practice. For quite some time, scholars in the field have effectively and convincingly argued that it is not the technology itself but what people do with it that gives life and determines effects among people, our practices, and our mediating tools (du Gay, Hall, Janes, Mackay, & Negus, 1997; Hawkins, 1991; Mehan, 1989; Vasudevan, 2006). Yet, frequently, the storytellers—the humans—get lost amid the love affair with emerging technologies. While many in the humanities and social sciences have advanced this argument in multiple domains and disciplines, in the world of practice new technologies are like flashing, shiny red buttons that command our attention. And, so, it has been difficult for theory to adequately inform practice. Together, border crossing and convergence may give our attention the anchor, the focus on what happens when human social and cultural practices meet with forms of technology. The emerging technologies are, after all, artifacts of previous human practices, and their physical embodiment can make them irresistible. But resist we must, if we want to maintain our human connection. Storytellers have a unique power in this regard. This is where border crossing and convergence reveal key aspects of practice in digital storytelling.

1.4.1 Convergence and Possibilities for Reciprocity

What is more seductive than the promise of emerging [digital] technologies? Why is it important to pose the question? If new technologies were universally good, perhaps this question would be unimportant. But, human hands and minds guide technologies in social and cultural worlds, and the systems we have inherited and created are uneven in their effects at best. So, the question becomes critical. Storytelling, which can also be understood as a human technology, is one of the answers to this question. As technology continues to advance, so has storytelling. Stories have been told across media—from oral traditions to books, radio, film, television, the internet, and so on. Stories travel. They are excellent tools for reflection, developing identities, persuading potential allies, organizing around shared needs, finding our common humanity, distinguishing our common enemies, etc. At times, it seems a well-told story can build, destroy, hide, reveal, or repair just about anything. In this volume, we have taken up digital storytelling to develop our understandings of the dual power of storytelling and digital media in creating conditions for convergence. Here, we are describing a broader conception of convergence that extends beyond consumption and production to dynamics of people's identities and practices as they cross borders.

It is tempting to distill best practices for convergence from a volume like this, yet we reject this approach. Taken together, the chapters affirm that practices are situated. In addition, processes of digital storytelling reveal opportunities for convergence and reciprocity in concert with finalized media projects taken as objects. The drawback to articulating best practices, as we see it, is in the reifying result and settling phenomenon, which Allor (1987) described as a problematic of success, particularly where critical inquiry is a goal. If there is a best practice it is in committing to 'asking again'—an active practice of respecting people's experiences and sense making about experience. These chapters address when and how digital storytelling practices and processes sustained dynamic engagement that invited participation, inquiry, and change. In so doing, these processes allow us to "redefine old research questions," helping us critically examine relations of power and epistemology (Slack & Allor, 1983) that build borders but also can be mobilized for convergence. In this regard, the chapters offer practical insights for using digital storytelling in pedagogy or methodology for supporting or studying convergence.

The *process* of digital storytelling can serve as a method for a sustainable social practice: reciprocity. As we cross borders, we can become storytellers for each other. If convergence gives us some conceptual purchase on *what* people are doing when they open themselves, together, to new possibilities, it also suggests *how* convergence might yield an ongoing practice that is distinct from the practices of border crossing. Convergence points us to practices for reciprocity. That is, that learning is mutual, that research and practice act as two parts of a dialogic whole, that the responsibility taken on by teachers and students, scholars and practitioners, institutions and communities is shared—thoughtfully, intentionally, and in ongoing negotiation. Paulo Freire described a method for praxis that provides a foundation for ongoing dialogue in participatory action research:

> Instead of taking people here as the object of my research, I must try, on the contrary, to have the people dialogically involved also as subjects, as researchers with me. If I am interested in knowing the people's ways of thinking and levels of perception, then the people have to think about their thinking and not be only the objects of my thinking. This method of investigation which involves study—and criticism of the study—by the people is at the same time a learning process. Through this process of investigation, examination, criticism and reinvestigation, the level of critical thinking is raised among all those involved.... Thus, there is a dynamic movement between researching and acting on the results of the research. (1982, p. 30)

Scholars have continued to explore practices like this as a core inquiry in their work because while the idea is powerful, discourses of power are resilient. In other words, reciprocity—like all attempts to achieve equity and justice—is an idea that requires ongoing effort to make progress. For example, Downing-Wilson, Lecuasy, & Cole (2011) have described a university and community partnership that yielded mutual appropriation. In a discussion of Mike Rose's proposed methods for designing "expansive forms of learning for all students" and how they relate to Cultural Historical Activity Theory, Gutiérrez (2012) again invoked reciprocity as a key ingredient in developing an imagined future that is equitable and just. Mariela Nuñez-Janes and Alicia Re Cruz (2013) suggest the possibilities of digital storytelling in disrupting the researcher-informant binary and propose the idea of a digital storytelling praxis— "the use of media technology and stories to reflect (research) and change (act upon) the educational lives of Latino/a students" (Implications for Research and Practice section, para. 5). In their chapter in this volume, Nuñez-Janes and Franco also extend discussions of praxis by emphasizing the dialogic encounters that digital storytelling facilitates among high school youth. Reciprocity is a hopeful remedy to the problem of unintended replication of the status quo, but it is persistently far from a certainty.

Processes of digital storytelling are like wayfarers in an uncertain search for powerful roles for humans' cycles of inquiry, learning, practice, production, and reflection. Digital storytelling is a promising arena for advancing theoretical knowledge that can be constructed reciprocally and socially by people in the many roles they inhabit in the process: student, teacher, adult, child, researcher, anthropologist, storyteller, listener, interpreter, etc. In our cases, emerging media supported the possibility of inviting people to theorize together, to practice together, to imagine together. Gloria Anzaldúa, whose vulnerable exploration of *Borderlands* lends her a powerful voice across disciplines, made an effort to liberate theory from elite practice and to recognize theorizing as human practice. In reviewing her work, Tara Lockhart (2007) reminds us of the possibility of "theorizing the personal and deploying it not only as singular reality, but instead as a framing and narrating tool" (Arguments Otherwise section, para. 3). Digital storytelling is one such framing and narrating tool. Within the hands of storytellers, borderlands can become spaces for convergence, and in turn, reciprocity.

1.5 Content Organization

This volume is comprised of 11 chapters broken up into two sections. Each section emphasizes border crossings and convergences as they relate to educational programs and practicing anthropology in classrooms or in the context of ethnographic research. The first section is comprised of six contributions detailing uses of digital storytelling and like digital media production processes in education programs and projects. The second section contains five contributions focusing on examples of digital storytelling being used in the practice and/or teaching of anthropology. Each of the contributions highlights digital storytelling's ability to facilitate the bridging of divides of various kinds.

1.5.1 Section 1: Instruction, Involvement, Inclusion, and More

The first chapter, by Angela N. Booker, Kindra F. Montgomery-Block, and Adabel Reyes, details a Summer and Social Justice program in which students transitioning to high school produced collaborative digital story projects about local and school programs or issues that affected them. Two of the 21 projects—one addressing how students experienced the effects of significant budget cuts and one documenting ways students tried to appropriate school grounds and resources to challenge the limited power of youth at school—were chosen to illustrate border crossings present in the projects and the process of making them. Ultimately, the students involved changed their perceptions of their place in their communities and their own potential agency to affect local conditions, thus crossing a border from being subjects to their circumstances to being actors within their school communities. Teachers involved in the program also learned ways of bringing community-based knowledge into the classroom through digital storytelling practice, to the benefit of their students. The process of producing digital stories in the Summer and Social Justice program helped students discern the politics of their educational environments and begin to reflect, analyze, and act on them.

In a description of another out-of-the-classroom program that positively affected classroom teaching and learning, Shelley Goldman and Molly Bullock Zielezinski describe a weeklong science, technology, engineering, and math (STEM) camp for middle school students. The camp participants used the digital comic production software *Comic Life* to produce group projects about their experiences in the camp. This process, Goldman and Zielezinski suggest, led to the integration of work in the areas of STEM, which are often treated separately in classroom environments. Thus, bridges are formed between areas of learning that are often compartmentalized in traditional teaching through application in the digital media projects. In particular, Goldman and Zielezinski's chapter speaks to how honoring the social lives of young people was integral to their learning in the realm of engineering practice. Digital storytelling processes helped young people learn through reflection and, in turn, showed promise for the potential of sustained participation.

Ernesto Colín and Philip Molebash also highlight an instance in which traditional separations are complicated through digital media practice. In this case, pre-service and in-service teachers produced 5-10 minute "micro-documentary films" on particular classrooms as final assignments in a course on cultural sensitivity and student diversity in K-12 classrooms. The teachers and future teachers making the videos learned much about students in the classrooms they filmed, but they got more than just information. "[T]hey left with much more than data," Colín and Molebash suggest, "they left with the human lives that touched them and human connection for which they now felt reciprocity and mutuality" (this volume, p. 67). In this way, commonly held distinctions between teachers and students were undone. This chapter puts anthropology in dialogue with teacher preparation with a particular focus on closing an opportunity gap (read, social justice). Colín and Molebash show how digital storytelling, compared to conventional research papers, offers tremendous potential to positively impact teacher attitudes and equity pedagogy because they require ethnography and instructional technology tools. With only an essential orientation in ethnographic methods, human subjects ethics, and movie editing, teachers who engaged in reflexive and intentional gathering of community experiences and perspectives developed a habit of practice which enhanced their culturally responsive pedagogy.

The distinction between teachers and learners was likewise complicated in the program detailed by Mong Thi T. Nguyen. Nguyen details a Vietnamese heritage language learning assignment in which groups of 11- to 14-year-olds produced a Vietnamese-language digital story based on a children's book, *Frog, Where Are You?*, by Mercer Mayer. The resulting projects were then screened to 5- to 7-year-olds. The role of teacher was taken on by the students producing the video projects both during the production process and in the screening of their final projects to their younger schoolmates. For the heritage language learners in Nguyen's study, digital storytelling invited a kind of commitment to their own language practices and engagement that the students recognized as supportive and unique in helping them contend with twin cultural and historical commitments.

Christine Fairless, a seasoned middle school educator and school leader, also describes an instance of students acting as teacher/mentors through digital media through her *iveBeenThere* website. This website and mobile app serves as a repository for short recorded narratives by high school students or recent high school graduates on a range of topics of concern to incoming high-school students, including drug/alcohol use, peer pressure, eating disorders, and more. Used as resources in middle school Social Emotional Learning classes, these video projects help to prepare transitioning youths, 8th graders who will be moving to high school in the next academic year, for the socially and academically demanding change from one institution to the other. Fairless examines design decisions that led to digital storytelling as an important resource for providing the peer-to-peer support—for which young people express a consistent need—when working through complex and high-stakes times of transition. In addition, the chapter affirms that curating a space for young people to share personal stories also provides a role for adults to play in holding space for young people to do the social and emotional work that traverses borders between daily life and schooling.

The transition from one education level to another is also highlighted in Mariela Nuñez-Janes and David Franco's description of the *IamWe* program associated with a Peer Assistance Leadership (PALs) class in a Texas high school, in that the cooperation between the high school and the University North Texas helped prepare the participating students for higher education. Further, students participating in the program produced personal digital stories resulting from a story circle process. This process facilitated trust and sharing between the diverse student participants, furthering the goals of the PALs curriculum, "to create a service oriented, diverse, and empowered group of young leaders ready to build relationships between students and tear down the boundaries between diverse groups with the school" (this volume, p. 102). Nuñez-Janes and Franco's emphasis on praxis anchors the practice of digital storytelling in a pedagogical process that invites high school youth to learn about each other's lives. In the case of the *IamWe* program, digital storytelling facilitated multiple dialogic encounters that helped the youth venture into emotional spaces while challenging the research and teaching practices of the educators and researchers involved in the program.

1.5.2 Section 2: Anthropology, Activism, and Autoethnography

Like in all the contributions to the first section of this volume, those in second section of the text, which detail uses of digital storytelling in anthropological research and teaching, highlight the crossing of accepted boundaries and borders. Darcy Alexandra's contribution, for example, focuses on a program that used digital storytelling practices to help undocumented workers, asylum seekers, and refugees in Dublin, Ireland, to tell their stories. In so doing, Alexandra's project bridges the gap that separates ethnographic research and activism, in its attempt to make Irish nationals aware of the daily struggles these immigrant populations face. At the same time, the projects facilitated a co-creative documentary practice that unsettled commonly held distinctions between researcher and participant. Alexandra's longitudinal and inquiry-based approach to digital storytelling reveals the importance of process together with artifact that center participants as emergent media practitioners—attending to people's circumstances and the city's systems and politics alongside the role of sound and montage in the craft of documentary filmmaking. Allowing that time led to the development of shared expertise through the production of heterogeneous, nuanced stories. Importantly, the longitudinal approach also allowed for an intentional, if unpredictable, consideration of possible outcomes, where a given story could travel, who would hear it, and what social or political impacts it might have. Alexandra's chapter suggests that this approach can ground a scholarship of engagement, making our shared endeavors visible and open to reflection.

Jason Miller's description of his doctoral dissertation research, in which he facilitated the creation of digital stories by native Spanish speaking immigrants in Florida, some of who were undocumented, also evokes border crossings of multiple kinds. The resulting digital stories, no doubt, would serve activist ends by facilitating communication between populations that might not otherwise communicate, not unlike the projects produced in Alexandra's program. At the end of his project, Miller had five completed projects, and two more that were very near completion. However, for reasons that often related to their immigrant and/or undocumented status, only one of the participants agreed to have their digital story screened publicly. This opens up an important discussion about the ethics of participant visual research projects and the reciprocal researcher-participant relationships they entail.

Edward González-Tennant's contribution makes a perfect piece for the transition from discussion of anthropological research projects to discussion of teaching anthropology, as he addresses both an historical anthropology project he produced, *Remembering Rosewood*, and his use of digital storytelling in teaching introductory anthropology classes. By way of screening *Remembering Rosewood* and having his student produce their own digital story, González-Tennant attempts to effect an engaged pedagogy that breaks down barriers between teacher and student, engages with students in majors other than anthropology, and more. González-Tennant shows the relevance of digital storytelling to pedagogical practices of engagement in college classrooms.

Barriers between the academy and the community were broken down by Nina Shapiro-Perl's students as they worked with Washington D.C. residents and institutions as part of the Community Voice Project. "This project set out to capture, through filmmaking, stories of *unseen* and *unheard* Washington, and in the process help train a new generation of documentarians," Shapiro-Perl claims (this volume, p. 173). In the process, connections between regularly separated groups of people and institutions were fostered. In this way, digital storytelling provided meaningful ways to make transformative moments for the storytellers visual and lasting. For Shapiro-Perl, bringing people together to listen to each other, through storytelling, provided an important bridge between people at a critical time of class, racial, and ethnic division.

Finally, Aaron Thornburg's use of digital storytelling in media anthropology classes complicates the in-school/out-of-school divide as his students construct ethnographic stories of their own media environments in a medium that is arguably more "their own" than written assignments. It is the self-referential, or autoethnographic, element of a range of digital storytelling assignments Thornburg received that he credits to the format's ability to cross this boundary, perhaps pointing to a key element in all the projects described in the volume that may help to facilitate crossings.

1.5.3 Conclusion: Countless Crossings and Copious Convergences

This brief summary of the book's chapters provides multiple examples of border crossings and bridgings that we see coming out of the contributions that comprise this volume, but it is hardly an exhaustive list. Each of the pieces that make up this volume highlights the many ways in which digital storytelling and like digital media production practices foster connections. We invite you to find additional instances of border crossings and convergence in each of the contributions and in all of them as a group.

The open access and digital format of this book opens the opportunity for the story of this volume to continue to develop in a manner guided by the reader. The book can be read chapter by chapter, as each one reflects in its own way the contributions of this volume. Each chapter is its own deep story. However, they can also be read as a combination of multiple chapters. Most importantly, as an individual reading through this practice, one can build his/her own deep story. We opted for this open access format in an attempt to facilitate this process. The digital format creates a space for readers, with or without experience with digital storytelling, to engage the qualities of digital storytelling discussed in the chapters. We are excited about the possibilities that the open access format of this book can generate for furthering the mission of engaging multiple audiences to which all the volume's contributors are committed.

References

Alexander, B. (2011). *The new digital storytelling: Creating narratives with new media.* Santa Barbara, CA: Praeger.

Allor, M. (1987). Projective readings: Cultural studies from here. *Canadian Journal of Political and Social Theory/Revue Canadienne de théorie politique et sociale, 11*(1-2), 134-138.

Alvarez Jr., R. R. (1995). The Mexican-US border: The making of an anthropology of borderlands. *Annual Review of Anthropology, 24,* 447-470.

Anzaldúa, G. (1987). *Borderlands/la frontera: The new mestiza.* San Francisco, CA: Aunt Lute Book Company.

Anzaldúa, G. (1990). Haciendo caras, una entrada. In G. Anzaldúa (Ed.), *Making face, making soul, haciendo caras: Creative and critical perspectives by feminists of color* (pp. xv-xxviii). San Francisco, CA: Aunt Lute Books.

Barth, F. (1969). *Ethnic groups and boundaries: The social organization of culture difference.* London, UK: George Allen and Unwin.

Bird, S. E. (2011). Are we all produsers now? Convergence and media audience practices. *Cultural Studies, 25,* 502-516.

Donnan, H., & Wilson, T. M. (1999). *Borders: Frontiers of identity, nation, and state.* Oxford, UK: Berg.

Downing-Wilson, D., Lecusay, R., & Cole, M. (2011). Design experimentation and mutual appropriation: Two strategies for university/community collaborative after-school interventions. *Theory and Psychology, 21*(5), 656-680.

du Gay, P., Hall, S., Janes, L., Mackay, H., & Negus, K. (1997). *Doing cultural studies: The story of the Sony Walkman.* London: SAGE Publications.

Erstad, O., & Silseth, K. (2008). Agency in digital storytelling: Challenging the educational context. In K. Lundby (Ed.), *Digital storytelling, mediatized stories: Self representations in new media* (pp. 213-232). New York, NY: Peter Lang.

Freire, P. (1982). Creating alternative research messages: Learning to do it by doing it. In B. Hall, A. Gillette, & R. Tandon (Eds.), *Creating knowledge: A monopoly? Participatory research in development. Participatory Research Network Series no. 1.* Society for Participatory Research in Asia. Toronto: International Council for Adult Education.

Goldman, S., Booker, A., & McDermott, M. (2008). Mixing the digital, social and cultural: Learning, identity and agency in youth participation. In D. Buckingham (Ed.), *Youth, identity, and digital media* (pp. 185-206). MacArthur Foundation Series on Digital Media and Learning. Cambridge, MA: The MIT Press.

Greenwood, D. J., & Levin, M. (2007). *Introduction to action research: Social research for social change* (2nd ed.). Thousand Oaks, CA: SAGE Publications.

Gutiérrez, K. (2012). Re-mediating current activity for the future. *Mind, Culture, and Activity, 19*(1), 17-21.

Hawkins, J. (1991). Technology-mediated communities for learning: Designs and consequences. *The ANNALS of the American Academy of Political and Social Science, 514,* 159-174.

Jenkins, H., & Carpentier, N. (2013). Theorizing participatory intensities: A conversation about participation and politics. *Convergence, 19*(3), 265-286.

Lambert, J. (2013). *Digital storytelling: Capturing lives, creating community* (4th ed.). New York, NY: Routledge.

Lockhart, T. (2006). Writing the self: Gloria Anzaldúa, textual form, and feminist Epistemology. *Michigan Feminist Studies, 20.* http://hdl.handle.net/2027/spo.ark5583.0020.002.

McClaurin, I. (2001). Theorizing a black feminist self in anthropology: Toward an autoethnographic approach. In I. McClaurin (Ed.), *Black feminist anthropology: Theory, politics, praxis, and poetics* (pp. 49-76). New Brunswick, NJ: Rutgers University Press.

Mehan, H. (1989). Microcomputers in classrooms: Educational technology or social practice? *Anthropology & Education Quarterly, 20,* 4-22.

Nuñez-Janes, M., & Re Cruz, A. (2013). Latino/a students and the power of digital storytelling. *Radical Pedagogy, 10*(2) http://www.radicalpedagogy.org/radicalpedagogy8/Latino_a_Students_and_the_Power_of_Digital_Storytelling.html

Rosaldo, R. (1989). *Culture & truth: The remaking of social analysis.* Boston, MA: Beacon Press.

Rosaldo, R. (1993). *Culture & truth: The remaking of social analysis.* Boston, MA: Beacon Press.

Slack, J. D., & Allor, M. (1983). The political and epistemological constituents of critical communication research. *Journal of Communication, 33*(3), 208-218.

StoryCenter. (n.d.a) Core Principles. Retrieved May 12, 2016, from http://static1.squarespace.com/static/55368c08e4b0d419e1c011f7/t/55f25885e4b0afb1e83b98fd/1441945733158/Principles.pdf.

StoryCenter. (n.d.b) Our Story. Retrieved May 12, 2016, from http://www.storycenter.org/press/.

University of Houston. (n.d.). What is digital storytelling? Retrieved July 11, 2014, from http://digital-storytelling.coe.uh.edu/page.cfm?id=27&cid=27.

Vasudevan, L. (2006). Making known differently: Engaging visual modalitites as spaces to author new selves. *E-learning, 3*(2), 207-216. doi: 10.2304/elea.2006.3.2.207.

Angela Booker, Kindra F. Montgomery-Block, and Adabel Reyes

2 Youth Claiming Media Practices to Perceive and Cross Borders

"Well, I like how our project is affecting us."

—First interview w/Mashal, Age 14 at time of interview

"It's changing me. It might not change the situation, but it's changing me. It's gonna change my thought processes about what's going on."

—First Interview w/Ariana, Age 13 at time of interview

2.1 Introduction

In the above interview quotes, Mashal and Ariana[3] privileged their own understanding and thinking practices and those of their peers. They held this as a key benefit to their participation in the production of a digital story. The story addressed impacts of budget cuts on students in their school district. Specifically, they wanted to shine a light on the decision to cut freshman sports at the high school. As they explored the decisions that led to the cuts and what would be given up, they considered their own positionality, imagined how they might handle such decisions themselves, and strategized about how they might effectively stave off the effects by mobilizing student and community support.

But before they could engage in those ways, they had to find an access point where their knowledge and experience could guide their learning. At the start, their team of 13 students had chosen a project about how the city's budget cuts affected the local homeless population. Yet, as they did their research their engagement remained more technical: they focused on surprising statistics and thought about how policy makers might be able to improve the situation. At that point, their role was limited to reporting the facts they had researched and to brainstorming ways to get their message in front of local policymakers. In our analysis, one question we asked was, how did they make a shift that resulted in the opening quotes? How did a technical task become something that changed them personally?

This chapter presents data from two collaborative digital storytelling projects: (1) Budget Cuts, and (2) Each One Teach One. These examples illustrate how students navigated between technical and political engagement as they produced digital stories, and the ways this shaped their learning (Booker, 2010). The two examples come from a data set of 21 digital stories and are representative of the kinds of practices occurring across projects.

---

3 All names of students and program sites are pseudonyms.

2.1.1 The Summer and Social Justice Program

The digital stories were among many projects produced by students participating in a summer program—Summer and Social Justice (SSJ)— that used a service-learning and social justice framework to help young people address community concerns. The framework combined three stances in working with youth in order to address individual, institutional, and community goals. One stance, positive youth development (PYD), that emerged as a response to deficit-based views of young people, has a more individual and cognitive focus and identifies assets and resources necessary for any young person to thrive (Benson, et al. 2006). A second was the *K-12 Service Learning Standards for Quality Practice*, published by the National Youth Leadership Council. It defines eight standards of practice to improve the quality of service learning in schools. These include meaningful service, youth voice, links to curriculum, partnerships, and diversity (Billig & Weah, 2008). A third stance provided a social justice orientation based in youth activism and collective work. In this way, young people were recognized as members and contributors in communities, shaping their own goals and leadership (Ginwright & James, 2002).

The program was developed by the Youth Development Department in a unified school district in Northern California. The department was responding to findings from a survey of district students indicating that only 11% of middle school students experienced a meaningful relationship between school and the rest of their lives. By ninth grade, this number dropped to 9%. The district prioritized serving students most susceptible to the effects of systemic inequities. Their goal was to help students develop meaningful connections between schools and communities by merging the frameworks described above. The frameworks were integrated to create a meaningful youth-adult partnership experience in which students strengthened their community through service projects as a way to address root causes to the challenges or issues existing in their community. Rising seventh and ninth graders who were transitioning to their new campus were able to meet new teachers and peers before the start of the school year.

2.2 Masking and Unmasking Politics

The digital stories in SSJ were produced by young people between the ages of 12 and 15 over 3 annual cycles of the program. What emerged during their production was a set of practices that made the politics of educational environments accessible for students' reflection and analysis—not just resistance or indifference. They did not do this by taking up explicitly political topics, though some of the stories addressed such topics. The *process* of creating digital stories supported a particular kind of learning environment—one in which young people were central actors and contributors of knowledge and practice. They did this while working directly with school staff and community partners. Heath's (2000) description of constrained institutional spaces explains why this was a unique circumstance:

> Within institutions such as schools, opportunities to think and act outside the constraints of the expected role of student or the structure of curricular and extra-curricular requirements come rarely. Moreover, schools in many post-industrial nations increasingly require standardization of product or outcome, determined by quantifiable measures of performance on standardized tests. Thus the agency of individuals in undertaking learning outside expected roles and structures must be submerged. (p. 39)

In general, American schools have operated in ways that mask politics for students in classrooms, though this may be unintentional[4]. For our purposes, the term 'politics' aligns with the dictionary definitions that follow: "the assumptions or principles relating to or inherent in a sphere, theory, or thing, especially when concerned with power and status in a society" ("Politics," 2013a); a broader alternative encompasses human interaction, described as, "the total complex of relations between people living in a society" ("Politics," 2013b). The first definition helps us distinguish formal education as a sphere where status in society could be negotiated. The second definition helps us think about how young people are primarily conceived in relation to their position in schools: as students. Formal education can be seen as a technical activity with discipline-based standards, pedagogies, and mechanisms for assessment. In this regard, the activity of schooling attempts to transcend the conditions of particular, localized contexts—to become universal, to make standard. In so doing, it also masks politics involved in selecting relevant knowledge and forms of practice. This is not to suggest that students in schools are altogether unaware of politics in the classroom. Classroom practice, however, tends to proceed as if decisions about what is to be learned, which practices will be used, or what ideologies will be welcomed do not represent a politically defined set of conditions (Eckert, 1989; Willis, 1977). There is a remarkably constrained set of disciplines that make up school content that is by no means comprehensive. Attempts to expand the content covered tend to meet with intense scrutiny and resistance[5]. Yet, what is taught is not typically examined or contested in these ways by youth in schools. Students have been given a seemingly apolitical task. However, opportunities to engage with politics offer important investigations within a learning environment.

---

4 James Ferguson (1990) presents a compelling case describing the instrumental effects of international development that simultaneously serve to increase the presence of the bureaucratic state and reframe political problems as technical ones that can be addressed by development. This chapter explores a similar approach to technical and political framing of learning environments.

5 Consider Stanford University's decision to change its Western Culture curriculum (see Lindenberger, 1990) or the attempts to take African American Vernacular English—known widely as Ebonics—into account when teaching Standard English in Oakland, CA public schools in 1996 (see Rickford, 1999). Both met with heated national debate and criticism.

2.2.1 Politics and Border Crossing

Erickson (1996) described learning as political assent, stating, "Here, I want to consider learning as a matter of politics; of assent that can be withheld, not necessarily with conscious awareness or intent. The notion of learning as a political act of assent directs our attention to the social conditions in which such assent is granted or withheld" (p. 91). Young people, then, have borders set up for them and patrolled by others, but they also have their own borders, and they patrol those themselves. Here, we refer to borders that govern conditions for participation (Rosaldo, 1997) and negotiating identities (Anzaldúa, 1999[1987]). Data from this study cannot reveal origination of these borders. What it reveals, instead, are encounters with them. The encounters detailed here make periods of review, negotiation, and inquiry visible. Processes of sense making and meaning negotiation were prevalent across these projects, and in particular, they were captured, edited, and refined specifically in a format intended to be shared with others.

Students in the study indicated a desire to contribute to their peers, something that can be difficult to accomplish in school classrooms. They were also pleased at their discovery that they could be transformed into change makers. These practices helped young people and educators gain access to borders that were visible (e.g., the demarcation between school grounds and surrounding communities) and virtual (e.g., identifying as a student or a change agent). They supported reflection and opportunities for retelling and reinventing.

2.2.2 A Particularly Persistent Border

Scholars have also examined practices for learning that are culturally informed and taking place in homes, community organizations, museums, and schools (Bell, et al., 2009; Booker, 2010; Cassell, 2002; Civil, 2002; González, et al., 2005; Gutiérrez & Rogoff, 2003; Lave, 1998; Rogoff, et al., 2003; Soep, 2006). In this body of work, practices for learning and problem solving in these environments are related to school and disciplinary practices. Sustaining effective links between them has proved challenging but not impossible (Goldman & Booker, 2009; Ito, 2008; Nasir, 2000). Sociocultural research highlights the importance for learners to access these cross-contextual links:

> Learning to see heterogeneous – and often unfamiliar – meaning-making practices as being intellectually related to those in academic domains entails two related moves: expanding conventional views of these domains and deepening understanding of the intellectual power inherent in varied discursive and reasoning practices that youth from nondominant groups bring to school....To take up the intellectual resources embedded in youth's everyday practices requires us to reorganize school practices in ways that actually make explicit the linkages between everyday and school-based knowledge and discourse. (Nasir, et al., 2006)

SSJ attempted to make those explicit linkages. Interestingly, even though these projects were largely developed on school campuses, with school resources, and supported by the school's teachers and after-school program managers, interviews revealed that most students did not easily recognize links back to what they could do during the school year. While teachers we interviewed consistently reported that SSJ helped students participate in classroom discourse by opening up links between their lives in community and their classrooms[6], students we interviewed consistently experienced the division between the two. For students, some borders remained unexamined. In an interview with Vien, whose digital story was based on a walking audit of the school's surrounding neighborhood, he shared a commonly held sentiment among young people who participated in the 6-week program:

> **Interviewer**: Have you been able to continue any of the work you started in [the summer]?
> **Vien**: Uh, no. Well, I would need to like have someone to like tell me or lead me...
> **Interviewer**: Have there been any connections between what you learned in [the summer program] and what you're doing in school?
> **Vien**: Well, I gotta say, kinda. I could teach my friends or my peers how to, like, help the community. Just pass it on. I haven't done it, but I could. First of all, I have a ton of homework, and everyday kicks in with these quiz[zes] and tests. So, I don't really have that much time.
> **Interviewer**: What kinds of things are you currently involved in that are important to you—in and out of school?
> **Vien**: Well, testing, yeah. Everyday, we gotta listen and pay attention to teachers because the STAR test is really important to us....It determines what class we'll get put into when going to 9th grade, and it's really important to me because it will put me in a good class or a bad class....I'm hoping it will be a good class.
> ....
> **Interviewer**: Can you tell a story about an accomplishment you've experienced since beginning the year and how you feel about it?
> **Vien**: I feel really good about doing the walk audit. We're speaking out. I never speak out. I feel proud. That's my first time doing it.
>
> — Second interview w/ Vien, Age 13 at time of interview

---

6 Unlike students, teachers consistently saw important ties between what young people did during the summer projects and what they needed to do during the school year. During individual interviews and focus groups, teachers consistently expressed a desire to incorporate their summer practices into the school year. While this discussion is beyond the scope of this paper, it is worth a brief mention here as an indicator that the persistence of the border is not a sign of its necessity.

He described what turned out to be a very difficult border to identify and cross. He was able to cross the border between school campus and surrounding neighborhood, camera in hand, and begin to see himself as a person who can "speak out." Yet, his point of view reveals how schoolwork and community work were not well aligned. His comments imply he had to choose one or the other, given the time constraints associated with prepping for quizzes and tests. This was consistent with responses from other student interviews. For Vien and others, during the school year the complex of social relations persisted. Yet, power and status were in play in community spaces and during summer. Processes of digital storytelling provide some insight here.

2.2.3 Digital Media and Politics

Educators and scholars concerned with youth civic engagement and political participation—specifically those engaged with youth organizing, youth activism, positive youth development, and service learning—have attended to modern forms of media production as participation. Studies about the ways youth engage digital media in realms that range from social to political have described how digital media has become embedded in ecologies for learning (Barron, 2006), practices of citizenship (Bennett, Wells, & Rank 2009; Kahne, Feezell, & Lee, 2012), community organizing (Goldman, Booker, & McDermott, 2008), and modes of creative expression and identity development (Ito, et al., 2010).

During the production of digital stories—which will be discussed in the findings section in more detail—the work involved examining ways that power, knowledge, and participation interacted. This is arranged, in part, through the program structure. But it also emerged because students tried to cross borders. On the surface, students produced a wide range of digital stories that minimally addressed their issues of concern and did little to affect the conditions they investigated and sought to change (i.e., sharing their concerns with anti-immigration legislation or reporting about plastic pollution in oceans). However, a close analysis of their practice shows that young people began to tread within their learning environments as political actors, where the present politics could be examined, played with, joked about and generally confronted. This is in contrast to more typically sanitized learning experiences on school grounds, where politics could be ignored or resisted, but not openly examined (Booker, 2010). The argument here is *not* that digital stories or digital tools themselves were the cause for these encounters. Rather, the ways young people oriented to their task and their medium created conditions necessary for learners to engage themselves as political actors.

2.3 About the Study

This study draws from a 3-year data set gathered to examine when and how young people were working alongside teachers, afterschool program leaders, and community partners to address a community concern. Four research questions framed the broader study: What are the practices in which young people are engaged that give them a sense of contribution and accomplishment in different contexts? In what ways are those practices shared among participants? When and how do those practices connect peers and adults? What are the tools and resources young people and site leaders use to support those practices? The sub-study focused on digital stories and uses of digital media. It investigated the following question: Can processes for producing digital stories help youth producers identify and address borders that circumscribe learning and access to participation?

Each summer between 500 and 800 young people participated in a 6-week program hosted at up to 6 middle schools and 8 high schools in the school district. At times, the program was also extended to community center sites that hosted local students who would be attending a nearby school. Twenty-one digital media projects comprise the data for this analysis[7]. These were all group projects, and each was produced by between 4 and 15 young people. Roughly 170 young people participated in the observed projects over a 3-year period. Nineteen of the 21 projects in the digital media data set involved video-based forms of media, while two others involved use of scientific equipment for measurement or robotics equipment.

Each year, program facilitators, teachers, and students negotiated areas of focus for the projects. Regardless of project focus, each group of participating students was facilitated through a power analysis process by a team of program managers, teachers, peer mentors, and at times recent college graduates who also served as program assistants. Having generated a list of issues, concerns, or opportunities that students identified as important, the students would then work through a roots-and-branches activity to begin distinguishing outcomes from causes and to identify decision makers and partners who might be able to aid in moving their projects forward. The result was a set of wide-ranging projects including but not limited to environmental degradation, homelessness, financial crises, multicultural education, nutrition, child safety, immigration reform, depression, etc. During project development, students grappled with whether they could establish and maintain a personal connection with a broadly framed social issue. It typically proved challenging.

Of the 21 projects included in the data set, 17 had an outward focus—they raised concerns in the community surrounding the school or sought to organize community participation. The other 4 focused more directly on the school

---

7 Digital media showed up in most projects in SSJ in some form such as internet research, etc. However, those uses were distinct from programs where media played an *organizing* role in the activity.

community or the local youth community itself. It is noteworthy that these more locally focused projects appeared in years 2 and 3. They may indicate a shift among students toward a more personalized focus. This occurred as the broader program went through its early cycles of development and implementation[8]. The study began with the first year of the program's inception, and cycles of program development were informed by the previous year's challenges and successes. As such, students were encouraged to seriously consider what was personally compelling and not just socially compelling. Processes of review and reflection weaved throughout the program could also lead a group to change tack once a project was underway.

The analysis presented here also draws on data collected in the broader study. Each year, we gathered field notes and artifacts during observations. In Year 1, 4 high schools and 1 community center site were observed, and roughly 500 students participated in projects across those sites. In Year 2, we observed 3 high schools and 3 middle schools where roughly 700 students participated across sites. In Year 3 we gathered field notes at 2 middle school sites, with roughly 200 participants. One of the sites was hosting students from 3 schools on one campus—including 2 high schools—due to budget and enrollment constraints for the program.

In Year 2 we also began a series of 3 interviews with 21 students. The students were enrolled in one of the 6 middle or high schools that were observed during that year's program. Twelve were in middle school and 9 were in high school. There were 6 boys and 15 girls. They self reported their gender, ethnic, and racial backgrounds during their initial interviews, which were representative of the district's overall enrollment[9]. Socio-economic status and academic performance for students were reported by the districts' program staff. Interviews were conducted in English and were gathered three times during the year: once at the end of the 6-week program, once mid-year, and once at the end of the school year. In Year 3, we also conducted 2 focus groups with program staff—teachers, after school program managers/site managers, facilitators, and peer mentors. In addition we completed 9 interviews with program staff at each site about their personal take on and stake in the SSJ program.

---

8 When SSJ initially began, many students expressed their concern that it was summer school in disguise. As they came to recognize that it was *not* summer school, many participants began to take more ownership over spreading the word about the program to other students. In the process, more projects that addressed local youth concerns began to emerge.

9 From the district website (accessed on August 5, 2014): "Our student population is 37.1 percent Hispanic or Latino; 17.4 percent Asian; 17.7 percent African American; and 18.8 percent white. About 5.3 percent of students are of two or more races or ethnicities. Residents within [the district] speak more than 40 languages; 38 percent of students do not speak English at home.

2.4 Findings

SSJ offered a wide range of practices for service and social justice. Some students in the program signed up explicitly to produce digital stories (e.g., producing a cultural heritage project based on interviews of local elders in a community). Others signed up for science projects, community gardens, local business outreach, disaster preparedness, etc. Interestingly, many teams ultimately lobbied to add a digital component to their projects, even though their chosen theme had not originally included a digital component. For example, in a cooking and nutrition project, the students decided to produce a zombie movie about environmental degradation as a side project. This was common for digital media but not for writing, music, or poetry. In the SSJ program, it seems, digital storytelling was a favored way to reach out to peers. The following two examples reveal practices that were consistently facilitated when groups produced digital stories.

2.4.1 Each One Teach One

In Year 3, a middle school site with roughly 100 students had originally organized itself into 7 project themes. They adopted a combination of projects and clinics that allowed students to participate in a camp-style model that included basketball, soccer, breakdancing, film editing, gardening and cooking, and a STEM themed robotics project. The site coordinator explained during Week 1 of that year that the students were seeking a way to be more active while also doing their project work. In his view, the students were having more fun as a result. He said he saw improvement in engagement with annual activities like the Change Agent Tree[10] that set the tone for social justice-oriented service work that was the hallmark of the program. He attributed the improvement to this blend of physical activity and the production-style aspects of the project work (Field Note, Week 1, Day 4). The site also eventually hosted students from two nearby high school sites that had smaller enrollments and due to budget constraints, were asked to share site and staffing resources. The addition of those sites led to 2 additional projects bringing the total to 9: a multicultural fair and a marketing project. Students included rising 7th graders who were preparing to enter middle school, and rising 9th graders who were preparing to enter high school. Some

---

10 The Change Agent Tree was an activity completed in the first week of the program in which students brainstormed strengths and weaknesses about their communities. They wrote the topics down on cutouts of leaves, and posted them collectively on a large, paper tree. Program educators then facilitated students in a discussion of the causes that could have led to the strengths and weaknesses, helping students distinguish between causes and outcomes. Causes were posted on the roots. Students then discussed ways to address causes and not just outcomes.

participants were not in transition (e.g., incoming 8th graders or 10th graders) who wanted to join the program. While the program focus was on transitions to middle and high school, doors were open to any interested students. Several of the rising 9th grade students had participated in the program in a previous year, and they started to recognize that although each summer session lasted only 6-weeks, it was likely to be offered again in future summers.

During Year 3, while some sites were heavily subscribed, other sites were challenged to reach their enrollment goals. As a result, the rising 9th graders in particular, were aware of the challenge faced with getting the word out to potential participants, and getting it out persuasively. They began to ask questions about how the program was "marketed" to students, and they examined the materials that had been given out. Their response to the recruitment materials and application for the program was that it did not look fun, and so of course it did not engage kids. Their facilitator asked what they planned to do about it, and they generated ideas like hosting a flash mob or developing youth-designed advertisements for the program. They began with sketches and attempts at logo designs they hoped would more effectively convey why the program was exciting. The images depicted things like a deserted island paradise that played off of the program name's acronym – SSJ[11] – and featured some of the activities, like a basketball hoop attached to a palm tree. Another sketch featured a worm bin to highlight the gardening project. Others emphasized project activities like media production and breakdancing. The clear goal of the sketches was to bring to students' attention the kinds of experiences they could be having over the summer. As the marketing group's project emerged, they decided to develop two videos that highlighted a site-wide service goal. That is, the marketing team took on the task of developing a narrative about all of the projects taking place at the middle school that summer. As the site coordinator described it, "the kids want to share the knowledge."

The entire site decided to host students from nearby elementary schools for a day, and to teach them some of what they had learned by participating in the program. They called it "Each One Teach One." Their perspective was that most kids in their community could not afford to pay for sports camps or attend enrichment programs, but with access to the school resources and adult staff support, older students could fulfill that need. During the daily sports and dance clinics, more experienced students were either teaching their peers (e.g., introducing breakdancing styles and moves such as top rocks and flares) or they were learning from adult staff (e.g., basketball drills for ball handling, shooting, and passing). In the cooking, gardening, and recycling group, students were harvesting food from the garden (e.g., peppers, tomatoes, peaches) to use in the kitchen to make tasty meals and treats while learning basic nutritional information about their ingredients (e.g., making spring rolls, peach

---

11 Because SSJ is a pseudonym, the play on words is lost in translation.

cobbler, or smoothies and learning about antioxidants, etc.). While each individual project developed individual goals, the entire site contributed to this broader service project by planning to offer a similar clinic-style experience to the elementary school students (2nd and 3rd grade students). On that day, the students took the lead in teaching children from 3 nearby elementary schools. The marketing and film editing groups then united to produce a digital story to showcase their work and to develop a resource for inviting future participation. In addition, the marketing group developed a second video that was playful. Rather than emphasizing the specific activities of the program, this second video emphasized this was a space for having a good time together. The two videos taken together showed participants' willingness to invest in and represent SSJ program goals with care while insisting on a way to put a personal stamp on their presentation.

The first video included an overview of how the students viewed the program and what was offered: "...where kids get the opportunity to help out the community and get new experiences to enter a new way of life." Three rising 9th grade girls provided the introduction, highlighting both the service aspects of the program and the opportunity for participants to get familiar with their new school and peers. Their description of the program's approach to service emphasized the opportunity to contribute to others: "The program gets kids to address community conflict concerns and help solve these issues by challenging themselves to learn more about the problem they are helping to resolve while having the most memorable and fantastic time of their lives." Following that introduction, the video featured each activity available at the site: breakdancing, basketball, film and editing, robotics, gardening and the art of cooking, and marketing and promotion. Students from each project provided voice-overs stating why their particular project was engaging, and these were played over b-roll of students engaged in the activities. The voice-overs were brief pitches to unseen peers. The Film and Editing project, for instance, tried to appeal to a desire to share your own story: "Have you ever wanted to learn how to record the different events happening in your life? Well, now you can. With Film and Editing, you can record and edit with your very own editing class. Give it a try."

The framing of this digital story reflected how students were taught a framework for social justice and a service-oriented approach to action. In creating the film, students specifically focused on reaching out to their peers. Rather than treating it as a final project or summary, they produced it with the idea that future students would have the opportunity to see it and be persuaded to join the program. The digital story even featured light, generic background music that is typical in this type of brief promotional video. This effort to communicate with and persuade peers was consistently evident in media projects throughout the data set. The two projects described here highlight an important distinction the student producers were making between perceived expectations and personal ones.

The first story ended with an admonition: "Why be bored all summer when you can join [SSJ] and have FUN?!" Still, the makers of this promotional piece seemed to know that the challenge to actually convey the fun they promised had not quite been met. The second digital story practically screamed, "this isn't summer school!" A sentiment we heard from nearly every student interviewed between Years 2 and 3 indicated students were happily surprised to discover the program was not summer school after-all. Since the program was relatively new, students knew little about what to expect when signing up. The second film was decidedly playful. It began with a chess match between a student and her teacher. When she won, in frustration and dramatic slow motion, the teacher threw the chess board and pieces across the room. This scene was then followed by a hand drawn puppet scene and a live-action story featuring a coveted new obsession among the students called Kendama. The Kendama story featured a video editing and effects showcase that highlighted students' attention to detail and their developing skills with storytelling and film production. While the video is clearly carefully crafted, its content represents a decidedly non-classroom experience. The students made jokes about Justin Bieber by creating a paper-pencil-puppet called Justin Beaver who keeps repeating a refrain from one of Bieber's hit songs that turns out to be another puppet's worst nightmare. The film is a sequence of non-sequiturs. While there was a scene specifically dedicated to modeling the choice to attend the SSJ program, it was presented in the puppet style as an exaggerated conversation between two narwhals – a reference to a YouTube cartoon – and a dinosaur from the first puppet short. The question at hand was what to do with your time over the summer. The dinosaur recommended SSJ prompting a third narwhal from outer space to jump into the conversation and go along to check out SSJ. The Justin Beaver joke soon followed, complete with a hand drawn puppet that looked like a beaver holding a microphone. The video closed with a Star Wars-like text scroll that said, "The End: Thanks for watching. We hope you enjoyed our silly video and we encourage you to come and join the [Summer and Social Justice] program. [SSJ], where the sun doesn't stop us from having fun!"

It is clear that this film was made by the students to meet their own goals and to freely express their humor, creativity, and interests. This notion of prioritizing the students' ways of being and lightheartedness while secondarily satisfying a program goal was particularly salient in the media projects. In the process, they crossed a virtual border – a border between what was expected of them and what they expected of themselves. The two films taken together make the border strikingly visible. In sharing them together, the students demonstrated their ability to travel in each domain. At first glance, it appears that they have not transformed either domain, but have simply crossed between the two. This, in and of itself, represents a unique experience on school grounds—both the more formally structured *and* the "silly" digital story coexist.

An analysis of the practices conveyed in the videos reveals the ways in which the students tried to transform the school and summer domains by blending the two. The content of the first one, for instance, featured scenes of students in various stages of learning to breakdance, attempting a new skill, and laughing together in the process.

The digital story, though formal in structure and presentation, attempted to capture students learning together and attempting to perfect a skill they valued personally. Notably, no program staff appeared in this video. In the second digital story, one staff member was featured at the start and his presence conveyed a flipped script. That is, during SSJ, youth hold the primary authority. Having established this at the start, the rest of the film pays homage to youth ideas, creativity, and popular culture. What each digital story supports—in terms of the practices of production—is an investigation of visible borders that demarcate school and virtual borders that maintain adult authority.

It is in the investigation of these borders that students worked thoughtfully and actively with the politics of these spaces and activities. This is where transformation became possible. Students who produced these stories used narrative and visual form to take up politics that limited the power of youth at school. In the process, they privileged forms of knowledge and practice—on school grounds—that extended beyond academic standards and adult expectations. They blended school and youth-based approaches to learning and participation to present SSJ as an unexpected, pleasant surprise. They used digital narratives to reach out to their peers and invite them into this set of practices. They also challenged educators and program managers to seek partnerships with students in crafting communication.

2.4.2 Budget Cuts and Freshman Sports

Briefly, we will return to Ariana and Mashal and their digital story team. Ariana and Mashal helped produce a digital story about how budget cuts in their school district had led to the dissolution of freshman sports and threatened more cuts in the future. They worked together with a team of 13 students, supported by 2 adult facilitators from a local community organization and a high school English teacher willing to spend his summer with incoming 9th graders doing community-based projects with an eye toward critical reflection about social justice. Because they changed their project halfway through the program, they had a big task in a short period of time. When they were attending to city-level cuts and their effects on the local homeless population, their digital story was shaping up like a traditional public service announcement, providing surprising statistics and highlighting local organizations that were providing support. Their hope had been to tell stories about how people became homeless to begin with, but they had trouble developing the concept for their project. They were new to this form of video production, and SSJ sent a media specialist named Dana who met with them. When she came to meet with them, the specialist suspected that there was little the students were willing to do to change this problem beyond producing their digital story. After some back and forth with the students about how they could move from concept to script, she posed this question:

> **Dana:** Let's make it real. How many of you really care about how budget cuts affect the homeless? [of 13 students at the table, 2 raised their hands]
> **Jermaine:** I'm maybe more interested in budget cuts affecting sports.
> **Dana:**...You guys, this is *action* right now. You need to do something you care about.

She went on to talk about how she believed they cared about homelessness but not enough to take action. Many students then began to jump in with ideas about sports and after school programs. The energy in the room bumped up.

> **Dana:** Now does that mess you guys up?
> **Tyrone:** Yes, because we've already spent a week on research and letters. We don't have time to go change the decision.
> **Mashal:** Isn't our video supposed to matter to the community?
> **Dana:** You're just thinking about the statewide community, but there are lots of communities.

They continued to debate the change for a while, considering the extra work and what they cared about in a way that they could see how to take action. Once they shifted their attention to cutting freshman sports, Dana guided them through a process of identifying actions and how those actions would support their digital story. She described her own experience as a cheerleader when she was a student in the same district, equating its importance with the book, movie, and television show, *Friday Night Lights*. By the end of the session, the students had plans to review the Superintendent's budget, contact school board members, student athletes, and coaches for interviews and to start generating their own fundraising ideas. They were discussing the legality of "pay to play" approaches, and discussing the social and academic costs of the cuts. Dana gave a parting suggestion for a tagline: "We dedicated our summer to saving our sports. Now, what will you do?" One girl responded, "Yeah, we gon' copyright that! Don't sue us!" Everyone laughed.

Once they were discussing a topic that touched each of them personally, the politics could emerge as part of their production process. They considered the way hierarchy was valued (e.g., Varsity sports would not be cut), and they debated about who had power to affect the situation (e.g., students, administrators, parents). These discussions went hand in hand with decisions about audience (e.g., policymakers or students) and tone for their digital story. Ultimately, they sought to organize young people, parents, coaches, and teachers to push for the reinstatement of freshman sports while presenting ideas to move forward on their own. They wanted to work with the existing structure for decision making while also working around it. As they imagined their digital story into being, they took up discourses of power as related to money and access to resources. It was the lever for their learning, and they were anxious to share their digital story as an organizing tool.

2.5 Discussion: Claiming Media Practices

This study sits at an intersection between learning and the political aspects of education. In addition to the student-driven desire to contribute to their present and imagined peers, media projects also provided extended periods of time for participants to explore, examine, reflect, frame and reframe, and discuss. During these processes, students further developed their perceptions of their environments, activities, and their possible roles within them. If they wanted to participate in change that might reach others, they had to participate in change that reached themselves first. Their processes during production cast them as potential actors on a previously inaccessible stage. In their view, they had become the subjects of their own actions, something they suggested was unique in their experiences as students in school.

What of the divide between summer and the school year? In each case, SSJ activities were ultimately understood as summer activities. Yet, a core goal for the program was to influence the nature of activity in classrooms throughout the school year. While this effort was more successful among educators[12], this was a persistent challenge among students. While young people stated they learned that they could participate in community change and "make a difference," they also found it difficult to see how this related to their coursework. Two students out of 21 interviewed expressed awareness of the relationship, and both had discovered ways to remain steeped in what they had learned in SSJ, mainly through extracurricular activities. But they saw those activities as contributing to their overall academic experience and opening doors to new opportunities for their learning; for the others, the benefits seemed to remain tied to "out-of-school time." Educators and program staff, on the other hand, saw direct influences for classroom and learning practice among students. This is a border that remains in tact for the majority of students, and this is a critical area for investigation. Digital stories did not appear any more effective in crossing that border than did other types of projects in SSJ. However, the production of digital stories opened a door that other projects and practices did not. Digital stories revealed choices about whose practices to privilege, whose voices to privilege, and whose agenda to follow.

The consistent appeal of contributing to peers—real and imagined—provides an indication of how digital storytelling can play a role in this ongoing effort. Digital storytelling supported opportunities to contribute to peers in ways that emerged *from* students. That is to say, peer contribution was both a goal and a practice across the SSJ program. This was evident in projects that ran the gamut from community gardens to establishing ready resources for students contending with depression. SSJ became a space for contribution not only to surrounding communities or public

---

12 Discussion of educators' experiences with SSJ is beyond the scope of this chapter but will be addressed in a future publication.

discourse, but to present and imagined peers. In the projects where digital media played an organizing role, students used their media resources to bring imagined connections to life. Media projects, in particular, allowed students to attempt forms of bi-directional engagement and at times, to establish a meaningful exchange among peers and educators alike.

References

Anzaldúa, G. (1999[1987]). *Borderlands/la frontera: The new mesitza* (2nd ed.). San Francisco, CA: Aunt Lute Book Company.

Barron, B. J. (2006). Interest and self-sustained learning as catalysts of development: A learning ecology perspective. *Human Development, 49*, 193-224.

Bell, P., Lewenstein, B., Shouse, A., & Feder, M. (2009). *Learning science in informal environments: People, places, and pursuits.* Washington, DC: National Academies Press.

Bennett, W. L., Wells, C., & Rank, A. (2009). Young citizens and civic learning: Two paradigms of citizenship in the digital age. *Citizenship Studies, 13*(2), 105-120.

Benson, P. L., Scales, P. C., Hamilton, S. F., & Sesma, A., Jr., (with Hong, K. L. & Roehlkepartain, E. C.). (2006). Positive youth development so far: Core hypotheses and their implications for policy and practice. *Search Institute Insights & Evidence, 3*(1), 1-13.

Billig, S., & Weah, W. (2008). K-12 service-learning standards for quality practice. *Growing to greatness, 6*, 8-15.

Booker, A. (2010). Framing youth civic participation: Technical, pragmatic, and political learning. In L. Lin, H. Varenne, & E. W. Gordon, (Eds.), *Educating comprehensively: Varieties of educational experiences* (pp. 209-231). Lewiston, NY: Edwin Mellen Press.

Cassell, J. (2002). "We have these rules inside": The effects of exercising voice in a children's online forum. In S. Calvert, A. Jordan, & R. Cocking (Eds.), *Children in the digital age: Influences of electronic media on development* (pp. 123-144). Westport, CT: Praeger.

Civil, M. (2002). Culture and mathematics: A community approach. *Journal of Intercultural Studies, 22*(2), 133–148.

Eckert, P. (1989) *Jocks & burnouts: Social categories and identity in the high school.* New York: Teachers College Press.

Erickson, F. (1996). Inclusion into what? Thoughts on the construction of learning, identity, and affiliation in the general education classroom. In D. L. Speece & B. K. Keogh, (Eds.), *Classroom ecologies: Implications for inclusion of children with learning disabilities* (pp. 91-105). Mahwah, NJ: Lawrence Erlbaum Associates, Inc.

Ferguson, J. (1990). *The anti-politics machine: "Development," depoliticization, and bureaucratic power in Lesotho.* Cambridge: Cambridge University Press.

Ginwright, S., & James, T. (2002). From assets to agents of change: Social justice, organizing, and youth development. *New Directions for Youth Development, 96*, 27-46.

Goldman, S., & Booker, A. (2009) Making math a definition of the situation: Families as sites for mathematical practices. *Anthropology and Education Quarterly, 40* (4), 369-387.

Goldman, S., Booker, A., & McDermott, M. (2008). Mixing the digital, social and cultural: Learning, identity and agency in youth participation. In D. Buckingham, (Ed.). *Youth, identity, and digital media* (pp. 185-206). MacArthur Foundation Series on Digital Media and Learning. Cambridge, MA: The MIT Press.

Gutiérrez, K., & Rogoff, B. (2003). Cultural ways of learning: Individual traits or repertoires of practice. *Educational Researcher, 32*(5), 19-25.

Heath, S. B. (2000). Making learning work. *Afterschool Matters, 1*, 33-45.

Ito, M. (2008). Education vs. entertainment: A cultural history of children's software. In K. Salen (Ed.). *The ecology of games: Connecting youth, games, and learning* (pp. 89-116). The John D. and Catherine T. MacArthur Foundation Series on Digital Media and Learning. Cambridge, MA: The MIT Press.

Ito, M., Baumer, S., Bittanti, M., boyd, d., Cody, R., Herr-Stephenson, B., Horst, H. A., Lange, P. G., Mahendran, D., Martínez, K. Z., Pascoe, C. J., Perkel, D., Robinson, L., Sims, C., & Tripp, L. (2010). *Hanging out, messing around, and geeking out: Kids living and learning with new media*. Cambridge, MA: The MIT Press.

Kahne, J., Feezell, J., & Lee, N. (2012). Digital media literacy education and online civic and political participation. *International Journal of Communication, 6*, 1-24.

Lave, J. (1988). *Cognition in practice: Mind, mathematics and culture in everyday life*. Cambridge: Cambridge University Press.

Lindenberger, H. (1990). On the sacrality of reading lists: The Western Culture debate at Stanford University. In *The history in literature: On value, genre, institutions* http://www.pbs.org/shattering/lindenberger.html (accessed on 12/16/13).

Nasir, N. (2000). "Points ain't everything": Emergent goals and average percent understandings in the play of basketball among African-American students. *Anthropology and Education Quarterly, 31*(3), 283-305.

Nasir, N. S., Roseberry, A. S., Warren, B., & Lee, C. D. (2006). Learning as a cultural process: Achieving equity through diversity. In R. Keith Sawyer (Ed.). *The Cambridge handbook of the learning sciences* (pp. 489-504). Cambridge: Cambridge University Press.

"Politics." *Merriam-Webster.com*. Merriam-Webster, n.d. Web. 16 Dec. 2013. <http://www.merriam-webster.com/dictionary/politics>.

Rickford, J. R. (1999). The Ebonics controversy in my backyard: A sociolinguist's experiences and reflections. *Journal of Sociolinguistics, 3*(2), 267-275.

Rogoff, B., Paradise, R., Arauz, R. M., Correa-Chávez, M., & Angelillo, C. (2003). Firsthand learning through intent participation. *Annual Review of Psychology, 54*, 174-203.

Rosaldo, R. (1997). Cultural citizenship, inequality, multiculturalism. In W. F. Flores & R. Benmayor (Eds.), *Latino cultural citizenship* (pp. 27-38). Boston: Beacon Press.

Soep, E. (2006). Beyond literacy and voice in youth media production. *McGill Journal of Education, 41*(3), 197-213.

Willis, P. (1977). *Learning to Labour*. Farnborough, England: Saxon House.

Shelley Goldman and Molly Bullock Zielezinski

3 The Production of Learning Stories Through Comic Making

3.1 Introduction

We work to introduce middle-school children to science, technology, engineering and math (STEM) through *Design for the Other 90%* activities in a project called *d.loft* STEM Learning (*d.loft*).[13] The design movement focuses on designing solutions to address the most basic needs of 90% of the world's population. We are inspired by the engineers, designers, scientists, technologists, architects, and mathematicians engaged in designing low-cost innovative solutions for the large portion of the world's population who do not have access to basic needs, services and products (Smith, 2007). Our work takes place in after-school, summer school, and camp venues. We introduce middle schoolers to local and global needs through design thinking challenges that are user-centered, empathy driven, and integrated with related STEM learning experiences. The approach aims to help them imagine themselves as innovators and problem solvers who can cross disciplinary and contextual borders to address issues in their own communities and globally. Each year the project takes up an interdisciplinary challenge relating to issues affecting people worldwide such as access to water, energy, and shelter.

We conduct a variety of intense challenges with the children wherein they use design-thinking methods to create solutions for specific people who they can affect positively. We use this design thinking approach with a user-centered focus because even those at a young age can come up with responsive and actionable solutions. Design thinking involves a process that includes understanding the problem and related needs from the perspective of a participant, developing an empathetic point of view, brainstorming solution ideas, prototyping a solution, and engaging in feedback on the design and further refinement. The process is repeatable and not necessarily linear. Design thinking also involves mindsets that we believe benefit young learners such as: failing forward, taking action, working in deep collaboration with others, and building on others' ideas (Carroll, Britos & Goldman, 2012). Design and design thinking are methods of engineering, art and design, and share some similarities with

---

13 This material is based upon work supported by the National Science Foundation under Grant No. 101029929. Opinions are those of the authors and not the NSF. d.loft STEM Learning is a project of the Research in Education and Design lab at the Stanford Graduate School of Education. For more information see dloft.stanford.edu.

problem-based learning and the scientific method. By integrating a focus on STEM and technology into the design thinking process, learners and educators have the opportunity to actively engage in a hands-on process for creative problem solving that both models and makes explicit 21st century ways of thinking and learning. As pedagogy, design thinking complements views of learning suggested by John Dewey (1938), Jerome Bruner (1977/1960) and Lev Vygotsky (1980). It is an intensely social, hands-on, actionable, and experience-based approach, with the expectation that learning occurs through practical, playful, and symbolic activity.

One aspect of our research involves how middle school-aged children think about and represent the experiences they are having while in a design thinking camp. We explore the roles that digital media access and production can have in this fast moving comprehensive learning experience. We want the middle schoolers to have ways to capture their experiences, reflect on them, and express what they might have found significant during their design experiences. We also want the youth to have resources for communicating their work in a range of activities when they went home (Bouillion & Gomez, 2001).

We chose to explore how creating comic books might fit the bill. We conceived of the comic books as a user-friendly version of journal writing. Journal writing is considered to be a way to aid learning that can be culturally relevant (Collins, 1993; Ladson-Billings, 1995; Tippins & Dana, 1992). Journals and notebooks are common in science classrooms, and it is recognized that students have familiarity with the genre. They can involve writing about feelings, observations, reflections, or ideas. They can also help students express their STEM work using disciplinary representations and have documents from which they can communicate with others (Dahl & Franzen, 1998).

We decided to put the idea of a comic-based journal to the test by introducing it as a feature in a one-week design thinking camp. We put a twist on typical journal writing by having the campers chronicle or comment on their experiences through creating media-based comics. The choice to engage in digital comic making and storytelling came in concert with the movement in education to give youth access to and experience with media and technology tools. Recent advances in research and practice surrounding youth and digital media aims to find ways to involve youth in making and producing media that enables them to learn, develop, and apply technology in the development of critical literacy, innovation, and citizenship skills. This work with youth and digital media is proliferating in school and out of school, and research is showing its value in the learning process (Barron, Gomez, Pinkard & Martin, 2014; Buckingham, 2007; Collins & Halverson, 2009; Goldman, Booker & McDermott, 2008; Ito et al., 2010; Ito, 2013). Storytelling, the focus of this volume, is one important area of inquiry in the digital media movement, and we thought that comic making might provide relevant ways for the campers to tell their learning stories and engage in digitally mediated literacy activity. We also thought the process might support young learners in crossing disciplinary borders and merging academic practices and social life.

We chose to experiment with comics because they have been recognized as a medium for artistic and literary expression, and are used for boosting children into reading (Liu, 2004), English language learning (Ranker, 2008), and literacy (Bitz, 2004). The recognition of comics as art and literary form has been established through scholarship (McCloud, 1993) and awards such as the Pulitzer Prize (1992 to Art Spiegelman for *Maus*). Scholarship has focused mostly on the positives that come from consumption of comics rather than on their production. With our interests in youth and media, we turned the middle schoolers into producers of comics, and studied how they told their stories. We hoped to make contributions to a better understanding of the potential of media literacy in connecting youth to STEM topics, processes and futures.

The campers were told that the comics would be their take away product and a way for them to chronicle and communicate their experiences. The campers generated an installment of their comic each day during the camp, and each final comic was printed for campers to take home on the last day. Our goal was to understand what the campers captured and produced with the charge we gave them as well as to explore the potential of the media to help them capture their learning.

Twenty-three youths who attended the camp completed a design challenge about water access and conservation as well as several additional STEM activities that were water-related. They used an application called *Comic Life*, and media they collected or generated using an *iPod touch* that we provided them.

We conducted analyses of 22 comics produced by youth. Because a sample of comics will give you an idea of what the campers produced, a few frames are shown below. These are frame examples from two campers' comics. The first frame illustrates how the camper included one of the engineering activities to build a water tower that met specified criteria. The activity, *Bear Tower*, was adapted from one given to undergraduate engineering students. It required students to use all the materials given to build a 14-inch tower that could survive high winds (provided by a hair dryer on high power). The activity was a team challenge that was very popular with the campers, even though several of the groups' towers failed to stand. Comic panels dedicated to this activity appeared in 16 of the 22 comics, making it one of the most represented activities in the camp.

While *Bear Tower* was a popular activity to depict, the comics also reflected other STEM activities and the social and play interactions that the young designers engaged in at camp. The second pane of Figure 3.1 shows a group's notes from the design challenge empathy activity, which was another dominant activity represented throughout the set of journals. Figure 3.2 shows sketches before building *Bear Tower*. Figure 3.3 shows how campers documented the social and emotional side of the camp. In this paper our analyses are concentrated on the ways STEM topics were depicted and the ways the youth represented themselves and others because they were both dominant themes in the comic books.

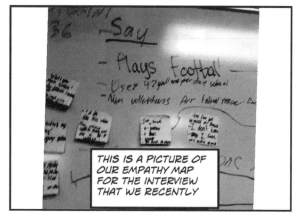

Figure 3.1: Samples of comic frames depicting camp activities.

Figure 3.2: Bear Tower comic frames illustrating the "idea" stage of the design challenge.

Figure 3.3: The social experience depicted.

3.2 Setting and Methods

3.2.1 Shoreline Academy of STEM

The research presented in this paper was conducted at a single site, the Shoreline Academy of STEM[14], a public middle school in Northern California. Shoreline Academy, a small school with just over 500 students in grades six through eight, provided a unique "magnet school" context given the dual focus set forth by the administration. The dual focus included a commitment to exposing students to both meaningful content in science, technology, engineering, and mathematics (STEM) as well as experience with design thinking as a human-centered approach to problem solving. The school strove to implement the standards of an aligned curriculum in conjunction with best practices related to STEM and design thinking. Additionally, Shoreline Academy offered a Gifted and Talented Education Program (GATE) through the provision of accelerated and supplementary classes for those students who were GATE designated.

While the school provided a unique programmatic experience for the students enrolled, the population they served was considered slightly more at-risk than the other schools in the surrounding district. Shoreline had 33% English Language Learners relative to 28% district wide and 69% on free and reduced lunch relative to only 32% district wide. Additionally, this school had 15% fewer Caucasian and 20% more Hispanic/Latino students than the surrounding district. It is a Title 1 School serving a fairly diverse population. The school was in its sixth year of the dire "program improvement" designation under federal No Child Left Behind requirements based on test scores in spite of the fact that it housed the school district's GATE program.

Shoreline followed a year-round calendar, including the typical 180 days observed by public schools with traditional schedules. The difference between the traditional calendar and the year-round schedule was the distribution of the days and breaks throughout the year. Breaks include several weeks in October, December/ January, and March/April followed by an abbreviated summer break in July. During these three week breaks called intersessions, Shoreline provides extra programming such as camps, academic support, and other extra-curricular activities. It was at one such camp that the following research was conducted.

3.2.2 Participants: Collaboration Across Contexts

Our team conducted a one-week intersession camp at Shoreline Academy in March of 2012. To recruit participants for this camp, the *d.loft* team offered an abbreviated

---

14 All names have been changed to ensure the anonymity of cooperating organizations and participants.

workshop at a parent meeting scheduled in the weeks prior to the intersession camp. As a result of this meeting and the resulting word-of-mouth between parents, 24 students were signed up for the Design Camp.

Whether by chance or particular interest in the content of the camp, 19 out of 24 campers enrolled were male with only five females in attendance. To maintain confidentiality and an even playing field, no information about the campers' student records was afforded to the facilitators prior to meeting the campers. At the completion of camp, the school staff informed us that as a student group, the youth had bifurcated demographics. In school categories, the group was a mix of Gifted and Talented Education students who attended camp for enrichment, low-income students designated as English language learners, and students whose parents sought a safe place for their children to spend intersession while they were at work. This information was only interesting to us post analysis, when we did not see these student labels making a difference in the comic texts. Two teachers from the school participated in the camp, supporting the Stanford design team by playing the role of coaches to camper groups. The Stanford team planned, facilitated, and observed the camp with the collaboration of several undergraduate students, alumni, and local volunteers. With ample staffing, it was possible for each camper team to be assigned a coach, who supported the team throughout the camp proceedings.

3.2.3 Design Camp

Design Camp was conducted during five sessions over the course of one week. This included daily sessions from 9:00 am to 2:00 pm. Each day was comprised of a combination of team building activities, design thinking activities, technology activities and STEM specific activities. Although these categories appear distinct, overlap within and between the types of activities was evident. The water studies topic was used to motivate and focus all STEM and design activities conducted during the camp. While the use of technology was embedded throughout the activities, additional technology specific time was afforded each afternoon. This time was used for campers to document their experiences at design camp through digital comic book making.

3.2.4 Use of Technology Towards Construction of Design Comics

On Day One of camp, campers were randomly assigned to six teams of four. One early camp activity included orientation to the use of *iPod touches*. One *touch* was assigned to each group and was designated for use towards one of two purposes. The first was for campers to rate the effectiveness and enjoyableness of camp activities throughout the days using the website *Poll Everywhere*. The poll let the campers rate each camp activity anonymously and see the real time results compile on the

Interactive White Board screen. The second use was for documentation of design camp through photography using the built in camera app that was standard to the *iPod touches*. The groups were asked to decide on one photographer for each day with one group member repeated on two days during the camp. The team photographer of each day was responsible for carrying, charging, and caring for the hardware for the duration of their day. They were told to take as many pictures as they wanted and we encouraged them to have many photos.

Each afternoon, campers were given 45-60 minutes in a computer lab using the software *Comic Life*. Just prior to this time, a camp facilitator brought the *iPod touches* to the computer lab and uploaded the photos collected by the group photographer to the computers used by the members of the group. Over the course of the camp, the designated photographers captured 2,198 unique photographs. While this is true, each group was only given direct access to those taken by their group photographers for the day. This amounted to roughly 92 photos per team per day for use in the comics. Campers were allowed free choice regarding which photos and how many to include in their comic retelling of the design camp experience.

Similarly, little structure was offered regarding the construction and content of the comics. Campers were afforded the freedom to retell their camp experience through daily entries in their design camp comic. To offer some support for the process, the following structure was provided orally at the onset of comic making for each day:

Table 3.1: Suggestions for the Creation of Comics

Day of Camp	Specific Suggestions/Scaffold Provided in Comic Making
Day 1:	Camp facilitator offered brief orientation to the comic application Campers were informed that this would be a take-away artifact of camp and that a printed copy would be given to them at the end of camp to share the story of design camp with family and friends. Campers directed to introduce self Campers directed to introduce team
Day 2:	Class discussion on what it means to tell a story Camp facilitator supported campers in generating list of elements of a story (ex. introduction of characters such as protagonist and antagonist, plot including conflict and resolution, etc.).
Day 3:	Campers observed and discussed three comics sampled to illustrate the arc of a story across frames. Groups identified elements of the comic that support readers understanding from frame to frame (ex. using similar setting between frames and varying only the speaker) Suggestions to connect content between frames and across days to tell a continuous story. Facilitator requested that campers ask and be granted permission if they chose to use a peer or instructor as the antagonist in their story.
Day 4:	No additional scaffolds given, campers continued working. Campers completed comics to be submitted for printing

Each day during comic construction, camp facilitators (but generally not team coaches) were present throughout work times to answer questions about the *Comic Life* application. While this is true, campers rarely asked the adults present about the rich variety of features available in the software application. Although none had previous experience using *Comic Life*, they were encouraged to explore its capabilities and began helping one another immediately. Most frequently, youth answered one another's technology related questions without the need for assistance from camp facilitators.

3.3 Data and Analysis

The final 22 comics analyzed are a collection from 18 males and 4 females in grades six, seven, and eight. Together these include 167 pages of comics generated during the four days of the camp. Individual comics range in length from three pages to 14 pages with a mean length of seven pages.

To begin the analysis, a random sample of 8 comics was open-coded by multiple researchers. A process to assure inter-rater calibration was created that included discussing similar and different codes, setting definitions for codes, and agreeing to combine some code labels where appropriate. The emergent codes from each researcher were combined and synthesized into eight code categories. The categories included: activities, affordances of technology, social displays, identity of self and group, who's included, evaluation, parts of a story, and holistic comic classification. For a graphic display of all codes, see Appendix 1.

To illustrate the themes, we present two that spoke with intensity and frequency to how the campers expressed and represented their camp experiences and activities–– identity of the self and the group, and activities that were STEM-related.

3.4 Themes Arising from Expressions of Experience

3.4.1 Being There, Being a Team Member, and Doing it in Peer-sanctioned Ways

One predominant theme in the comic books emerged around the campers establishing and representing themselves as both individuals and members of a team. The comic book form enabled the campers to express these constructions through playful representations and textual moves. The facilitator suggested introduction of the self appeared at the front of all but three of the comic books. One of the three got to it on page four. Eleven comic books were coded as providing a neutral introduction with no commentary or embellishment (e.g., "My name is...."). Each self-introduction included a picture of the author. Several provided negative comments about themselves, and two indicated they were confused. One of the campers expressed the opinion that during camp activities he had stage fright, and it also appeared in his comic. The most common pattern was to introduce themselves first, then quickly move on to introducing their group members. In comic books where campers did not introduce themselves, they did introduce the group and its activities. We had suggested that campers introduce themselves and others, so that was expected. Of interest was that the campers moved so quickly to their teammates both in terms of page and comic real estate.

Expressions about the group dominated. There was a quick movement from use of the pronoun "I" to the pronouns "we" and "our" in the comic books. Expressions about activities being untaken were predominantly group referenced, and from the comic books an analyst would be hard pressed to figure out what any individual did apart from their team members during camp activities. If design thinking is meant to be an intensely collaborative process, the middle school campers fell right into place (see Carroll, M., Goldman, Britos, Koh, Royalty, et al., 2010 for similar report on design collaboration by middle school students). Being a member of the group and being part of the group's activities were extremely present. Group membership was a huge theme for the youths. Because the campers could choose layouts, photos to put in frames, provide captions, and overlay speech and thought bubbles, they could present their team members, activities, and add commentary. The expressions about others in the group were flattering, derogatory, and neutral in tone. In our coding, comments about others in the groups were coded as positive, negative and neutral in equal numbers. However, it was difficult to see the negative barbs as representative of bad feelings, and we judged these as attempts at humor and playfulness. We will take up this mix of stances again momentarily. Many positive expressions of the camper's feelings about the group appeared in their texts. For example, one boy spoke for himself and the group in his last frame of the week when he posted a group picture after a successful tower building activity. His caption:

> *EVERYONE IN MY AWESOME GROUP HAD A LOT OF FUN. EVERYTHING WE LEARNED WAS FASCINATING!! DESIGN THINKING RULES!!!!*

Positive expressions about the group appeared throughout the comics, making it an indisputable highlight for the middle schoolers (see Figure 3.4 below as an example where the picture of the group is captioned with the label, "Happy Times With Our Group!").

EVERYONE IN MY
AWESOME GROUP
HAD A LOT OF
FUN. EVERYTHING
WE LEARNED WAS
FASINATING!!!
DESIGN
THIINKING
RULES!!!!

Figure 3.4: Positive Expressions about the Group.

3.4.2 Jokes, Humor and Playfulness as Expressions by the Youth

Expressions about the group and social relations were of importance to the campers, and the layering affordances of the *Comic Life* software and the visual media they used made it possible for campers to craft complex representations of themselves and others. Much of this was done with humor and jocularity. Sanford and Eder (1984) described how humor is a vehicle for communication and bonding among adolescent peers, and how different kinds of humor are linked to both group size and closeness. Among the campers, humor and playfulness were drivers of social interaction, communications, and collaborations, and it carried over into the comic books. It was delightful to us and seen as a positive that the comic book medium made it possible for humor to move seamlessly into their composed records of the campers experiences.

During the camp week, the youth joked with each other as a matter of course and, as mentioned earlier, these same humorous and playful comments found their way into their comic books. Humor was certainly not a required feature of the comic book making, yet it turned out to be a defining characteristic of the texts. One or two seemed to attempt to maintain humor throughout their comic books, and most accomplished intermittent humor alongside more narrative descriptions of their experiences. For many, humor alternated with more descriptive accounts. This is similar to what Holcomb (1992) described and called "nodal points of humor" (p. 224)—the places where humor is concentrated, yet still connected to the general narrative and context. We saw humor take several forms, which we describe. We saw: (1) humor about self and peers (some of which was similar in style and form to the "live" social banter in the camp); (2) playfulness; (3) joke telling; and (4), integration of humor relating to the STEM activities of the camp.

3.4.2.1 Humor About Self and Peers

Youth used humor, and in some cases with just a single comic frame, to express both positives and negatives about themselves. One boy posted a picture of himself in a frame and labeled it with two thought bubbles: "I think that I am really funny" and "This kid is a maroon" [sic]. This type of frame appeared frequently across the group's comic books. Of course, there was much play about others in the group as well. Campers placed individual photos of their team members and friends into frames, and then commented with thought and talk bubbles or captions. Neutral comments most often were speech or think bubbles saying: "I'm Jack", "and I'm Juan." A more playful version included photos with thought bubbles such as, "I am weird by the way", "I am lost", "I am cool", or "My armpits are stinky!!!" Some of the narrative overlay tended toward sarcasm such as, "I am trying to stop your thinking." Others asked questions such as, "What am I doing?"

3.4.2.2 Playfulness

Some of these textual moves tended to mimic the negative talk the middle schoolers engaged in during face-to-face social banter, where some comments were harsh to the ears of adults, but mostly self-managed, handled, and reciprocated by the young teens. Most of what was said in even the more negative live or comic-based banter was untrue. This pattern of untrue verbal, social banter was documented by Labov (1973) when he studied Black English vernacular in action. Put downs and ritual insults among peers tend to be constructed of benign accusations and it was actually a violation to speak hurtful truths. Although provoking of reciprocation, these verbal accusations are considered verbal play by those engaged. On paper, where there was no response to comments coming from peers, the one-sided comments were less harsh in nature. On the positive side, the comic books were also full of fun comments about others and the power of the group. An example is one frame that featured a speech bubble assigned to three in the group that says, "We are awesome."

The campers used drawing overlay on photos to create light-hearted frames about themselves and others. These were less related to any narrative description, so we classified them as "playful." One boy drew red scribbles on his head and labeled it, "I am Katy Perry" (a pop singer), while another put white dots over his eyes and noted, "I used to wear contacts." The example in Figure 3.5 below illustrates this playfulness in practice. The boy puts himself upside down in the first frame and his speech bubble asks, "Why am I upside down?" When the next bubble shows him correctly positioned, he comments, "I am very dizzy." He is having fun with the capabilities in the software and having fun with himself. He uses text and image to create this playful moment.

Figure 3.5: Playfulness in practice

3.4.2.3 Joke Telling

Much of the humor we saw represented jokes using the comic frame as a form. Many consisted of a single frame combined with a context reference, or commentary. Some used a theme such as superhero or detective as a narrative device. A couple of them managed to set up a context for jokes that did not build off of the camp content, yet were completely related to the social banter among their campmates. Jokes in these classic forms have been studied by scholars including Harvey Saks (1989). Saks claimed that the telling of a joke involves adopting a preface, the telling, and the response sequences. The joke we profile has all three components.

Let's look at the example of a joke that builds off of camp social conversations. The joke featured in Figure 3.6 invokes two mass-culture references: Snickers candy bars and pop star, Justin Bieber. The middle schoolers know both.

I LIKE JUSTIN BEIBER!!!! AND THIS SNICKERS BUT MOSTLY THE SNICKERS BAR.

This is followed by a text frame that tells the joke:

HEY GUYS WHAT'S THE DIFFERENCE BETWEEN A SNICKERS BAR AND JUSTIN BEIBER.

Punch Line: SNICKERS BAR HAVE NUTS: D

Figure 3.6: Joke telling

The joke itself may be a re-telling of a joke heard elsewhere. Nevertheless, it is in the comic book for the enjoyment of the readers. The joke is a "put-down" of the pop star that is mitigated slightly by the speech bubble that admits, "I like Justin Beiber" [sic]. It is also risqué, given the teller is a girl, the ages of the campers, and how it comments on Bieber's anatomical correctness. This joke was very popular with the other campers when comics were shared.

Jokes reached beyond being strictly social and became integrated with the camps' STEM activities. In Figure 3.7 below, one girl shows a thought bubble attached to a photo of petri dishes from a comparison condition experiment the campers completed concerning the roles that water, bleach, and no intervention has on bacterial growth. The bubble says, "WHY AM I SO DORMANT? This speaks directly to the investigation she was conducting, as observations determined that the bacteria was less visible for the condition where the hands were washed with water or sprayed with bleach before imprinting in the petri dish. It's not a joke per se or obvious humor, but it is playful, clever, and connected directly to one of the major science investigations the campers completed during the camp. We saw a second version of this joke in another comic book where the photo showed the petri dishes and the bubble read, "Shut your trap Bacteria. I can kill you." These represent one of several kinds of jokes that appeared across the comic books that were directly informed by the STEM-related activities.

3.4.2.4 Integration of Humor Relating to the STEM Activities

Fourteen campers introduced jokes about the STEM activities. In quite a few cases, they employed a thought bubble to be humorous. In these instances, the campers took a visual from the STEM activities and their understanding of them, and set up thought bubbles that made them humorous. An example is shown in Figure 3.7.

Figure 3.7: The thought bubble conveys science humor.

A second, narrative account that included both humor and the STEM activities of the camp was the "superhero" approach. Several campers described themselves as superheroes that could save the world, their designs, or their group. Several chose to highlight this around a science experiment that was conducted to see the power of water in slowing down bacterial growth. One boy is both superhero and scientist as he "disintegrates" bacteria by spraying them with bleach. Of course, he is a superhero who saves the day. Another saves the "bears of Bear Valley" by his group's construction of a tower that withstands high winds. These boys employed super hero or super saviors through which the stories of their camp week could be told and through which they could be playful, humorous, and display their competence.

Figure 3.8 shows a camp coach asking a camper why he is drawing many pictures of penguins on Sticky Note papers. The response is that he was "doing penguins to give." This boy spent a good deal of time drawing cartoons of penguins, and the frame indicates his reflection about how he was drawing them to give them to others. While not directly related to the STEM goals of the camp, it was a reflection about how he spent some of his time and his intentions. We saw a mix of ways the comics were used to highlight commentary about campers' socialness.

These presentations of self and others dominated the comic books, taking form in deep connection to the social life and group activities of the camp. The campers exercised their freedoms to personalize their comic books, and from the analysts' points of view, they succeeded in carrying their social experiences of the camp into their comic books. Appreciating and celebrating their teams and friends was made possible by the technology, the intensely team-based nature of the camp activity, and the "outside of school" nature of the camp.

What we saw in the data was consistent with theories of the "self" as emergent in social interaction (Goffman, 1971; Mead, 1934). These conceptions suggest that as people transact with language, play, and aspects of experience (including controls) in the course of activities with others, the self is continually emergent. The social participation unit of the camp was the team, so it is not surprising that students represented the group experience, taking the quick jump to integrate "self" and "team" in their representations. The camp structure had many supports for "teamness." Each group had a name, a team cheer, a stock of materials, tools, and a designated workspace. Facilitators helped groups establish group routines, ground rules for team behavior, and shared solutions. The design challenges and the hands-on STEM activities transacted through objects such as STEM tools, prototyping materials and products (models and conceptual prototypes of solutions) that acted as boundary objects through which communication, camaraderie, and meaning were generated (Star & Griesemer, 1989). With pressure for grades, achievement and individual accountability not in play, the comic books reflected and celebrated the self-consciousness and socialness of the middle school camper experiences.

Figure 3.8: Campers engaging in social behavior

3.4.3 Doing STEM

In addition to numerous displays of identity in a myriad of ways, the analysis also revealed a high frequency of kids "doing STEM." By this, we mean accounts of being engaged in actions and behaviors related to the content, concepts, methods, skills, or mindsets related to the STEM professions. We present this in contrast to K-12 school learning of STEM subjects that are predominantly taught in isolation. To reveal this contrast, begin by picturing yourself in your seventh grade science class. Think about the assignments you worked on, your learning materials, and the arrangement of your seats. If you have received an education influenced by the age of accountability brought on by the federal government's No child Left Behind (NCLB) regulations or a prior accountability or back to basics movement, it is likely that you pictured seatwork at a single desk amidst a sea of rows and columns. Maybe you completed your work alone but had the occasional excitement of a pre-determined step-by-step "lab" done with a partner or lab group that was aimed at the "re-discovery" of a well-known concept or process. This is the way that many students in the United States learn "STEM" subjects, but this is not the way that scientists and engineers solve problems in the real world. In a study of students' conceptions of engineering, Brenda Capobianco and her colleagues determined that most students have misconceptions about the work of engineers. The students' notions completely missed "the essential characteristics of engineering, such as creativity, teamwork, an ethic of care, and communication" (Capobianco, Diefes-Dux, Mena, & Weller, 2011; National Academy of Engineering [NAE] & National Research Council [NRC], 2009). Through analysis of the comics it is clear that our learners had the experience of doing STEM that was more aligned with the work of professionals and focused on a "community of practice" model of learning (Lave & Wenger, 1991) than on individual-achievement, or in the transfer-of-knowledge model that exists in many schools.

3.4.4 Integrated Subject Matter

While our emergent coding structure distinguished between and coded for STEM activities and design thinking activities, a more holistic look at entire comic pages (rather than individual frames) revealed that the young designers did not apply these superficial borders in the same way. On the comic excerpt in Figure 3.9, we see a boy narrating his experiences in the camp seamlessly. In frames one, two, and three, he presents both experimentation and design activities together. The boy refers to the prototype designed by his group as an experiment. While a prototype is essentially experimenting with a solution to a problem, this is not the language we presented to the campers, making it a rather revealing insight into the way that this boy was applying labels across boundaries. In frame four, he mentions the comic making, but does so alongside a joke about bacteria found in a water fountain. This is one reference to technology use, but its appearance on the page alongside the other content types illustrates the integrated nature of the experience for this boy. Integration of science, technology, engineering, and mathematics is a representation that appears in several of the comics.

Figure 3.9: Camper narration integrating STEM and design principles

3.4.5 Absence of the Teacher and Presence of the Group

Coding also revealed information about who is included in these comics and thus whom the children valued as integral in the design camp experience. Campers appeared alone infrequently throughout the comics. They most often appeared with their groups and very rarely featured the presence of an instructor or coach. When coaches and instructors were pictured they were often in the background. They infrequently garnered reference in thought bubbles, speech bubbles, or captions. In fact, in the texts alone (putting playful representations aside for a moment), the words "team" and "group" were used

39 times where the combined total of teacher, instructor, and coach appeared in only two instances. These were not solely to introduce team members (per the prompt on Day One). Mentions of team and group work stretched throughout the narratives. The pictures used as illustrations were also focused on collaboration. Note how, in Figure 3.10 in the pane on the left, both the picture and text reinforced the camper's value that was placed on the collaborative process. In Figure 3.10 in the pane on the right, a second camper places shared emphasis on collaboration in the text and the photograph. Not only does he mention working "together", but the picture illustrates this as well. In both examples, the members of the team appeared to be contributing to the project at the moment the picture was taken. Furthermore, the young authors chose to include these group pictures to illustrate the experience rather than pictures of themselves alone with the final product. This may illustrate that the collaboration of team members was a more salient experience for campers than instruction by teachers and coaches during design camp. While orientation and collaborative team work is a goal of problem solving with design thinking and a valued skill for STEM professionals, we have reason to believe that the comic creation process enabled the middle schoolers to show evidence that collaboration was a salient part of the their experience.

Figure 3.10: Demonstrates the value of collaborative process

3.4.6 Creativity and Communication

Research by Capobianco et al. (2011) stressed the importance of collaboration for STEM professionals and also introduced creativity and communication as part of their skillsets. A recent publication by the National Research Council (NRC) also described communication and collaboration as interpersonal and intrapersonal competencies that contribute to a 21st century skillset (NRC, 2012). The NRC report indicates that there is little research to link these skills to cognitive educational outcomes, but opens the conversation about the ways researchers can begin to determine unique ways to measure these non-cognitive skills that are highly valued in the workforce. Young people's creation of media rich comics to retell their experiences might be one way to begin to interrogate young people's experiences of collaboration, communication, and creativity.

In the design process, the young designers engage in the human-centered process to identify creative solutions to complex problems. They plan and prototype solutions for particular users and then communicate these solutions in numerous ways. Both prototyping and communicating appeared in nearly all the comics indicating that these experiences held a particular value to the campers throughout design camp. Figure 3.11 shows examples from four different campers that illustrate their use of prototyping and presentation to solve a problem in the world. Four of the frames mention some aspect of the prototyping process. The campers brainstormed ideas, made prototypes, presented them to users, revised the prototypes based on feedback, and showed them to an audience of their parents and peers. Prototyping activities were rated highly by the campers, and from the comic depictions, appeared to hold prominence for them. Communication within and outside of the group also gained some currency. While campers did not have the opportunity to include their final water-related designs or their final presentations in their comics, several referenced the team communications and the public service announcements they created about water access and conservation.

The analysis of the comics reveals that the campers presented their design camp experiences and highlighted their STEM experiences. By identifying instances of integrated subject matter, team and peer-centered collaboration, and creativity and communication, it became clear that campers saw themselves as engaged in the process of being young STEM designers who worked collaboratively. Their choice of pictures and words in their comics indicated that STEM related work was an important part of design camp, and that they participated in and understood those activities. This was captured both in the way they shared their experiences and by the particular experiences they chose to share. In the end, it was these STEM experiences that garnered the most comic real estate in retelling and will ultimately comprise the memory record the comics provide.

Figure 3.11: Prototyping and presentation of work.

3.5 Discussion

The fact that less and less women and diverse young people are entering STEM fields raises concerns and requires new kinds of positive, formative experiences. The *d.loft* project joins this effort to increase the number of teens with access to and knowledge of STEM and STEM careers through intensive camp experiences that take a design for the other 90% approach. Through STEM introductions outside of the regular school program, we have been able to provide youth with low-stakes and more organic experiences that connect them to real-world problem solving processes. We also see the value in teaching them through design thinking, which is an intensely collaborative problem solving and innovation process.

One of our goals was to better understand the ways youth can create representations of their learning experiences, and comic book making seemed a possibility that would highlight the connections they were making through the digital media they interact with outside of the classroom. The comic books were successful in enabling creative expression and a record of what STEM content connections they made.

In the comics, the story of the design experience as narrative through time was the dominant form. Telling stories of events, with commentary and critique predominated. Whether or not that may have been due to the way the comic bookmaking sessions were spaced throughout the week or the ways access to media was available, we cannot say. Future studies wherein we vary the access might reveal a departure from narrative form.

The open coding process revealed several patterns and themes that were predominant in the comics. Youth depicted themselves and their teammates, and for most, there was a strong orientation to and representation of the team. Others told of personal journeys through the design challenges. Storytelling elements that were central included time-based narratives, characters, significant events, socialness, and problem resolutions.

The comic book making process enabled the campers to capture images of people, activities and products, share their images with others, and construct representations of their experiences. The campers made style and content choices, and were free to innovate in how they represented their experiences. They were free to choose narratives, montages, poems, jokes, and other literacy forms. These activities provided meaning-making experiences.

The findings indicate that the comic form allowed the campers to be extremely expressive and creative while representing the socialness of camp, the daily activities, the STEM content, and their own emotions and evaluations of their experiences. Central to their products were profiles of campers, with pictures of themselves and their team members, and their peers at work on their activities, prototypes, and products. The comics also generated excitement and a desire among campers to share them with friends and family. The mentions of the STEM-based activities were substantial and high in number, yet less frequent than social or identity-relevant comic panes.

We will have the opportunity to have middle school youth create comic books again, and we will set up the process to encourage even more fidelity between them, their camp experiences, and the comic books they create. One direction we have considered is seeing if we can easily prompt the campers in ways that might continually yield the vital, joyful, developmental, and social expression while creating STEM learning connections.

Ultimately, we seek to learn how an accessible media-based storytelling activity such as comic book making offers middle school youth ways to express and reinforce their experiences while learning. We also hope to see if this form of expression of experience can become a tool for extending and reinforcing learning activities, and whether it serves both the youth and their learning facilitators in productive ways. We see the potential for digital comic making to provide opportunities to engage youth with multiple media forms, artistic expression, language play, and experiences with technology for relating their experiences and finding convergence between STEM identities and youth social identities. We see the digital comic experience as an activity that might mitigate structural disparities among young people through production opportunities that fit their developmental and social readiness and preferences. In this regard, reflection through digital comic storytelling may offer aid to young people who encounter socially-reproduced relations of power that limit access to STEM participation.

References

Barron, B., Gomez, K., Pinkard, N., & Martin, K. (2014). The digital youth network: Cultivating digital media citizenship in urban communities. Cambridge, MA: MIT Press.

Bitz, M. (2004). The comic book project: Forging alternative pathways to literacy. *Journal of Adolescent & Adult Literacy*, *47*(7), 574-586.

Bouillion, L. M., & Gomez, L. M. (2001). Connecting school and community with science learning: Real world problems and school–community partnerships as contextual scaffolds. *Journal of Research in Science Teaching*, *38*(8), 878-898.

Bruner, J. (1977). *The process of education*. Cambridge, MA: Harvard University Press. (Original work published 1960).

Buckingham, D. (Ed.). (2007). *Youth, identity, and digital media*. Cambridge, MA: MIT Press.

Capobianco, B., Diefes-Dux, H. A., Mena, I., & Weller, J. (2011). What is an engineer? Implications of elementary school student conceptions for engineering education. *Journal of Engineering Education*, *100*(2), 304-328.

Carroll, M., Goldman, S., Britos, L., Koh, J., Royalty, A., & Hornstein, M. (2010). Destination, imagination & the fires within: Design thinking in a middle school classroom. *International Journal of Art & Design Education*, *29*(1), 37-53.

Carroll, M., Britos, L., & Goldman, S. (2012). Design thinking. In S. Garner & C. Evans (Eds.), *Design & designing: A critical introduction* (pp. 20-31). Oxford: Berg Publishers.

Collins, A. (1993). Issues in assessment: Purpose, alternative assessment and equity. *School of Education Review*, *5*, 68-77.

Collins, A., & Halverson, R. (2009). *Rethinking education in the age of technology: The digital revolution and schooling in America*. New York, NY: Teachers College Press.

Dahl, S., & Franzen, P. (1998). The science journal: Writing and inquiry development. *Sciencelines: A Newsletter From the Teacher Resource Center at Fermilab*, Fall 1997.

Dewey, J. (1938). *Experience & education*. New York, NY: Kappa Delta Pi.

Goffman, E. (1971). *Relations in public*. New Brunswick, NJ: Transaction Publishers.

Goldman, S., Booker, A., & McDermott, M. (2008). Mixing the digital, social and cultural: Learning, identity and agency in youth participation. In D. Buckingham, (Ed.). *Youth, identity, and digital media* (pp. 185-206). MacArthur Foundation Series on Digital Media and Learning. Cambridge, MA: The MIT Press.

Holcomb, C. (1992). Nodal humor in comic narrative: A semantic analysis of two stories by Twain and Wodehouse. *Humor: International Journal of Humor Research*, *5*(3), 233-250.

Ito, M., Baumer, S., Bittanti, M., boyd, d., Cody, R., Herr-Stephenson, B., Horst, H. A., Lange, P. G., Mahendran, D., Martínez, K. Z., Pascoe, C. J., Perkel, D., Robinson, L., Sims, C., & Tripp, L. (2010). *Hanging out, messing around, and geeking out: Kids living and learning with new media*. Cambridge, MA: The MIT Press.

Ito, M., Gutiérrez, K., Livingstone, S., Penuel, B., Rhodes, J., Salen, K., Schor, J., Sefton-Green, J., & Watkins, S. C. (2013). *Connected learning: An agenda for research and design*. Irvine, CA: Digital Media and Learning Research Hub. http://dmlhub.net/publications/connected-learning-agenda-research-and-design

Labov, W. (1973). *Language in the inner city: Studies in the Black English vernacular*. Philadelphia, PA: University of Pennsylvania Press.

Ladson-Billings, G. (1995). Toward a theory of culturally relevant pedagogy. *American Educational Research Journal*, *32*(3), 465-491.

Lave, J., & Wenger, E. (1991). *Situated learning: Legitimate peripheral participation*. Cambridge: Cambridge University Press.

Liu, J. (2004). Effects of comic strips on L2 learners' reading comprehension. *TESOL quarterly, 38*(2), 225-243.

McCloud, S. (1993). *Understanding comics: The invisible art.* Northampton, MA: Kitchen Sink Press, Inc.

Mead, G. H. (1934). *Mind, self, and society from the perspective of a social behaviorist.* Chicago: University of Chicago Press.

National Academy of Engineering & National Research Council. (2009). Engineering in K-12 education: Understanding the status and improving the prospectus. Washington, DC: National Academies Press.

National Research Council. (2012). Education for life and work: Developing transferable knowledge and skills in the 21st century. Washington, DC: The National Academies Press.

Ranker, J. (2008). Comic books as read-alouds: Insights on reading instruction from an English as a second language classroom. *The Reading Teacher, 61*(4), 296-305.

Saks, H. (1989). An analysis of the course of a joke's telling in conversation. In J. Sherzer, (Ed.). *Studies in the social and cultural foundations of language* (pp. 337-353). Cambridge: Cambridge University Press.

Sanford, S., & Eder, D. (1984). Adolescent humor during peer interaction. *Social Psychology Quarterly, 47*(3), 235-243.

Smith, C. E. (2007). *Design for the other 90%.* Editions Assouline.

Spiegelman, A. (1986). *Maus.* New York: Pantheon Books.

Star, S. L., & Griesemer, J. R. (1989). Institutional ecology, translations' and boundary objects: Amateurs and professionals in Berkeley's Museum of Vertebrate Zoology, 1907-39. *Social studies of science, 19*(3), 387-420.

Tippins, D. J., & Dana, F. N. (1992). Culturally relevant assessment. *Science Scope, 15*(6), 50-53.

Vygotsky, L. S. (1980). *Mind in society: The development of higher psychological processes.* Cambridge: Harvard University Press.

Appendix 1: Emergent Coding Scheme

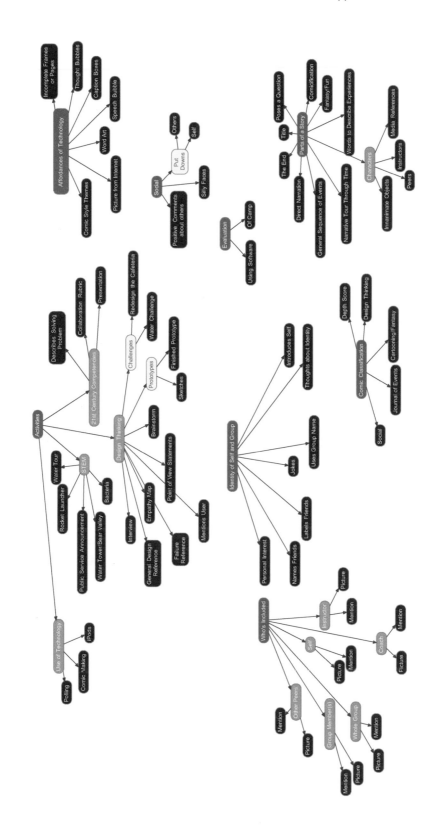

Ernesto Colín and Philip Molebash

4 Life, Camera, Action: Exploring Issues in Urban Education Through Edited Video Narratives

4.1 Introduction

Transformative cognitive and social relationships are potentialized in the careful crafting of the story of community dynamics that will be shared with an audience. In education contexts where teachers engage in ethnographic immersion or investigative reporting, the nature of the looking, asking, and telling invites teachers to confront the culture of their setting and consider the impact of observed power dynamics and social roles. Halstead (2008) would agree and argues that the experiences and encounters of reflexive knowledge construction through ethnography are transformative spaces; researchers actively negotiating the meaning of their observations are inevitably transformed. Beyond personal transformation, those concerned with social justice and teacher preparation can call on educators to traverse constructed boundaries with insights gained from reflexive practice. This chapter is an account of the impact that micro-documentary filmmaking and related ethnographic processes had on pre-service teachers. We celebrate what Robinson (1994) has called the *ethnography of empowerment*, or "an ethnography that will not only record but actually lead to transformative and re-humanizing action in the world" (p. 7).

Studies have revealed the potential of video technologies to document rich contexts of teaching and learning and provide teacher candidates with dynamic tools to observe and reflect carefully (Wang & Hartley, 2003). For example, two studies by Sherin and van Es (2005) examining how video can be used to assist pre-service and in-service teachers in "learning to notice" what was happening in classrooms found that teachers often re-center students in their focus of attention (and not their own positionality), and moreover, they found participants shifted away from being purely evaluative in their reflections (i.e., whether the activity went well or not) to more interpretive (i.e., why this may have occurred). Other studies involve pre-service teachers editing digital video of themselves (with user-friendly editing apps) in classroom settings as a means to promote reflection. Scholars are finding that engaging pre-service teachers in the process of editing digital videos to tell a personal narrative can be particularly effective in fostering teachers' reflections (Calandra, Dias, & Dias, 2006; Calandra, Dias, Lee, & Fox, 2009; Yerrick, Ross, & Molebash, 2005).

Our findings resonate with Lowenthal (2009) who reviews the various uses, benefits, and implementation issues of digital storytelling in education, citing that educators are using digital storytelling to increase student engagement, provide platforms for student voice, access multiple kinds of literacies, and inspire emotion and deep reflection. Given the importance of using reflection as a way to change teachers' beliefs and ensuing practice, and the promise of using digital video editing as a tool to scaffold this reflection, the authors of this paper submit that digital video editing can be developed as an intervention in teacher preparation, specifically as a tool to promote deep reflection that, in turn, positively changes future praxis.

Life, Camera, Action: A turn of phrase. Immense wisdom comes to teacher candidates embedded and interacting in the field, in real life. While near the nexus of theory and practice, the camera becomes a research tool, as well as a medium for reflection and digital storytelling. The examination of the field through the camera lens informs ideological and pedagogical shifts, depth of understanding, and a general impact on future practice. As this volume suggests, what emerge are deep stories facilitated by the field experience and the medium of analysis. In a manner unique to its medium, the micro-documentary films allow for intimacy, visual collage, non-verbal cues, multiple voices, archived moments, invitations to reflect, and a revelatory framing of the contexts portrayed.

4.2 About this Study

A teacher education course in our mid-sized university requires teacher candidates to produce ethnographic micro-documentary films (5-10 minute target length) as the culminating assignment. Colleagues who have taught this course have approached this required community engagement assignment in other ways (traditional research paper, community mapping study, etc.). We decided to institute a change and involve candidates in micro-documentary film production for this culminating project because we perceived great potential for digital/visual storytelling to impact teacher candidates and audiences. Since the change in assignment format and at the completion of the study, more than 80 micro-documentary films have been created (the course and film productions continue). The course in which they are produced centers on topics of (multi)cultural sensitivity and analysis of K-12 student diversity. In addition to course content, students receive introductory training in visual anthropology, human subjects protocols, social science research methods, and video editing. After designing, filming, editing, and production, the students also produce a complimentary written narrative describing the context for their film, and implications of their findings.

In the early phases of this research, we pondered whether the planning, filming, editing, and narrating processes involve intellectual modalities, reflection, and decisions that are distinct from those of traditional research papers. At its core, the research inquired about the impact of production of micro-documentaries on teacher candidates. Furthermore, given the current context of media and technology, the study explored how a multimedia project potentialized greater audience engagement and influence as it circulates, in contrast to a written paper, which is often turned in, graded, and forgotten.

We set out to include around 10% of course alumni/filmmakers in this small-scale qualitative study (n=7). Our target participants were teacher candidates at the time of the course/film production who had graduated from the university with credentials to now teach in their own classrooms. Study participants would then be 6-18 months removed from participation in the course/film making. Lapsed university email accounts, varying employment statuses, and other factors narrowed the pool of available participants. We included the first seven students who responded to email recruitment. The study gathered interview data regarding: (1) teacher candidate reflections on the process of digital storytelling; (2) self assessment of the impact of the course content—especially the process of creating micro-documentaries—on their professional practice; and (3) an assessment of the value of the assignment in the course.

4.2.1 Participants

Six females and one male student participated in this study. They were the first seven students to respond to the call out of 15 invited to participate through randomized selection. A review of records demonstrated that study participants had all received high marks on the original scoring rubric for the film that took into account aesthetics, content, ethnographic connections, and connections to the course content. In a stroke of appropriateness, study participants reflect the heavily skewed gender ratio of the teacher education courses in our school of education. All participants are alumni of a teacher education certificate and degree program whose central framework involved the anthropological analysis of cultural diversity in schools. Participants had completed the micro-documentary film 1-4 semesters prior to the study. In alphabetical order:

- **Alana**. A student teacher in environmental and natural sciences for a local comprehensive high school in the Los Angeles Unified School District. Her film focused on student aspirations and anxieties regarding college attendance at an urban charter high school in Los Angeles.
- **Ingrid**. A graduate student researcher and a long-term substitute in a local public school district. Her film focused on the gendered perspectives of several female high school students in urban Los Angeles.
- **Jenna**. A teacher and former public relations professional. Her film was an auto-ethnography exploring her bi-racial identity in relation to the African American community.
- **Jeremy**. A middle school teacher who has just left public school service to join the seminary in preparation for pastoral work. His film centered representations of the home/community and school context of one special education student in an urban public school.
- **Marissa**. A social science high school teacher in south Los Angeles. Her film explored the events surrounding the election of a transgender homecoming king at a local high school.

- **Randi**. A veteran Catholic schoolteacher and performing artist who returned to school to complete two teaching credentials in order to teach in public schools. Her film focused on an exploration of Special Education teachers and classroom practices.
- **Tara**. A middle school teacher of 5 years in urban Los Angeles. Her film was a "day in the life" piece focused on two of her students, their friends and neighborhood.

4.3 Patterns

Each participant was shown their own film, asked questions about their professional experience, and asked to recall the film making process, especially the production, challenges, possible impact, and circulation of the micro-documentary films. In addition, participants were asked to relay their understanding of the objectives of the course from which the films emerged and discuss their evaluation of the amount of fit between the course and the ethnographic project.

The interviews were done in person except for two participants who had moved away from the area. All interviews were transcribed and coded in two passes, separately, by two of the project researchers who later reconciled their findings. The following is a conceptual map (Figure 4.1), or graphic representation of the data presented in the text of this paper (colors representing participants).

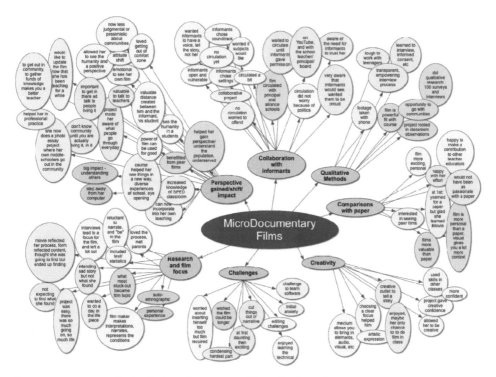

Figure 4.1: Pattern analysis of micro-documentary filmmaker interview comments

4.4 Findings: Micro-Documentaries as Tools for Research and Reflection

Three general types of comments emerged from participants in this study. Discussed below, participant comments deal with (a) evaluation of the micro-documentary film project in general, (b) the project as a tool for ethnographic research and reflection, and (c) the shifts in perspective in or impact of the process on their professional development.

4.4.1 General Evaluation of the Assignment

Filmmakers in the study were asked to reflect on the assignment in general and in relation to the goals and objectives of the course. They offered generally positive evaluations of the assignment and discussed how the challenges they faced were mitigated by satisfaction with the outcome, the opportunity to be creative with their research product, and agreement that this project offers advantages over a traditional paper produced after small-scale ethnography. Each of these is discussed in turn and in detail below.

4.4.1.1 Challenges

Participants discussed many challenges in the design, execution, and post-production of the micro-documentary. For most students, this project came in their very first graduate course, teacher education course. Many participants discussed having a great deal of anxiety about the assignment because it required research in schools and communities and because it required film production software with which they were unfamiliar. Students were initially daunted by the task. Once underway, students commented most frequently about navigating challenges with keeping the film to the target length, overcoming disorientation coming with the first attempts at social science research, narrowing the focus, crafting a coherent narrative, transcending the lament of excluding elements from the final cut, and making decisions about how much to insert themselves in the produced work. Ingrid, for example, stated "I knew I did not want to be narrating it because I felt that it would create myself, I would be inserting myself as a character and it's not necessary."

Challenges notwithstanding, most participants reported feeling a great deal of satisfaction after overcoming the big obstacles and difficulties of the project. After discussing her toil, Marissa represents that sentiment: "I am really proud of the end product and at the end of the day it was all worth it…"

4.4.1.2 Opportunities for Creativity

An area of commentary we did not anticipate when we set out on this research but which emerged throughout the interviews was that this project resulted in opportunities for creativity. Mentioned often, the participants revealed that this project allowed them to be creative, to have a creative outlet for their classwork, to tell an engaging story, and to gain creative confidence. Jeremy remarked that the medium of film allows us to use many elements (visual, audio, etc.) to craft a narrative. "When you are making a video you have the opportunity to kind of bring in more [creative elements]. . . I think any artistic medium is a really great way to kind of approach a situation with a different lens and so I think that's very powerful." For many, this was their first experience making a short film. Also noteworthy was the mention made by several participants that they went on to use filmmaking experience in other school projects. In other words, they transferred skills acquired through this project in either film editing, or social science research, or both, to projects in other classes.

4.4.1.3 Comparisons to Conventional Written Ethnographies

We asked study participants explicitly to compare their experience of creating a film after undergoing research with their experiences of writing papers as culminating projects for other teacher education courses. Participants were unanimous in asserting that filmmaking was a more personal, more engaging endeavor than the typical research paper. Some explained that it required more passion. Some went further to describe the film as being the most memorable assignment in their graduate career. Overall, they agreed that a film carried more potential for impact—on different audiences—and for making a contribution to the field of education, especially other educators. Despite it requiring quite a bit more time and potential frustration, participants reported feeling deep satisfaction, and having their care for the work and for their informants amplified. Furthermore, they mention benefitting not only from their own process, but also from seeing the films screened by their peers in class. Ingrid explained, "I felt good in bringing these voices into the classroom...I felt good that [my classmates] got to see these girls." Confirming that statement, Alana shared, "Getting to see everyone's film in class was, again, really valuable."

Overall, the students see a powerful assignment that extends the influence and fulfills the objectives of the course.

4.4.2 Micro-Documentaries as a Research/Reflection Tool

This study explored procedural effects of completing an ethnographic film project. By its nature, the micro-documentary film project requires teacher education candidates to engage communities, to venture out to collect experiences and voices. Though specific social science methods were not required, candidates did receive targeted guidance in human subjects, informed consent, and effective interviewing techniques. This study found that filmmakers, in developing and executing their filmic explorations, had important occasions to develop their repertoire of qualitative research methods, as well as collaborations with informants marked by respect and mutuality. The following explains this set of findings.

4.4.2.1 An Occasion for Training in Qualitative Research

The micro-documentary films became occasions for extending experience with qualitative research methods. Alana prepared for her film about high school student attitudes about college with a preproduction questionnaire: "I had a survey for students to fill out that was how likely do you think you will go to college and how likely did you feel about this before you started this high school to compare how much being at that high school had changed their perceptions." Participants noted that their films were rooted in classroom, school, and community observations. They learned about taking human subjects into account in research design and execution, about consent procedures and limitations, surveys and statistics, interviews and transparency, and film editing as a form of data analysis. As many a social science researcher has discovered, participants learned to expect the unexpected, and to adjust in mid process. For example, Tara commented, "I got a little experimental with my data collection. I started as a day-in-the-life film about one student and I just walked around with a camera, but then I started taking pictures of the environment and at one point [my informant's] little sister started giving me a tour of the neighborhood. It [the data collection] developed." Ingrid also noted, "I loved the process. They invited me into their homes . . . I had a set of questions asked to all the girls but every interview was different because the conversation might have lead to different questions being asked."

4.4.2.2 Developing Research and Film Foci

Teacher candidates were told at the beginning of the semester that the films had to be about the topics of diversity covered in the course, but each developed their research focus independently. It was interesting to hear how each of their topics and foci emerged. For one, the focus was personal and auto-ethnographic, with the self in the center. Others were extremely reluctant to insert themselves in the work too much, hoping to de-center themselves and disappear behind the camera and editing keyboard, thereby lifting their informants into first position. Sometimes, filmmakers designed their focus from the outset, electing to capture a "day in the life" or a set of advice for teen peers. For others, the film's narrative focus emerged in the field, after noticing what stood out in observations, or in surveys, or after interviews with a few informants. For Marissa, whose film addressed the crowning of a transgender homecoming king, the film she ended up producing reflected her own research process.

Hers was a film with two halves starting with a narrative about what she expected to find on her research journey and ending with what she actually, unexpectedly found: "The film is also not just the finished product, but it's my evolution about my own thoughts of homophobia in high school and not everything, and not everyone is victimized."

Overall, participants enjoyed the process, the bonds formed with informants, meeting parents, and so forth. However, they left with more than data; they left with the human lives that touched them and human connections for which they now felt reciprocity and mutuality. In the process, they took responsibility for representing the conditions and voices they encountered, and for interpreting the stories of their research context. Marissa described the importance of garnering consent and working with high school students from marginalized school communities. "If they didn't not trust me, I felt like they weren't going to 'lay it all out there' for me, so to speak." The need for trust in the relationship with the informants was a recurring theme.

4.4.2.3 On the Relationship with Informants

As we mentioned above, many of the filmmakers were intentional about considering their informants' voices and decentering their own. They wanted their informants to lead with their voice, tell their story. In some cases, informants chose the interview locations, and chose the soundtrack for the films. The projects became occasions for fruitful collaborations.

Above, Marissa talked about how aware she was of the need to develop trust with informants in order for the research (and film) to be effective. She also mentioned that she was transparent with everyone involved (teachers, administrators, parents, informants) about the topic of her research (homophobia in public high schools), and clear with informants that they had control over the final cut of the film and could ask that any part of their testimony be left out. Study participants stated that either they wanted the informants to be proud of the film or worried their informants would not like what they created: two sides of the same coin.

As teacher educators, we contend that there exists a great deal of potential for impact and circulation through these films, more than with papers that are too often turned in and never revisited. Teacher candidates are encouraged to secure consent and to circulate their films. We expected to find that all filmmakers had done so, but found that not all did circulate or screen their films beyond our class section. Of the seven, four did share their films with informants, and some also with the school staff and administration, the school board, the informants, and on video sharing sites like YouTube. Those who refrained did so because of the fear of politics at school sites, for fear of offending informants, or because they did not have confidence that their films were good enough for circulation. In any case, consideration for informants factored into circulation amounts.

4.4.3 Impact: Perspectives Gained or Shifted

The most important finding of this study has to do with the impact the ethnographic filmmaking exercise had on the formation of the teacher candidates. We were very interested in the intersection of visual anthropology and teacher preparation. We found that the micro-documentary filmmakers were able to complete films successfully in one semester and that they had valuable experiences along the way. Study participants remark how the project was emotional, valuable, and provided important occasions to reflect on the context of schools. The following is an account of the understandings that teacher candidates came to as a result of the project.

4.4.3.1 Understanding Community Contexts

Study participants consistently appreciate that the project compelled them to get out in the field, out from behind the computer, where they get to know the communities they will serve. Like most of the participants, Marissa explicitly identified that one cannot know a community fully without being there with them, immersed: "Getting into the community, seeing what's its like first hand which is why its better then writing a paper because you actually get to talk to these people that are living through it…" Many participants discussed how getting out of one's comfort zone produces transformative learning, and eye opening occasions to comprehend people's diverse experiences of schooling. Marissa added, "we are preparing to go into this world and what better way than to talk to the people that are already going through it."

4.4.3.2 Understanding Others

In addition to understanding contexts, the lenses of the project allowed filmmakers to view people differently. Several participants relayed that the ethnographic films allowed them to see the humanity of people who were dimensionally abstracted before the project. The project allowed them to be aware of what people go through every day, especially in underserved communities. After completing her film on the perspective of young urban females navigating school, Ingrid experienced an attitude shift, from one built upon negative experiences as a public school substitute teacher to one less judgmental and less pessimistic about the community she serves. She stated, "[the project] gave a more positive perspective of the area and in turn, you know, made me more willing to go out to [substituting] assignments. . . it made me be a little bit more, like, positive and up beat working with these kids." The project put teacher candidates in contact with people, rather than readings about people, and through this dialogue and interaction, filmmakers came to care more deeply about their informants. Informants became experts, guides, teachers, and inspirations for the filmmakers. Not only do filmmakers understand other communities more holistically, they often understand themselves at a deeper level. Jenna's film involved a cultural plunge into the African American community from which she was estranged as a biracial person. She explained, "the best way to understand someone is really to become a part of their community even if only temporarily."

4.4.3.3 Professional Practice

The main objective of the micro-documentary film project is to make a positive impact on the formation of teacher candidates through the exploration of critical issues of diversity through film research and film production. Study participants gained valuable experience that serves them in their professional practice. Repeatedly, participants explained that they gleaned a great deal from being in the field. After talking with teachers, getting a feel for classrooms, and observing settings like Special Education classrooms, charter schools, and schools with progressive extracurricular programs, they are better prepared for their own teaching.

Tara explained that the project has made a big impact, because gathering her student's community-based knowledge makes her a better teacher:

> I just felt more connected with the students and what their lives look like outside of, you know, the walls of the school building. And I think that's so important in our jobs, to consider that, as far as instruction goes . . . to know that things that are going on outside of school are really important and help you be a better teacher.

Additionally, Tara has incorporated the film into her teaching. She has her students do an annual photo essay project. She uses her own film as an example to show her students.

Randi teaches theatre arts and plans to incorporate digital story telling into her teaching. She now has students produce short films of famous mono/dialogues, of their improvisation, or of their live theatre productions.

4.5 Life, Camera, Action

Findings indicate that digital storytelling connected to ethnographic field experiences enhance transformative reflection in teacher education. These components compel teacher candidates to cross borders—socioeconomic, linguistic, racial/ethnic, etc.— in the communities they will serve as PK-12 schoolteachers. In the films, two parties claim a voice. On the one hand, filmmakers articulate their research and reflections through deep digital stories, and on the other the films give informants from these communities a voice before audiences. Most important perhaps, conceptual change around diversity gains momentum early in a teacher candidate's career. These formative experiences, deep engagements, reflections, and border crossings, lead to affirmative actions in their professional practice.

Cook-Sather (2006) discusses how embracing a "paradoxical model leadership" is vital for pre-service teachers. In her study, teachers learn to adapt their pedagogy and advocacy by listening to the concerns and lived experiences of highs school students in their teacher preparation courses. There they contemplate a model of leadership that is neither hierarchical nor centered on the teacher. In a similar way, our findings reveal that new perspectives emerging from the micro-documentary project served to flatten social hierarchies between teachers and students, filmmaker and informant. The reflexive research and emotional intelligence fostered by the micro-documentary project allows for a more equitable power dynamic between students and teachers or teachers and community members.

Also worth noting is an important "side effect" that emerges as a result of film production: increased circulation. Study participants reported an increased circulation of the digital narrative beyond informants with stakeholders, partners, and university audiences for professional development. Given a current context of video sharing, social visual engagement, online training and professional networks, and the like, these micro-documentary films have a significant potential for circulation and impact.

In the end, the entire process becomes an exquisite medium for complex looking, experiencing, thinking, and presenting issues of diversity. More than conventional projects, this presents an opportunity for genuine engagement with diverse communities where assumptions are laid to rest. Taking teacher candidates out of the university classroom and into the field also accomplishes a course goal of encountering diversity, not through second hand accounts, but through authentic community experiences.

These findings support the need for further integration of new forms of digital media in teacher preparation.

References

Calandra, B., Brantley-Dias, L., Lee, J. K., & Fox, D. L. (2009). Using video editing to cultivate novice teachers practice. *Journal of Research on Technology in Education, 42*(1), 73-94.

Calandra, B., Brantley-Dias, L., & Dias, M. (2006). Using digital video for professional development in urban schools: A preservice teacher's experience with reflection. *Journal of Computing in Teacher Education, 22*(4), 125-133.

Cook-Sather, A. (2006). 'Change based on what students say:' Preparing teachers for a paradoxical model of leadership. *International Journal of Leadership in Education, 9*(4), 345-358.

Halstead, N. (2008). Introduction. In N. Halstead, E. Hirsch, & J. Oakley (Eds.), *Knowing how to know: Fieldwork and the ethnographic present* (pp. 1-20). New York: Berghahn Books.

Lowenthal, P. (2009). Digital storytelling in education: An emerging institutional technology? In J. Hartley & K. McWilliam (Eds), *Story circle: Storytelling around the world* (pp. 253-259). Malden, MA: Wiley-Blackwell.

Robinson, H. A. (1994). *The ethnography of empowerment: The transformative power of classroom interaction*. Washington D.C.: The Falmer Press.

Sherin, M. G., & van Es, E. A. (2005).Using video to support teachers' ability to notice classroom interactions. *Journal of Technology and Teacher Education, 13*(3), 475-491.

Wang, J., & Hartley, K. (2003). Video technology as a support for teacher education reform. *Journal of Technology and Teacher Education, 11*(1), 105-138.

Yerrick, R., Ross, D & Molebash, P. (2005). Too close for comfort: Real-time science teaching reflections via digital video editing. *Journal of Science Teacher Education, 16*(4), 351-375.

Mong Thi T. Nguyen

5 The Digital and Story in Digital Storytelling

5.1 Introduction

Advances in technology and software development have made digital storytelling easily accessible via movie editing programs, websites, and apps. These user-friendly programs offer intuitive interfaces and powerful editing tools that can result in simple voice-overs across digital images to cinematic quality short films. These technologies have led many educators to explore the possibilities of digital storytelling to facilitate authentic and meaningful learning experiences. In formal and informal classrooms, digital storytelling has provided opportunities for students to engage in critical literacies such as theorizing research, reexamining institutional practice, (re)positioning individual identities, and sharing life experiences (Benmayor, 2008; DeGennaro, 2010; Goodman, 2003; Rolón-Dow, 2011).

I broadly define digital storytelling as (in its simplest form) the telling and sharing of short stories (3-5 minute) accompanied with recorded sound (such as narration or music) and digital images. The process is comprised of two essential components, the story and the digitalization of the story. Separately considered, the story involves opportunities for reading and writing literacies, and the digitalizing of artifacts involves visual and performative literacies. Together under the guise of digital storytelling, students have opportunities to engage in multiliteracies (Group, 1996) through multimodalities (Bezemer, 2008; Kress, 2001) as they (re)present "multilayered and multichanneled" stories (Coventry, 2008); hence, the written and technological composition of digital storytelling can potentially create literacy learning space(s).

This chapter builds on efforts that centered on how digital storytelling challenges and engages students in language and literacy development. I explore the ways the structure of digital storytelling (both composition and digitalization) provided students with opportunities for Vietnamese heritage language (HL) learning, discussion, awareness, and use. Students (ages 11-14 years old) produced digital stories based on Mercer Mayer's wordless picture book, *Frog, Where Are You?* The stories were written, recorded, and screened in Vietnamese and were screened to grade 1 students (5-7 years old) at a community-based language school. Through this project, I propose that the use of digital storytelling in the language classroom provided students with opportunities to develop and engage with Vietnamese (listening, reading, writing, speaking etc.) in ways that differ from literacy and language practices associated with traditional storytelling.

5.2 Literature Review

The advancement and accessibility of digital media and technology[15] has fostered practitioners' and researchers' investigation of its potential for teaching and learning (Resnick et al., 1998; Roschelle, Pea, Hoadley, Gordin, & Means, 2000; Schwartz, Blair, Biswas, Leelawong, & Davis, 2007). Scholars have also recognized that learning with and through digital tools transcends hardware capabilities (and intended purpose) as users creatively (re)purpose them to meet their needs and express their identities (Goodman, 2003; Soep & Chávez, 2010; Goldman, Booker, & McDermott, 2008). Further, Gee (2005) argued that the appeal and success of technology to engage and sustain interest resulted in making learning enjoyable. Gee proposed that long and complicated video games engaged learners by incorporating good learning principles throughout the game's infrastructure, including: empowering the learner through manipulation and distributed knowledge and scaffolding problem-solving (Gee, 2005). For Gee, instead of moving through the cyclic process of education reforms— recycling the old as new—examining ways students already engage and solve complex issues in their daily lives can provide insight regarding ways to reimagine teaching and learning practice in the classroom. One area in technology that educators have focused on is digital storytelling, specifically how students use, learn from, and communicate through this medium. In the following section I discuss the learning documented from digital storytelling projects and then focus on how the story and digital components are rich environments for language learning.

5.2.1 Digital Storytelling: The Story and the Storyteller

Digital storytelling offers multiple entry points for students to share their voice and to express their identities (Hull, 2003; Alexandra, 2008). As students produced personal and meaningful stories they drew powerful connections between how they understood the world and the world that surrounded them. This can be a starting point for students to think deeply (Sadik, 2008), theorize (Benmayor, 2008; DeGennaro, 2010; Leon, 2008), and engage in critical literacies (Goodman, 2003; Rolón-Dow, 2011). Goodman (2003) defined critical literacies as "the ability to analyze, evaluate, and produce print, aural, and visual forms of communication" (Goodman, 2003, p. 3). As high school students produced documentaries, Goodman argued that reviewing and logging videos allowed students to distance themselves and critically reflect on the content, to subsequently "explore deeper levels of truth and hope" (98). Additionally, Goodman cautioned against the assumption that learning how to produce compelling

---

15 I recognize that these terms are often not use interchangeably, however, I use them together to represent the phenomena of the technological advances that result in digital media and artifacts.

stories with technology equates to developing and producing well-researched arguments (Goodman, 2003). Hence, combining the possibilities of technology with pedagogical considerations can both challenge and support students to move beyond the immediacy of their stories and engage in reflective and critical literacies.

5.2.2 The Story in Storytelling: Writing My Stories

Storytelling encompasses many aspects of everyday life, and can function as a way to share knowledge, connect with others, and build community (Heller, 1997). However, the rules for storytelling can change across contexts and cultures. Norms in one situation may be inappropriate in others, resulting in conflict or misunderstandings (Heath, 1983). Particularly in the language classroom, researchers recognize that explicitly teaching storytelling is just as important as teaching language and linguistics (Essig, 2005; Jones, 2001). Cortazzi and Jin (2007) suggest that the telling and retelling of stories from keywords and story maps can provide (English) language learners with opportunities to recall and reflect on the story and storytelling process (2007). Additionally, in Nicholas, Rossiter, and Abbott's (2011) case study of adult ESL students and instructors, the authors argue that personal storytelling was an effective way to engage students in language practice, learn about the storytelling genre, and contributed to the classroom culture. As elements of storytelling (plot, characters, setting etc.) were repeated and systematically applied to subsequent lessons, students had multiple opportunities to speak, listen, read, and write stories. Personal stories allowed students to "find their own voice in their new language, first by listening to others' stories and then by telling their own" (Nicholas, Rossiter, & Abbott, 2011, p. 254).

Storytelling is not limited to text and speech, but elements of visual and audio performance can enhance the experience for both the narrator and audience. Early and Yeung (2007) explored the potential for language learning through student-produced storybooks in a Canadian French immersion school. Grade 9 students wrote and illustrated a children's book in French, and then developed a script to perform for younger students. The stories allowed students to attend to "certain aspects of the story when deciding how to physically embody the texts through action, gesture, gaze, and stance" (314). The authors argued that the multimodal and multi-stage nature of the project enabled students to practice and learn French. Additionally, the authors reported that students' engagement throughout the project facilitated their attention to language features such as pronunciation, grammar, and language patterns in oral and written modes (Early & Yeung, 2009).

The above studies highlight opportunities for language learning through storytelling. That is, storytelling is more than sharing stories. Rather, as students composed their stories they practiced and attended to their own language development. And, finally, as Early and Yeung (2007) discussed, the multimodal nature of storytelling allowed students to engage with language learning through multiple entry points. In the following section I discuss how digital storytelling, a multimodal genre, can provide students with additional avenues for language learning via its digital capabilities.

5.2.3 The Digital in Digital Storytelling: User Control and Student-Centered

Digital storytelling includes the compositional aspect of traditional storytelling as students write and narrate their stories, however it also includes visual and audio components unique to the digitalization of the story. Similar to traditional storytelling, digital storytelling engages students in language learning as students produce their personal stories, but also provided opportunities for students to choose meaningful digital artifacts (Peng, 2006; Vassilikopoulou, 2011; Vinogradova, 2011), and engage in authentic language learning during the navigation of digital media (Goulah, 2007). Meaning-making opportunities are embedded throughout the digital storytelling process because students are often afforded the opportunity to take ownership of the process through media and medium selection, the production and performance, and for language learners the ability to control their language and literacy experience.

The structure of digital storytelling often included the following: composition, digitalization, and finally the presentation of the stories. Sylvester (2009-2010) contends that this framework can appeal to struggling writers who have difficulty starting the writing process, using proper writing conventions, and including essential details in their writing. Sylvester suggests that prior to the digitalization of the stories, students can create storyboards that highlight omitted details and then diagram the sequencing of the storyline. Additionally, the use of digital visuals and auditory artifacts can also assist students in effectively communicating their stories without the distractions of errors found in writing. In this way, digital storytelling can reposition struggling writers as competent writers (Sylvester, 2009-2010). The digitalization of the stories can also illuminate the non-linearity of composition, as students move back and forth between visual and audio cues in their stories, they are constantly (re)evaluating how each component serves to effectively communicate their stories (Bruce, 2010; Leon, 2008). For language learners and struggling writers the (transparent) iterative process in digital storytelling of negotiating and representing meaning can emphasize the messy and recursive nature of the writing process.

The digitalization of images and audio also allows students to reflect on the content of their work in order to produce a meaningful story, particularly as students view and edit their products. Valkanova and Watts (2007) investigated the use of digital videos, as video diaries, to facilitate seven- to eight-year-olds language and self-reflection. Students produced a 3-minute short film from a lesson on light and shadows (after a forty-five minute lesson), and then produced a voice-over narration to explain what they were thinking and learning. The authors concluded that as students chose video segments and watched themselves, they expressed thoughtful, reflective, and evaluative statements about their science knowledge. Valkanova and Watts also proposed that narrating the stories facilitated students' oral language performance as students explained the events (Valkanova & Watts, 2007). Similarly, Goodman (2003) discussed how the logging processes of movie-making (writing summaries from a video—including details of what students saw and heard) allowed students to step back from the immediacy and familiarity of the situation to critically reflect on its content. In the above studies, the digital component of digital storytelling allowed students to review their videos and (re) consider ways to effectively tell their stories. Although the authors in the above studies do not specifically address language learning, the opportunity for reflection from studying video content to produce stories may transfer into the language classroom as students are immersed in authentic, complex, and meaningful language practice.

Additionally, digital stories include components of audio and visual input that can be controlled by the creator and user—especially multimedia that allow users to interact and manipulate content in their stories. The interactive nature of digital stories allows users control of their own language and literacy learning by navigating and replaying the stories. Verdugo and Belmonte (2007) investigated whether digital stories, selected from an educational website, would be more effective for young Spanish speaking students learning English as Foreign Language (EFL) than traditional text-based lesson plans. Digital stories were catalogued and selected for their interactive nature and emphasis on language skills. Pre- and post-tests revealed that students using digital stories outperformed the control (text-based) group in their listening comprehension. The authors attributed the difference to the nature of digital stories as a means to focus students' attention on oral input and the exposure students had with the language because of the option to play the stories multiple times (Verdugo, 2007). Tsou, Wang, and Tzeng (2006) also explored the language learning potential of a multimedia storytelling website. Students (EFL) composed multimedia stories by choosing backgrounds, still and animated subjects, sound effects and music from pull down menus, and then recorded and typed their stories. Once the stories were completed students could view, replay, and share their stories. Based on story recall (assessing students' understanding of the story by asking students to recall and recreate the story), the authors concluded that students using the multimedia website produced more complex sentences than non-website users. Further, the authors proposed that the audio and visual stimuli influenced students' creative inclusion of details and description in their story recalls (Tsou, Wang, and Tzeng, 2006). In these two studies, the ability to manipulate and control the stories provided additional opportunities for students to engage in language learning. The digital stories were part of an interactive learning environment that allowed students to control the length of time they were exposed to and the experience that they were immersed in the language.

Collectively the above studies suggest that storytelling and the digitalization of stories can create spaces for language learning. That is the digital and the story in digital storytelling separately promoted language learning in complementary and different ways. Together, the digital and the storytelling of digital storytelling offered students multiple opportunities for language and literacy practice. In concert with efforts to explore technology in instructional contexts, I explore how the structure of digital storytelling, including the compositional and digital nature, provided heritage language (HL) learners with opportunities to practice, use, and engage with language.

A unique aspect of HL learning is the cultural, familial, heritage ties that students may have with the language that transcends linguistic development. HL learners may experience and engage with language in ways that different from language learners studying a foreign or second language. I focus on each phase of the digital storytelling process: composition, narration, and performance, and propose that producing digital stories in a HL class provided multiple spaces for students to engage with the language in ways that differ from traditional storytelling.

The research questions guiding this chapter are: In what ways did the process of digital storytelling facilitate students' language learning with regards to the composition and digitalization of the digital story? And what limitations should be considered prior to adopting this approach in a language classroom?

5.3 Context, Participants, and Methodology

Digital storytelling was introduced to students through an in-class group project, *Frog Stories*. Students were then assigned a home project, *My Story*, in which they completed a traditional digital storytelling project about a topic of their choice. The in-class group project required students to produce a children's digital story based on Mercer Mayer's wordless picture book, *Frog, Where Are You?* Students were provided print outs from the Mayer's book and selected[16] images that they wanted to include in their story. This project was completed during students' language learning hour, across seven sessions for the duration of sixty to ninety minutes per session. During this time students composed their Vietnamese stories, practiced and recorded the narrative, designed their stories for production, and prepared for and screened the stories during the film festival. Language resources available to students included: myself (teacher), the teaching assistant (native speaker), bilingual Vietnamese-English dictionaries (one per group), and other adults at the school and in the home. Technological tools included: digital recorders (one per group), and one personal computer to review their edited movies and insert special effects in iMovie.

---

16 Although image selection plays an important role in digital telling it is beyond the scope of this chapter.

As the teacher of record for this class, my instruction was guided by the adopted curriculum, but I also took the liberty provided by the school to supplement lesson plans with outside resources, and incorporated activities such as the digital storytelling projects, poetry, research, films, and music for this project which stemmed from a two-year ethnographic study that focused on the Vietnamese-American experience, the relationship between language learning and identity, and possibilities of transformative education, specifically guided by "What does it mean to be a Vietnamese HL learner?"

Data collected and analyzed for this chapter included both the process and product of producing the digitals stories. Specifically, data included: students' written draft (English and Vietnamese), classroom audio during work days, practice and final digital narrations, reflective journal writings (quick writes) throughout the process, students' evaluation and assessment of the project after the screening, and my field notes. The different sources of data were analyzed individually and coded for themes of language learning, and then compared and contrasted collectively using Glaser and Strauss's constant comparative method to ensure that the "theories" from the analysis were grounded in the data that provided a conceptually dense explanation of themes (Heath & Street, 2008; Merriam, 1998).

5.4 Findings

5.4.1 The Story: Learning Vietnamese

In this section I discuss how composing the stories challenged students to engage with the language beyond literal translations, and therefore provided a space for Vietnamese language learning. The compositional component of digital storytelling naturally lends itself to language and literacy practice as students read, write, and tell their stories. It seems likely, then, that when the students produced their Vietnamese digital stories they would also use and learn Vietnamese. However, analyzing the students' final stories may not reveal nuances of language learning because of the range of knowledge and experience that HL learners have with the language. HL learners often relied on their English fluencies to complete class assignments and may have translated their stories from English to Vietnamese without meaningfully engaging with the language or attending to linguistics and language features. Further examining only the final product would make it difficult to understand the extent of how *using* Vietnamese actually resulted in *learning* Vietnamese. Rather, through the analysis of the process of making and screening the digital stories, students demonstrated their Vietnamese learning as expressed in their compositions, use of vocabulary, and in their discussions.

The class project required that students produce a final children's digital story in Vietnamese based on Mercer Mayer's *Frog, Where Are You?* In groups of three to four, students wrote stories that featured the boy's (main character) search for his frog, describing the characters, setting, plot, and resolution in Vietnamese. Students were free to use resources (bilingual dictionaries, two teachers, and numerous fluent Vietnamese speakers at the school and home) to compose their stories.

In addition to their group project, students also produced an individual "frog" story during their midterm exam. Under assessment conditions students did not have access to any of the above resources and were asked to write a short narrative based on four images from Mayer's book. The images were selected for two reasons, first because they were the most popular images in students' stories so it was assumed students would be familiar with the details and vocabulary, and because they followed a logical sequence and would allow students to produce a story during their exam. The images included: the frog escaping, the boy getting chased by bees, the boy falling down a cliff, and the boy in pond.

Table 5.1: Student responses to frog stories exam by language use

Language on Test	Count of Students	Written Exam Examples
Vietnamese	9	O: Một hôm, khi em đi <u>ngũ</u>, con <u>ếch</u> của em <u>dảy cửa</u> sổ vả đi mất tiêu …
		C: *Một hôm, khi em đi <u>ngủ</u>, con <u>ếch</u> của em <u>nhảy ra cửa</u> sổ và đi mất tiêu …*
		T: One day, while I was asleep, my frog jumped out the window and went away …
Vietnamese and English	3	O: Một ngày con ếch đi ra phòng của Billy. Billy <u>woke up</u>, Billy <u>nổi</u>…
		C: *Một ngày con ếch đi ra phòng của Billy. <u>Khi</u> Billy <u>dậy</u>, Billy <u>nói</u> …*
		T: One day the frog left Billy's room. When Billy woke up, Billy said …
English	4	O: There was once a boy who had a frog. One night when the boy was sleeping the frog got out of the jar.

Key: O – student's original; C – teacher corrected; T – translated ; <u>Underline</u> – Error

Twelve students used Vietnamese to write their stories, and four students used only English (Table 5.1). Of the twelve students who used Vietnamese, nine stories were written entirely in Vietnamese and three were written bilingually, using both Vietnamese and English. The Vietnamese-only stories were fairly complex in vocabulary used and details addressed because students incorporated details, events, and plots that went beyond the four pictures in order to compose a comprehensive story. Despite spelling errors, in general, the stories were easy to follow and were quite fluid to read. The Vietnamese-only example in Table 5.1 included details of what the character was doing when the frog left ("while I was asleep"), how the frog left "frog jumped out the window", and where the frog went ("and went away"). The Vietnamese-English stories substituted English for Vietnamese words that students could not recall during the exam or did not know. For example Table 1.1 shows that one student wrote, "woke up" in place of "*dậy*", when she described what her character (Billy) was going to do. And, finally, English-only stories were just that, stories written in English. However, one of the English-only students did substitute "*ếch*" in the place of "frog" throughout his story. The English-only students did not indicate why they wrote their stories in English rather than Vietnamese. However, these three students were very resistant to using Vietnamese in other class assignments and activities and often completed their work in English, despite encouragement to use Vietnamese. The analysis of the exams revealed that several students were able to compose a Vietnamese story without the aid of a bilingual dictionary, showcasing that Vietnamese language learning was possible through digital storytelling.

Excerpt 1:

Draft 1:	The boy goes to the forest to start his trip.
Draft 2:	*Cậu bé vào rừng để bắt <u>Dậu</u> chuyến của mình.*
Translation:	The boy goes into the forest to start his **trip**.
Draft 3:	*Cậu bé vào rừng để bắt đầu chuyến của mình*
Translation:	The boy goes into the forest to start his **trip**.
Draft 4:	*Cậu bé vào rừng để bắt đầu cuộc mạo hiểm của mình.*
Translation:	The boy goes into the forest to start his **dangerous adventure**.

Key: <u>Underline: Error</u>; **Bold: Revision changes**

Students also demonstrated their Vietnamese knowledge during the making of digital stories as represented in the revisions of their scripts. Students experimented with the Vietnamese language, expanding their own Vietnamese vocabulary by incorporating words that are less commonly used in daily conversations, and using words that more accurately capture elements in their stories. For example, uncommon words included *nhanh chóng*–quickly, instead of *nhanh*—fast, and *tuần lộc*—reindeer, instead of *nai*—deer. Multiple revisions also helped students write more concisely. In Excerpt 1, students used *chuyến* for "trip", which is a correct and literal translation of their character's plans to take a trip in search of his missing frog. However, after three revisions students settled on *cuộc mạo hiểm*, which translates to a dangerous adventure. Switching from "trip" to "adventure" changes how the audience understands the boy's plans and sets the tone for the type of trip he is embarking on. In this case, instead of going on a "casual" trip the boy is now going on an exciting and "dangerous adventure" to find his missing frog. By writing and rewriting their stories students used (and learned new) Vietnamese words that more accurately reflected the sentiment of their story. The multiple revisions resulted in students' engagement with Vietnamese beyond conversational language and allowed students to express their complex ideas in Vietnamese.

Excerpt 2:

Cindy: No it's just *kể chuyện,* not *người kể*
Translation: *tell story   person who tells*

Thuy: Narrator is a person when there is an "or" means a person,

we need a *người* for mean person
Translation: *person*

kể chuyện is tell story, this one is a person
Translation: *tell story*

Key: *Italics: Vietnamese English translation*

Writing the stories in groups allowed students to teach and learn Vietnamese from each other. Students who were more fluent and proficient in Vietnamese often provided insight to their peers about Vietnamese language features, such as spelling, pronunciation, and word order. Excerpt 2 is an example of one group's discussion about nouns and verbs in the Vietnamese language. The students in this group were in the process of writing their script and wanted to indicate the narrator's lines in the script. Cindy begins by stating that narrator should be *kể chuyện* not *người kể*. Her adamant proposal to use *kể chuyện* instead of *người kể* could have resulted from using a Vietnamese-English bilingual dictionary to translate "narrator" without recognizing that the dictionary translated both "narrator" and "to narrate" with the same word, *kể chuyện*. Thuy however, recognizes that because the narrator is a person, *người* (literally means person) would need to be placed before *kể chuyện*. By including *người* she is differentiating between the noun and verb forms of narrate in Vietnamese, and because the group intended to write narrator, the person telling the story, *người kể chuyện* is the most appropriate choice. In this case, Thuy challenges Cindy to move beyond the literal translation and consider the context of what they wanted to convey, a Vietnamese word for a storyteller. Ultimately, students agreed to use *người kể chuyện* for narrator, and then later confirmed it by asking me. Excerpt 2 illustrates how writing stories in groups facilitated discussion about the Vietnamese language and ultimately the opportunity to teach and learn from one another.

In the above section I discussed how composing Vietnamese stories resulted HL learning and use. Specifically, I focused on how the compositional process led to opportunities for students explore and engage with the language beyond literal translations. Composing the stories created spaces for students to consider alternative ways to express their complex ideas and considering the unique language and linguistic structures of the HL. In the next section I examine language learning opportunities available through the digitalization of the digital storytelling process, attending to spaces that are not readily available during the composition phase.

5.4.2 The Digital and Performance: Assessment and Sharing

The structure of digital storytelling involves telling a story via text, voice, images, and music—all presented in a short film. After students completed their written script they recorded and screened their stories. Although much has been written about the learning possibilities from having students navigate and use technology (Goodman, 2003; Goulan, 2007), in this project students did not make their digital stories on a computer because the class only had access to one computer, my personal computer. However, students did record their narration via a digital recorder, wrote notes in English along the margins of their script regarding how they wanted their films to be edited including: pacing, transitions, sound effects, title, placement of subtitles, etc., and reviewed the movie for any changes before it was screened during the film festival. Each group was given a digital recorder and sent to the playground to record their narrative. It was up to each group to determine what was worthy of their final recording. In this section, I focus on the ways that digitally recording narratives facilitated students' language assessment (their own and their peers). In particular, I discuss how the digital recordings encouraged language practice, language feedback, and repositioned students as competent Vietnamese speakers.

Unique to digital storytelling is the ability to pre-record multiple "final" recordings, providing speaking practice. Instead of just practicing for one live performance or final presentation, students can practice and record as many final (live) recordings as they feel is necessary to produce a polished narrative. The number of practice recordings ranged from four to twenty-four times (of which fifteen were practice final recordings and nine were "final" final recordings—as indicated by students). Students' criteria for keeping or re-recording their narratives included: performance (timing, fluidity of narration—forgetting lines, messing up), fluency (pronunciation), or professionalism (giggling, side conversations, background noise).

Excerpt 3:

Katie:	cám ơn gia đình ếch nhỏ. Cám ơn cho con Trực
Translation:	Thank you little frog's family, thank you for giving me Truc (the frog)

	Cho con –em, it's em,	I forgot, sorry
Translation:	Giving me—me, it's me,	
Van:	so it's *em*	
Translation:	me	
Katie:	cause it is not *con*	
Translation:	me	

A characteristic typical of some HL learners is their strong receptive and oral language abilities and therefore their ability to recognize errors in spoken Vietnamese. The multiple opportunities to practice Vietnamese via a digital recorder allowed students to receive self and peer feedback about their spoken Vietnamese during the live recordings and in playback mode. As students performed their live recordings they corrected each other's Vietnamese in real time, or during the playback. For example, in Excerpt 3 as Katie performed her script she self corrects when she uses *con* to indicate "me." The Vietnamese language includes a self-reference system in which the addressor and addressee are designated with social identifiers that are expressed with different self-referential terms. In this instance the use of *con* for "me" does not align with the character's social position in the story because the boy is talking to the frog family and wouldn't refer to himself as their child. Rather an appropriate word for "me" would be, *em*, which she recognizes and changes. Further, Katie confirms that she is aware of the changes when Van asks for clarification. The live recordings facilitated Katie's awareness of the discrepancies between the context and pronouns in her story by allowing Katie to assess her own Vietnamese. It is important to note that Katie did not recognize this discrepancy until after three practice rounds. Practicing multiple times does not ensure that students will notice all of their errors, however each additional recording can potentially attune students to different aspects of language use, and therefore be a source for language learning.

Students then submitted an audio track of their final narrative to be incorporated into their films. I placed the images that students selected according to their script, added sound effects, inserted final audio recordings, and timed the sequence according to students' editing notes in iMovie. Each group previewed a preliminary version during the following week and additional changes were added to the final version. After viewing the final version of their narrative during the review and film festival, several students were pleasantly surprised by their Vietnamese use and fluency. I differentiate between use and fluency because for some students speaking Vietnamese was already an accomplishment (use), and for others it was how fluently they spoke Vietnamese. For students, the multiple recordings and final presentation allowed them access their language development and positioned themselves as Vietnamese speakers and learners.

First, several students stated that it was "fun" to see (and hear) the stories that other students produced and it was nice to hear other students speak Vietnamese in the class. Students were also surprised by the ease and fluencies of their classmates' narration. Screening the movie served to reinforce that the class was a community of Vietnamese speakers, and that the school was a space that encouraged the use of Vietnamese.

Excerpt 4:

> Katie: "Today, I heard myself in Vietnamese I felt so out of place, because when I hear others read it, they sound so fluent, and I sounded uneven. I never heard myself, and I sounded more different then I usually am. I think overall I did a pretty decent job, but I will need to practice it, until I start sound[ing] like my parents."

Second, students were surprised by their own Vietnamese fluency, with reactions ranging from being happy to critical. In Excerpt 4 Katie wrote that listening to herself speak Vietnamese made her aware of her language development because she had not "heard [herself] in Vietnamese." Although she thought she "did a pretty decent job," she also acknowledged that she would need to practice more to sound like her parents and her fluent peers. Katie was critical of her Vietnamese even though she is one of the most proficient and fluent Vietnamese speakers and writers in the class. By her standards she still needed to practice more to reach her goals of speaking like her parents. For Katie, listening to her recordings allowed her to reflect on her position as a Vietnamese speaker and learner, and also articulate her personal goals for Vietnamese learning.

The students use of the digital recorder to narrate the digital stories provided another space to practice oral language and reflect on their positions as heritage language speakers and learners. Digitally pre-recording the performance allowed students to use Vietnamese under performance-like conditions without the pressure of it being the final (and only) performance. Practicing their scripts multiple times allowed students to assess and provide feedback to one another regarding their Vietnamese fluency by listening and reflecting on their Vietnamese language development; hence, positioning themselves as speakers and language learners. By listening to their narrations, students were giving the opportunity to self and peer assess their Vietnamese language development.

5.4.3 Digital Storytelling Considerations for the Language Classroom

The above findings suggest that digital storytelling, both the compositional and digital components, can provide students with different and multiple spaces for language learning. As students write their stories, produce, record, and screen their films, they take ownership for their own and their peers' Vietnamese language learning. Instead of having only one teacher in the classroom, students' experience and familiarity with the language (as heritage language learners) resulted in a room full of language teachers.

Digital storytelling can be appealing to both teachers and students as students become engaged in producing stories, and teachers can tailor the project for specific content learning. Despite the enthusiasm for digital storytelling, it is also important to acknowledge the ways in which this tool may limit or hinder language learning opportunities. In this section I present two incidences that illustrate how providing students with (complete) ownership of their language learning also resulted in missed opportunities for language instruction.

Students were given the freedom to creatively compose their children's story. On the one hand, this allowed students to take ownership of the language learning available through digital storytelling; on the other hand, it also resulted in missed opportunities. In the follow section, I discuss challenges that teachers should consider as they incorporate digital storytelling in their language classrooms.

5.4.4 Missed Opportunities for Language Learning

Excerpt 5:

Original English script:	tip toe	
Students' translated Vietnamese script:	*đầu ngón chân*	*tiếng ồn*
Translation:	the tip of toe	sound
Appropriate Vietnamese translation:	*đi*	*nhẹn nhàng*
	walk	softly

The first consideration I address is supporting students' understanding of the difference between translating words and translating ideas during composition. The majority of students initially wrote their stories in English and so relied on their Vietnamese knowledge, bilingual dictionaries, and Vietnamese speakers (teachers) to translate it into Vietnamese. Although there were two teachers in the classroom (myself and the teaching assistant) students seldom asked for assistance, rather choosing to complete the assignment in groups and with the use of dictionaries. In Excerpt 5, students literally translated "tip toe" to "the tip of toe," as *đầu ngón chân*, instead of translating the idea of tip-toe, that is to walk softly, which is *đi nhẹn nhàng* and would be the appropriate translation. Literal translations may be sufficient for some word-to-word translation, but often times translating words across languages and cultures requires the consideration of context. In general, most translations require students to first define the meaning (idea and context) and then translate the idea between languages in order to stay faithful to the original idea. Literally translating an idea can result in awkward, inappropriate, and often incorrect expressions of the idea between languages. In this situation, a class discussion about the limitations of literal translations, and the need to define ideas and context before translating would be helpful for students. Further, once students recognize the limitations of literal translations they can better attend to telling their stories in the target language by focusing on their message (thinking like the target speaker) rather than as a translation, and engage with the language in ways that facilitate language development. Although this incident is about dictionaries and translations, it highlights the need to supplement digital storytelling projects with discussion about language learning strategies.

Excerpt 6:

Practice: *"và **kê** cậu về nhà cậu sẽ kể **nũng** điều tốt đẹp cho những người **ban** của của **con**."*

Student Correction: *và **khi** cậu về nhà cậu sẽ kể **những** điều tốt đẹp cho những người **bạn** của **cậu**.*

Final Recording: *"và ky cáu về nhà cậu sẽ kỹ nững điều tốt đẹp cho những bạn của cau.*

Translation: "and when the boy went home he will tell his friends a wonderful story.

Key: **bold** = errors in during practice; underlined = errors in final; **bold underlined** = same errors

A second challenge to consider is maximizing students' language practice through multiple digital recordings. Specifically, helping students more accurately gauge their oral language so they can better use the practice opportunities available with multiple digital recordings. As I proposed earlier in this paper, digitally recording the narratives allowed students multiple opportunities to practice and get feedback about their oral language. Ideally, this would result in practicing to speak like a native speaker. This is especially important for the Vietnamese language because it is a tonal language, where any inflection can change the tone and subsequently the meaning of the word. Further, incorrect use of tones can make a sentence (spoken and written) unintelligible. Even though students often corrected each other, there were times when they did not, without corrective feedback students continued to make the same error. Excerpt 6 shows the repercussions of not getting corrective feedback during practice recordings. Between the practice and final recordings, this student made the same three errors, *khi, những,* and *cậu*. Without any corrective feedback on her oral language, this student continued to make the same errors. In this instance, it was a missed opportunity to inform, discuss, and practice the Vietnamese language, in ways that would attune students to the linguistic features of the Vietnamese language.

The considerations that I presented in this section are a few of several missed teaching moments during the digital storytelling project. I discuss these two examples in particular because they highlight the importance of using effective language teaching pedagogy alongside a student-centered project like digital storytelling to create a rich language-learning environment for students. Ideally, as the teacher in this class, I would monitor students' language output (written and oral), and address these issues as they arise. However, this would be nearly impossible to do (both to notice all of these teachable moments and then to address them in sufficient detail) in a full classroom. Additionally, attempting to micro-manage the project would not allow students the freedom to explore and experiment with the language in authentic ways. Ultimately, digital storytelling is one of many tools that can facilitate language learning and using it alongside effective teaching practice can provide students with multiple opportunities for language engagement.

5.5 Conclusion and Discussion

In this paper, I investigated the use of digital storytelling in a community-based heritage language class to facilitate language and literacy learning. I specifically explored how the structure of digital storytelling, both the storytelling and the digital components provided multiple spaces for heritage language learning. I argue that as the students composed their stories and produced digital artifacts for their digital storytelling projects they had opportunities to learn language by practicing, assessing, and reflecting on their language development. Further, I discussed pedagogical considerations of the story and digital components of digital storytelling in order to emphasize that tools (such as digital storytelling) alongside effective language teaching practice can produce a rich language-learning environment for students. The storytelling and digital in the digital storytelling project offered students multiple ways to learn and engage with their HL.

The most important experience of this project for students was not producing the digital storytelling project, but rather the personal and deeper connections students developed with the language through the digital storytelling process. Or, as one of the students, Thomas, stated, he learned the most Vietnamese in this class from the "frog stories", because he had to "use it (Vietnamese) the whole way."

References

Alexandra, D. (2008). Digital storytelling as transformative practice: Critical analysis and creative expression in the representation of migration in Ireland. *Journal of Media Practice, 9*(2), 101-112.

Benmayor, R. (2008). Digital storytellng as a signature pedagogy for the new humanities. *Arts and Humanities in Higher Education, 7*(2), 188-204.

Bezemer, J., & Kress, G. (2008). Writing in Multimodal Texts: A Social Semiotic Account of Designs for Learning. *Written Communication, 25*(2), 166-195. doi: 10.1177/0741088307313177

Bruce, D. L. (2010). Composing with DV in English language arts teacher education. *English Teaching; Practice and Critique, 9*(1), 14-124.

Cortazzi, M., & Jin, L. (2007). Narrative learning, EAL and metacognitive development. *Early Child Development and Care, 177*(6&7), 645-660.

Coventry, M. (2008). Engaging gender: Application of theory thorugh digital storytelling. *Arts and Humanities in Higher Education, 7*(2), 205-219.

DeGennaro, D. (2010). Grounded theory: Immersing preservice teachers in technology-mediated learning. *Contemporary Issues in Technology and Teacher Education, 10*(3), 338-359.

Early, M., & Yeung, C. (2009). Producing multimodal picture books and dramatic perforances in a core French classroom: An exploratory case study. *The Canadian Modern Language, 66*(2), 299-322.

Essig, W. (2005). Storytelling: Effects of planning, repetition, and context. In C. Edwards & J. Willis (Ed.), *Teachers exploring tasks in English language teaching.* (pp. 201-213). New York: Palgrave Macmillian.

Gee, J. P. (2005). Learning by design: Good video games as learning machines. *E-Learning, 2*(1), 5-16.

Goldman, S., Booker, A. N., & McDermott, M. (Eds.). (2008). *Mixing the digital, social, and cultural: Learning, identity, and agency in youth participation.* Cambridge, MA: The MIT Press.

Goodman, S. (2003). *Teaching youth media: A critical guide to literacy, video production, and social change.* New York: Teachers College Press.

Goulah, J. (2007). Village voices, global visions: Digital video as transformative foreign language learning tool. *Foreign Language Annals, 40*(1), 62-78.

Group, N. L. (1996). Pedagogy of multiliteracies: Designing social futures. *Harvard Educational Review, 66*(1), 60-92.

Heath, S. B. (1983). *Ways with words: Language, life, and work in communities and classrooms.* Cambridge: Cambridge University Press.

Heath, S. B., & Street, B. V. (2008). *On ethnography: Approaches to language and literacy research.* New York: Teacher College Press.

Heller, C. E. (1997). *Until we are strong together: Women writers in the Tenderloin.* New York: Teachers College Press.

Hull, G. A. (2003). At last: Youth culture and digital media: New literacies for new times. *Research in the Teaching of English, 38*(2), 229-233.

Jones, R. E. (2001). A consciousness-raising approach to the teaching of conversational storytelling skills. *ELT Journal, 55*(2), 155-163.

Kress, G., Jewitt, C., Ogborn, J., & Tsatsarelis, C. (2001). *Multimodal teaching and learning.* New York: Continuum

Leon, S. M. (2008). Slowing down, talking back, and moving forward: Some reflections on digital storytelling in the humanities curriculum. *Arts and Humanities in Higher Education, 7*(2), 220-223.

Merriam, S. B. (1998). *Qualitative research and case study applications in education.* San Francisco, CA: Jossey-Bass.

Nicholas, B. J., Rossiter, M. J., & Abbott, M. L. (2011). The power of story the ESL classroom. *The Canadian Modern Language Review, 67*(2), 247-268.

Peng, H., Fitzgerald, G., & Park, M. K. (2006). Producing multimedia stories with ESL children: A partnership approach. *Journal of Educational Multimedia and Hypermedia, 15*(3), 261-284.

Resnick, M., Martin, F., Berg, R., Borovov, R., Colella, V., Kramer, K., & Silverman, B. (1998). Digital manipulatives: New toys to think with. *CHI, 98*, 18-23.

Rolón-Dow, R. (2011). Race(ing) stories: Digital storytelling as a tool for critical race scholarship. *Race Ethnicity and Education, 14*(2), 159-173.

Roschelle, J. M., Pea, R. D., Hoadley, C. M., Gordin, D. N., & Means, B. M. (2000). Changing how and what children learn in school with computer-based technologies. *The Future of Children, 10*(2), 76-101.

Sadik, A. (2008). Digital storytelling: A meaningful technology integrated-approach for engaged student learning. *Education Technology Research and Development, 56*, 487-506.

Schwartz, R. L., Blair, K. P., Biswas, G., Leelawong, K., & Davis, J. (Eds.). (2007). *Animatins of thought: Interactivity in the teacheable agents paradigm.* Cambridge, UK: Cambridge University Press.

Soep, E., & Chávez, V. (2010). *Drop that knowledge: Youth radio stories.* Berkeley, CA: University of California Press.

Sylvester, R., & Greenidge, W-I. (2009-2010). Digital storyteling: Extending the potential for struggling writers. *The Reading Teacher, 63*(4), 284-295.

Tsou, W., Wang, W., & Tzeng, Y. (2006). Applying a multimedia storytelling website in foreign language learning. *Computers & Education, 47*, 17-28.

Valkanova, Y., & Watts, M. (2007). Digital storytelling in a science classroom: Reflective self-learning (RSL) in action. *Early Child Development and Care, 177*(6&7), 793-807.

Vassilikopoulou, M., Retalis, S., Nezi, M., & Boloudais, M. (2011). Pilot use of digital educational comics in language teaching. *Educational Media International, 48*(2), 115-126.

Verdugo, D. R., & Belmonte, I. A. (2007). Using digital stories to improve listening comprehension with Spanish young learners of English. *Language Learning & Technology, 11*(1), 87-101.

Vinogradova, P., Linville, H. A., & Bickel, B. (2011). "Listen to my story and you will know me": Digital stories as student-centered collaborative projects. *TESOL Journal, 2*(2), 173-202.

Christine Fairless

6 Exploring Social Issues Using Mobile Social Media: Dynamic Teaching and Learning Opportunities to Support Students Transitioning from Middle to High School

6.1 Introduction

The move from middle school to high school is a key moment in the lives of American young people and, as an 8th grade Math/Science teacher with 15 years of experience, I have seen young people grapple with fears and anxieties about this border crossing. While facing issues such as more demanding academics, peer pressure, drugs, sexuality, and body image are often rites of passage, grappling with these topics can also interfere with academic progress and overall wellbeing. Though there are many reliable resources available, such as TeensHealth (n.d.), young people mostly turn to their peers for advice and information, which may or may not be accurate. Furthermore, sometimes questions are withheld because they are perceived to be embarrassing or trivial. As a result, transitioning teens—crossing academic, cultural, and physical borders that distinguish middle and high school experiences—often make ill-informed decisions based on incomplete and/or incorrect information, despite the seeming availability and accessibility of trustworthy sources. This chapter is about iveBeenThere, an app designed to help teens through critical crossings by providing access to accurate information through digital stories, while respecting their need for peer knowledge.

This chapter focuses on the design of a digital storytelling app and describes why I made specific design decisions. These decisions were rooted in my experiences as a math and science educator working with young people. While students are required to learn the disciplines, they are also required to learn how to navigate social, cultural, and historical worlds. This plays out most acutely in their processes of social and emotional development. My students preparing for the transition to high school were anticipating and experiencing the real challenges that accompany change. As I worked with this pattern alongside my students, I created and implemented a class called Issues and Choices, which provided a safe space for 8th graders to learn about and discuss relevant social issues. iveBeenThere was developed in part as a result of my experiences teaching this class. Weekly classes provided students accurate information about a variety of issues and allowed them to talk openly with their peers about topics not typically covered in school such as race, self injury, and peer pressure. While feedback about the class was positive, I felt more could and should be done to create more effective classes like this in my and other schools.

I also wanted to find a way to reach young people who did not have access to this kind of class in school. There are programs available such as the app Destructive Issues and the website teenfaze.com. While both have positive aspects such as easy navigation and the use of video to engage the user, I felt that neither specifically addressed the student transitioning into high school and the kinds of border crossing they negotiate. iveBeenThere (n.d.)— my master's project for Stanford University's Learning, Design, and Technology program—was designed to not only allow for classes similar to mine to be more effective but also to create access to accurate information in a compelling format for students without classes like these in school. As an experienced educator who has worked throughout my career to bridge scholarship and practice, storytelling has been a critical resource for the task. Digital stories that convey iveBeenThere's content are intended to facilitate students' access to content outside of school in addition to classroom use.

The goal is also to incorporate it into already existing social, emotional and high school transition programs in as many schools as possible nationwide, while ensuring it contains content relevant to all students and not just those dealing with severe negative issues. Within schools, teachers can use the digital stories as discussion starters for sensitive topics, effectively allowing them to invite credible virtual guest teachers into their classrooms (and therefore allowing them to avoid initiating difficult conversations themselves). In so doing, iveBeenThere helps students cross the border from middle to high school, a transition that can be particularly difficult. The digital stories create a forum for students to consider multiple views, identify with mentor role models, and evaluate accurate information in a safe space. Additionally, students can access the videos outside of class any time as needed with confidence that they are getting accurate information and without fear of judgment by their peers, thereby problematizing the in-school/out-of-school dichotomy.

6.1.1 Classroom-Based Challenges to Supporting Students Transitioning to High School

Students leaving 8th grade to enter high school often do so with mixed feelings. On the one hand, they are excited to have more choices and freedom, make new friends, and become more mature. On the other hand, students are often fearful and anxious about the unknown, concerned about the challenge of more demanding academics, worried about peer pressure, and intimidated at the prospect of being the youngest on campus. In addition to school-based concerns, many transitioning teens will face new social concerns such as drugs and alcohol, body image and sexuality for the first time. Consequently, it is not surprising to find out that 9th grade is the grade with the highest dropout rate, a loss of 10.5% in 2005 (National High School Center, 2007).

At the same time this transition to high school is occurring, children typically start turning away from adults as their main source of support. Somewhere around the beginning of adolescence, peers replace adults as the primary influencers in most young teens' lives. While a natural occurrence, this shift could potentially have detrimental consequences as young teens go to their peers for information or advice about social issues (Harris, 1995). In light of the declining power of adult influence, even the best-intentioned school program could lose some of its effectiveness. When it comes to social issues, most teachers do not carry as much impact as older peers, who have more recently gone through what the transitioning students are experiencing.

Declining effectiveness notwithstanding, many schools do provide transition programs for eighth and ninth graders; however, these programs typically focus on only the academic transition. While this serves a good purpose, failing to address social concerns as well can result in decreased academic achievement and an increase in problem behavior (Smith, 2006), again highlighting the complexity of this systemic and social border crossing. In Smith's (2006) report for the National Middle School Association, students were aware that time management, ability to stay on task, social skills, and positive classroom behavior are essential to high school success, but many students noted that social matters and peer relationships overshadowed academic concerns, especially in the ninth grade.

An ideal comprehensive social emotional learning (SEL) program, together with a transition program would address both school-based and social concerns. The challenge is that it is difficult to implement a SEL program properly. Extensive teacher training and teacher buy-in are crucial to ensure the program is executed effectively. Poor execution of a social emotional learning program can have negative effects. Teachers need to be thoroughly comfortable with and conversant in the subject matter at hand in order for students to perceive them as credible. They must be vigilant about students treating the class with the level of seriousness it requires. One inappropriate comment that is not addressed by the teacher sends a message to the whole class and can seriously undermine overall program effectiveness. In addition, especially at the high school level, the school day is already filled with required classes, and it can be a hard sell to add something else to the academic load (Zins & Elias, 2006).

6.2 Learning Opportunities Afforded by iveBeenThere

The digital stories in iveBeenThere are accessible through the internet (n.d.) and a mobile application. The use of the mobile platform videos provided by older teen mentors provides a variety of learning opportunities, all of which are grounded in learning, design, and developmental theory. The mobile platform allows users to expand their learning beyond the classroom's four walls with access to the videos anytime and anywhere, particularly in 'safe' places free from judgmental or questioning classmates. Older teen mentors offer multiple perspectives on given topics, facilitating identity formation as users listen to their personal anecdotes. The potential for users eventually to become mentors by submitting their own digital stories provides a dynamic learning exchange as young people reflect on their own experiences and contribute to the lives of others.

With mobile technology, access to information, advice and resources are not dependent on time or place (Lai et al., 2007). A young teen can find answers to questions without being constrained by the school day or being able to find a reliable person and schedule an appointment. This immediate, on-demand access to information is especially important when dealing with potentially sensitive topics such as eating disorders, drug abuse, or self injury, and is especially valuable given teens' tendency toward impulsive actions. Beyond providing a resource for first-order self-help, iveBeenThere provides resources for peers supporting friends in crisis. For example, a teen with a friend in danger of harming himself can use the app to find help and information.

The variety of mentors with multiple perspectives allows for identity formation opportunities that would not be possible in a classroom with one teacher delivering the content. The addition of video to the mobile platform further adds to the expanded learning opportunities: "A signature quality of video is that it can help people see things they could not see before" (Schwartz & Hartman, 2007, p. 337). For example, a mentor might talk about the social status that being a designated driver at high school parties affords. The user may have never considered this as an option but now can begin to identify with this possible strategy for being a person who avoids drinking or doing drugs, yet is still socially accepted. Moreover, presenting a virtual community of diverse mentors may supplement limited in-person peer learning opportunities in homogeneous communities. Through listening to the personal experiences of older teens, users can project themselves into the future, already crossing that border that separates middle and high school and seeing themselves taking similar actions, which influences identity development.

To expand the dynamic nature of iveBeenThere, it was designed for young people to submit their own digital stories. Bringing the process full circle provides opportunities for students to reflect on their own experiences and to contribute to the lives of others. This feature embodies Lave and Wenger's (1991) theory of Legitimate Peripheral Participation (LPP), the process by which newcomers enter a community of practice (in this example, high school students) and become experienced members. Newcomers observe 'old timers,' and learn the roles, tasks, vocabulary, and organization of the community before they are even really a part of it. Users can learn about the academic and social culture of high school by selecting digital stories from a variety of mentors describing their experiences and offering perspectives and advice. LPP is a cyclical process, whereby newcomers work towards becoming active members of the community of practice, eventually becoming the 'old timers' themselves. Digital stories, both their content and reflective processes for producing them, make a low barrier to entry into new communities of practice while supporting movement toward full participation at a time when the complexities of border crossing can leave young people isolated and excluded.

6.3 How iveBeenThere Works

When users open the app, they see thumbnail images of the mentors. They can access digital stories by either selecting a mentor to see all videos from that mentor or by browsing by topic from a tab at the bottom of the screen.

There are two ways that digital stories are added to the site. The first is to have the site manager film interviews with mentors. The second is for mentors or other users to submit their self-made digital stories to the site. Before being uploaded to the site, all submitted videos are approved by the site manager.

As the designer and current site manager, I have personally uploaded most of the digital stories on the site. I reached out to former students in the age range of eighteen to twenty to see if they would be interested in contributing to the site by sharing their high school experiences and offering advice to students transitioning to high school. Then, I filmed interviews in which I asked questions related to common relevant social issues such as sexuality, race, peer pressure, etc. I edited the interviews to short digital stories that were then added to the site.

A few digital stories on the site were filmed by a mentor using a webcam. These videos were then uploaded to the site after my approval. This is a developing project, and the long-term goal is that digital stories will increasingly be added in this way as more users access the site and choose to share advice or personal experiences as contributions to the greater set of digital stories which make up iveBeenThere.

6.4 Feedback about iveBeenThere

Initial feedback about iveBeenThere has been positive. I collected feedback as I was creating the videos and putting together the site for my capstone master's project. I surveyed forty 8th graders after they watched the videos asking questions related to overall effectiveness: Did they learn anything by watching the videos? Would they watch more videos if given the opportunity? Most users expressed that iveBeenThere would be useful in alleviating high school social concerns. Here are a couple quotes highlighting reported learning from two students:

> The biggest things that you can learn from these videos is [sic] that you're not alone, and they really show you that people have the same experiences that may seem scary, and like you're isolated and nobody else has them, but really it's common, and there's a lot of ways to get help with it.

> I learned a lot about how different people deal with different experiences, for example peer pressure, how some people, they [sic] can succumb to it, and some people try and help their friends overcome it, and other people are not as affected by it.

The mentors themselves reported that the experience of sharing advice, reflections and personal stories related to high school was positive for them, even cathartic. They were thankful for the opportunity to support those going through the transition to high school.

6.5 iveBeenThere in Practice

At my school, an independent K-8 school in Oakland, iveBeenThere videos are used as part of our social emotional program. For example, videos about race have been shown to 8th graders as an entry point into potentially challenging conversations. It is developmentally appropriate for students this age to engage in conversations about race that include joking about race. It is often difficult for students to see that these jokes can be hurtful, and they are not always open to the opinions of their teachers on this particular topic. Older peers sharing their thoughts on this topic offer instant credibility. In the videos, a variety of mentors share that even though they might laugh at jokes about race, these jokes are often hurtful and not funny. A critical goal for sharing these digital stories is that students watching them who feel the same as the mentors in the videos will know they are not alone in their thoughts and feelings. Likewise, hopefully, students who are telling jokes about race will learn persuasive reasons to stop and alternatives for engaging in conversations exploring race in our society.

6.6 Conclusion

Even with the expanded and dynamic learning opportunities afforded by the combination of mentors and video on a mobile platform, additional information is needed to gauge the potential effectiveness of using iveBeenThere to address social issues in schools and in daily life. Initial learning studies have shown positive results, but in a relatively small scope. Is it possible for schools to embrace this type of social media as a way to address sensitive topics that are easily set aside for more traditional subjects? Are there enough teachers passionate enough to fight for this type of learning in schools? Can iveBeenThere gain enough traction to side step schools altogether and reach transitioning teens, especially the ones who really need accurate information and the knowledge that they are not alone in their experiences? I don't know the answers to these questions yet, but I believe that iveBeenThere has the potential to validate and empower young people in their transition to high school in making educated, healthy, and safe choices in their lives. At the heart of this potential is iveBeenThere's seeming ability to bridge gaps that exist between middle school and high school, middle schoolers and high schoolers, and the classroom and out-of-class learning. In my opinion, the possibility is most certainly worth pursuing.

References

Harris, J. (1995). Where is the child's environment? A group socialization theory of development. *Psychological Review, 102*(3), 458-489. http://faculty.weber.edu/eamsel/Classes/Child%203000/Lectures/3%20Childhood/SE%20development/JudithHarris.html

iveBeenThere. (n.d.) iveBeenThere. Retrieved on May, 11, 2016, from http://ivebeenthere-site.com/sHome/.

Lai, C. H., Yang, J. C., Chen, F. C., Ho, C. W., & Chan, T. W. (2007). Affordances of mobile technologies for experiential learning: The interplay of technology and pedagogical practices. *Journal of Computer Assisted Learning, 23*(4), 326-337. doi: 10.1111/j.1365-2729.2007.00237.x

Lave, J., & Wenger, E. (1991) *Situated learning: Legitimate peripheral participation*. Cambridge: Cambridge University Press.

National High School Center. (2007). The first year of high school: A quick stats fact sheet. Retrieved November 30, 2014 from http://www.betterhighschools.org/docs/NHSC_FirstYearof-HighSchool_032807.pdf

Schwartz, D. L., & Hartman, K. (2007). It's not video anymore: Designing digital video for learning and assessment. In R. Goldman, R. Pea, B. Barron, & S. J. Derry (Eds.), *Video research in the learning sciences* (pp. 335-348). Mahwah, NJ: Lawrence Erlbaum Associates, Inc.

Smith, J. S. (2006). Research summary: Transition from middle school to high school. Retrieved November 30, 2014 from http://www.nmsa.org/Research/ResearchSummaries/TransitionfromMStoHS/tabid/1087/Default.aspx

TeensHealth. (n.d.) For Teens. Retrieved May, 11, 2016, from https://kidshealth.org/en/teens.

Zins, J. E., & Elias, M. J. (2006). Social and emotional learning: Promoting the development of all students. *Journal of Educational and Psychological Consultation, 17*(2&3), 233-255.

Appendix 1: Features of iveBeenThere

1 Short Digital Stories

Short digital stories (one or two minutes) are unscripted and focused on one topic. In order for users to gain maximal benefits from the app and its mobile capabilities, they need to be able to use the app in a variety of time segments, ranging from watching just one digital story to watching a series of videos. This will depend on the time and place of use and the needs of the user.

2 Simple User Interface

Young people and educators can navigate to wanted videos easily and quickly. This is especially important for an urgent question or concern. A complicated interface might dissuade the user from using the app and instead go to peers for advice or information that may not necessarily be accurate. The main page has pictures of the mentors, almost like a yearbook. There are two tabs at the bottom, "Browse by Topic" and "Resources" (see below to read about the resources feature). The video pages contain small screen shots of the digital stories with the topic for each. After viewing the digital story, the user can choose to watch other videos by that mentor, that same topic, or go back to the main page. Here are some screenshots:

3 Links to Resources

Resources Page

The "Resources" page is accessible from every page in the app. Reputable resources are listed by topic. Each resource page contains the title of the resource and the URL, which links directly to the resource and a short description. Hotlines for emergency situations are also included. This connection to reliable, professional information and sometimes a live person is very important in case the user is in need of more information or immediate help beyond the scope of the content provided by the mentors' digital stories.

4 Users Uploading Their Own Videos

Users can upload their own digital stories, becoming the next generation of teen mentors. The site manager screens videos for reliability of the content as appropriate and accurate.

5 List of topics

Academics	LGBTQ
Alcohol	Making Friends
Birth Control	Parties
Body Image	Peer Pressure
Bullying	Race
Depression	Religion
Drugs	Sex
Extracurriculars	Self Injury
Fun Facts About the Mentors	Social Media
General Advice	Stereotypes
High School Transition	STD's

6 Current State of iveBeenThere

The mobile version can be found at: **ivebeenthere-mobile.com**
The web-site can be found at: **ivebeenthere-site.com**
There are eleven mentors and eighty seven digital stories covering twenty two topics. The main functionality of the app and web-site are complete, including a 'Resources' feature. In addition, there is an admin page from which mentors, videos, and resources can be added.

Mariela Nuñez-Janes and David Oliveira Franco, Jr.

7 IamWe: Digital Storytelling, Personal Journeys, and Praxis[17]

7.1 Introduction

In 2007 a college professor and a high school teacher began to forge connections between their high school and university by giving high school youth the opportunity to share their stories through digital storytelling. They developed a program named IamWe by the high-school youth who participated in a digital storytelling workshop. IamWe became part of a Texas high school PALs (Peer Assistance Leadership) class. Through this program over 100 high school students produced their own digital stories and developed Participatory Action Research (PAR) projects about their school and community.

In this chapter, we discuss the practice of digital storytelling as it relates to personal growth among high school youth who were part of the IamWe program. Our discussion draws on data collected for an assessment conducted during the 2010-2011 academic year, although examples are also drawn from observations and interviews gathered throughout a nine-year period. We analyze digital storytelling and contribute to scholarly discussions that emphasize the pedagogical opportunities that digital storytelling offers to integrate technology and meaningful learning activities in classroom settings (Heo, 2009; Kajder, 2004; Miller, 2010).

In the IamWe program the effectiveness of digital storytelling was integral to the process of creating a digital story – a series of activities that helped youth construct meaning and facilitate multiple border crossings or "personal journeys" that encouraged trust and empathy among the youth. As the high school youth participated in trust building activities, a story circle, and the process of digitizing their stories, they found commonalities and differences between their lives and the lives of their classmates. The activities fostered what we theorize as dialogical encounters or pedagogical opportunities for reflections and actions that helped the high school youth listen and share diverse experiences with the assistance of media technology.

---

17 We want to acknowledge Mr. Tim Sanchez (PALs advisor), Will Richey, and Alejandro Perez for their commitment to IamWe and their willingness to share their knowledge and talent over the years. Felipe Vargas introduced us to Campecine and his vision has been an inspiration. We are thankful to all of the University of North Texas students who were part of IamWe as mentors or volunteers in particular: Kimberly Davis, Nancy Gillis, Micaela Kline, Sara Masetti, Amy Zapien, Preston LaFarge, Nydia Sanchez, and Kaleb Hadenfeldt. We are also indebted to all the PALs for sharing their stories with us.

7.2 Putting Ideas to Practice: Theoretical Foundations

Many technology tools and techniques aimed at transforming teaching and learning are available for students and teachers. As a digital tool, digital storytelling has been used for a multitude of purposes including: community-based participatory research (Gubrium, 2009), alternative forms of literacy (Kajder, 2004; Miller, 2010), increasing teacher disposition towards technology integration (Heo, 2009), incorporating and legitimizing student knowledge in the classroom environment (Nuñez-Janes, 2009), new media literacy and IT skills (Sadik, 2008), and fostering moral values (Mukti & Hwa, 2004). Further, the use of this tool has also expanded from K-12 into higher education (McLellan, 2006).

Several methods and techniques are involved in the process of creating a digital story. These methods are considered the "...art and craft of exploring different media and software applications to communicate stories in new and powerful ways..." (McLellan, 2006, p. 66). The key to successful technology integration through digital storytelling is related to authentic, meaningful, and captivating learning activities rather than the actual use of hardware and software. Fundamentally, according to Sheneman (2010), digital storytelling incorporates these traits, and targets a generation that has the "... ability to weave together images, text and sound in a natural way" (p. 40).

We relied on the concept of digital storytelling praxis—"the use of media technology and stories to reflect (research) and change (act upon) the educational lives of [] students" (Nuñez-Janes & Re Cruz 2013) and introduce in this chapter the idea of dialogic encounters to theorize the opportunities that digital storytelling offers to foster authentic and meaningful connections between media technology and the lived experiences of high school youth. Narratives are embedded within stories, which are strung together through words, actions, thoughts, and in this particular case through digital media (Ochs, 2007). As stories were shared in the IamWe program through digital media, youth learned about their peers' past, their thoughts about the future, and their perspectives on a variety of topics. In this process, the practice of digital storytelling helped youth work against distrust and prejudicial judgment towards their peers.

IamWe relied on youth's existing familiarity with digital media to tell their stories (Gubrium, 2009; Kajder, 2004; Nuñez-Janes, 2009; Robin, 2008; Skouge & Rao, 2002). The curriculum for IamWe was developed as a result of a pilot study involving a three-day workshop conducted by the Center for Digital Storytelling (CDS) in 2006. CDS's, now StoryCenter's, emphasis on the story circle as shared dialogued was a key element of the IamWe program.

The IamWe curriculum was developed based on a series of theories related to pedagogy, social phenomenon, and research which were applied by integrating technology to the process of creating digital stories. With respect to pedagogy, IamWe was informed by the following theories: Latina/Chicana Feminist Pedagogy, a synthesis of every-day forms of teaching, learning, and community transformation (Delgado, Elenes, Godinez, & Villenas, 2006), and Critical Praxis, a dialogic practice of education for freedom (Freire, 2000/1968). Specifically, the curriculum was built around Latino/a cultural values such as *conversación* (dialogue) and *convivencia* (collective teaching and learning) practiced as culturally relevant educational tools with an ethnically diverse group of youth. These values were implemented through the use of media technology, storytelling, and action research. With respect to research, IamWe was informed by Participatory Action Research (PAR) and Youth Participatory Action Research (YPAR)—a research process in which youth act as researchers and engage in community action (Cammarota, 2008; Fals Borda & Rahman, 1991). Finally, with respect to social phenomenon, the idea of cultural wealth was also used as a framework. Cultural wealth, defined as accumulated assets and resources of marginalized communities that include different types of capital (aspirational, familial, social, linguistic, resistant, and navigational), guided the practice of storytelling (Yosso, 2006).

To this extent and based on these theories, the dialogue and communication created through a digital storytelling praxis resulted in what Paulo Freire called "element critic pedagogic," which is simultaneously creative and liberating. In this case youth were able to integrate their personal experiences or "personal journeys" to the learning process relevant to the PALs classroom. The activities that were part of the curriculum were primarily centered on dialogue and communication to engage youth in a dialogical process—a personal journey that involved themselves and others. A connection between digital media and personal narratives assisted the teacher and high school youth to "overcome some of the obstacles to productively using technology in the classroom" (Robin, 2008, p. 222) and improve the youth's attitudes towards each other. The activities that were part of IamWe were directed towards building bonds of trust and respect.

7.3 The IamWe Program

The program blended oral history, digital technologies, and culturally relevant pedagogies (Benmayor, 2000) to integrate "funds of knowledge" (Moll, 1992; Olmedo, 1997) into schooling. Some of the high school youth that participated in the initial pilot study "could not wait" to do more digital stories. This urgency launched a group effort between the PALs[18] advisor and the Anthropology department at the University of North Texas (UNT).

---

18 Part of a nationwide initiative, PALs strives to build tomorrow's leaders through peer assistance, peer helping, and leadership. It is an extra-curricular program, adopted as an accredited elective course by the Texas Education Agency reaching over 750 Texas school districts and over 1000 schools in the U.S. Based on recognizing youth's potential to effect change and make a difference in their schools and communities, the PALs curriculum focuses on teaching students skills such as group dynamics, self-esteem, and problem solving, while developing cultural awareness ("Peer Assistance and Leadership," 2014).

In 2008 the IamWe curriculum was revised to further facilitate the goals of PALs, particularly the need to create a service oriented, diverse, and empowered group of young leaders ready to build relationships between students and tear down the boundaries between diverse groups within the school. New activities were included and others were revised to prepare the high school youth for a diverse college environment. These activities emphasized personal growth and were designed to affect the youths' attitudes towards higher education while creating skills for college readiness. They focused on instilling in youth what one of the program collaborators, Will Richey, calls the "emotional literacy" necessary to navigate diversity. The idea was to assist students to better understand their peers. The curriculum revolved around three main activities: 1) a digital storytelling workshop, 2) participatory action research projects, and 3) an interactive film festival (Campecine). These activities were carried out in sequence during the academic school year.

The week prior to the digital storytelling workshop, PALs students met in a portable classroom in the back of the school's campus. A setting outside of the school building was chosen to help the youth share their experiences more freely. The story circle was designed to help students share stories with their peers and brainstorm which story they would choose to develop into a digital story. The story circle was often considered a highlight of the program by many of the youth, even when they found it difficult, surprising, and emotional. In addition, as the "heart" (Lambert, 2013) of the digital storytelling process the story circle helped participants find their story by sharing and listening to personal narratives. In the story circle the youths' life experiences were at the center of dialogue while youth "...lead with the authority of their own lives" (Lambert, 2013, p. 76). The circle was facilitated by the PALs teacher, and the participants included high school youth, the researchers, and college student volunteers.

The story circle began with questions used as prompts to foster reflection and dialogue among the youth. The questions included, "What was the happiest moment in your life?" "Can you share something about you that others don't know?" The majority of the youth talked about time spent with their families or friends and shared personal, emotional, funny, sad, traumatic, or joyful experiences. Many youth cried during the story circle and others hugged each other seeking comfort. This activity lasted for the entire period of the class, over an hour, and in some cases half a day. On the following days, the youth wrote their stories and created storyboards to begin planning their digital story.

The weekend long digital storytelling workshop and Campecine film festival took place at UNT. It was an opportunity for youth and their families to experience a college environment sometimes for the first time. Students spent three days digitizing their stories. This included recording voice over narrations, inserting photographs, video, and sound, editing, and sharing their digital stories for the first time with other PALs and family members in a celebration.

7.4 Context and Methods

Oscar Lewis High School[19], is part of the Oscar Lewis Independent School District founded in 1882. Accredited as one of 50 international baccalaureate schools in Texas, it serves 9th through 12th grades. It was ranked academically acceptable by the Texas Education Agency (TEA) in 2011, a rating it has maintained since 2006. In 2012, according to TEA, the district served 24, 738 students, 52% identified as white, 31% Hispanic, and 12% African American; 43.2% qualified as economically disadvantaged. One of three high schools in the district, Oscar Lewis High School serves over 1,500 students. The school's racial and ethnic student composition roughly mirrors that of the district: 47% white, 32% Hispanic, 17% African American, and 43.9% economically disadvantaged, a growing number. The percent of graduating students taking advanced courses at the high school, and considered college ready, is declining, while this percentage is increasing within the district.

Enrollment and participation in the PALs class occurs through a selection process. The process accesses a series of student characteristics and is led by PALs students from the previous academic year. It is done in two phases. Students from the previous year nominate other non-participating students based on their informal assessment of their leadership skills, maturity, and school involvement. Before the nomination, the prospective students fill out an application form. This application form provides the selection committee with a student profile that includes detailed information about their demographics, school year schedule, grades, school activities, interests, perceptions about the community, and thoughts about leadership, along with details about their personalities, life goals, and priorities. Once applications are collected and analyzed, students from the previous year's cohort vote on their preferred candidates. The process of voting is entirely anonymous. Once the candidates are selected, the PALs sponsor goes through the list of selected candidates and makes adjustments if deemed necessary. The program initiates its activities with a summer training that covers PALs, peer mentoring, and mediation.

The 2010-2011 PALs class was comprised of 28 students although in other years there were up to 35 juniors and seniors with ages ranging from 16- to 18-years-old. Ethnically, the composition for the 2010-2011 academic year was diverse, 29% Latinos/Hispanics, 25% African-Americans/Black, 25% white/Caucasian, 8% white/Hispanic, 4% Filipino, Albanian, and other. This demographic composition reflected the high school's overall ethnically diverse population.

Most of the data discussed in this chapter was collected between August 2010 and January 2011 as part of David Franco's Master's Practicum project in applied

---

19 The names of the school and high school youth are pseudonyms.

anthropology. Of the total population, 25 students answered a pre and post leadership skills assessment survey (Ellis, 1990), 22 students participated in initial semi-structured interviews, and 19 students participated in final semi-structured interviews. This chapter is also informed by seven years of collaboration with the PALs program during which youth produced over 125 digital stories http://www.youtube.com/user/DHSPALS/videos?view=0&sort=da&flow=grid and nine videos about their PAR projects.

The research questions that guided the 2010-2011 study were:

1. How does IamWe affect student participants' attitudes towards higher education?
2. How does the IamWe program prepare students to enter college?
3. How does the digital storytelling praxis implemented in IamWe, particularly the use of media and culturally relevant activities, affect students' personal growth?
4. In what ways and to what extent does the PAR component of IamWe effectively help promote students' leadership?

This chapter will focus on the findings relevant to question three.

Classroom ethnography was the main tool of data collection. This ethnography pays attention to "the covert, tacit or implicit cultural patterns that affect behavior and communication particularly in face-to-face social interaction, and that are largely outside the consciousness of the actor" (Spindler & Spindler, 1997, p. 60). Classroom ethnography elicits the youths' point of view and critical reflection of the cultural reality of the school and classroom. Data was collected through formal and informal interviews conducted before and after the completion of the IamWe program, surveys, and participant observation. The main focus was on the use of media and culturally relevant activities, as it related to students' personal growth and attitudes towards higher education. As participant observers, both of the authors actively participated as program facilitators with the assistance of college students, while the high school youth acted as researchers in their respective PAR projects.

The analytic practices used in this project draw from grounded theory (Glaser & Strauss, 1967). We continuously read through observation notes, rearranged codes, isolated themes that were predominant, and identified themes related to context, student interaction, and the implementation of IamWe. Themes included higher education as an envisioned goal, necessary, natural, and positive, preparing for college by recognizing that everyone has a story, realizing personal lessons through trust, and learning to be less judgmental. Memoing was used to assist in relating the data to the scholarly literature (Bernard, 2006, p. 492).

7.5 Findings and Discussion

7.5.1 Trust

> "My loved ones, my friends, my family, my teachers, I am sorry if I ever pushed you so far that it hurt. You loved me regardless. My loved ones, who would have given up their sanity to make me feel whole because they saw me in pieces. I broke down in the arms of my mentors, fell apart in the classroom of my instructors, and ran so far when I saw their arms reach out to help me. Never let me go!"—Maria

In her digital story Maria tells her story of recovery from trauma. Her story begins with her realization of recovery as a lonely journey. We see a black screen and only hear her voice as she admits, "I have to survive this!" Images of family and friends flash as she tells us about the trauma she experienced. "Because at the age of 16 I defy in silence!" is how Maria described the initial way she coped with the trauma she experienced. We then see images of family, teachers, and friends as Maria story unfolds from loneliness into her expression of her need for love and support, her cry to "Never let me go!" and her knowledge that "These people gave me butterflies in my stomach when I first felt that I was no longer alone." Through Maria's digital story we witness her personal journey of transformation from solitude to accompaniment, decline to recovery. While many factors outside of the IamWe program contributed to Maria's recovery, digital storytelling allowed Maria to share her journey by expressing through words, images, and sounds the complex emotions she felt during her road to recovery. Maria relied on her love for poetry and photography to communicate her experience and she was inspired by the trust she felt in her peers to share a story that most of them were not aware of.

Youth like Maria felt compelled to share very personal stories and felt that IamWe helped them to trust their peers. Learning to trust other PALs occurred in the context of the story circle and in relation to several trust building exercises designed to build rapport among the youth. The emphasis on sharing personal experiences in the story circle was critical to fostering trust among the high school youth. When asked about the process of digital storytelling, Tabatha said that her initial perceptions were that this activity was "sketchy." Tabatha's initial reaction towards the story circle was "I don't like it. I had just met these people I had only known for a couple of months barely and I was scared."

Despite this initial fear, Tabatha felt that the story circle helped her change her perspective. She told us "I think it [story circle] specifically helped me because I had to force myself to go out of my way to share something about myself and then listen to someone else about themselves." By the end of the story circle Tabatha's initial apprehensions changed. The people she initially characterized as strangers were now worthy of her trust. After sharing a very emotional and personal story with her peers during the story circle she felt that "It is a story I trust to tell PALs, but it's not something I would tell the general public." Similarly, Christen told us that she surprised herself during the process of creating her digital story because, as she put it, "I was really nervous to do it in first place but I was surprised on how much I trusted everyone in PALs and how trusting PALs can be. That is just not the norm in today's society to be trusting to anyone. That is how I was surprised."

For many youth, trust-building exercises practiced in the days prior to the story circle helped forge personal connections with other youth and prepare them for the emotions of the story circle. For example one youth explained that the trust building activities "...help[ed] a lot because it is hard to trust people you don't know." The combination of the story circle and trust building activities helped build trust among the youth and foster comradery. For Susan the best part of doing digital storytelling was uniting the PALs class. She explained that she experienced this group unity in the form of "...having a greater connection, friendship and trust."

As Delgado Gaitan (2005) suggests, the use of stories, in particular sharing stories, builds connections and trust. For Delgado Gaitan (2005) "community action and social change have roots in personal family narratives that connect members within the same household, between families and schools, and between families across national borders"(p. 265). In the same way, the practice of digital storytelling through the integration of pedagogy, storytelling, and media technology, helped foster trust among the youth who participated in the IamWe program. This combination was transformative for the youth helping them cross barriers that kept them from connecting to each other. Delgado Gaitan (2005) explains the transformative quality of integrating storytelling and media technology in the following way,

> "Yes, computer literacy is critical in accelerating communication. But the important lesson I glean from the families in these communities is that while our personal narratives may seem like small stories, small stories can be huge. They are a part of a longer narrative of survival, of wars in distant homelands, of isolation, of illness, of poverty, and of courage. In these people's stories, the recurring theme is about confronting and transcending the fear of not knowing and using personal stories to preserve the thread that defines us." (p. 271)

7.5.2 Being Less Judgmental

> "Hate, intolerance, isolation, hostility, revulsion, disgust, contempt, discrimination...so what is it that stops people hating? And how can we stop it? For me it was personal experience"—Carla

Carla's digital story was about challenging discrimination through personal experience. As we see images of demonstrators holding signs that say "Fags are beasts," "God hates you," "All gays go to hell," we hear Carla ask how homophobia can be stopped. She tells the story of a happy nuclear family that ended in divorce and we see pictures of her as a young child. She describes her parents' divorce as the end of her "innocence and ignorance." When her mom told her that she is gay Carla wondered how her mother would be able to endure the discrimination and hate towards people like her. Carla tells us in her digital story that she realized that her parents' divorce "...gave [her] more opportunities to receive love." As we hear this important lesson we see photographs of Carla's new extended family. Carla's personal journey into the love of a new family, as she shared it in her digital story, "...taught me how much the world can hate and how much I can love." Carla shared a deeply personal journey with ramifications for understanding and transforming social issues rooted in discrimination, racism, sexism, and homophobia. Carla expressed the implications of her personal story through a photograph of the New York City Twin Towers prior to the 9/11 terrorist attacks shown as the last image of her digital story.

As in Carla's case many youth were surprised to learn about each other's experiences. Learning about their peers' stories facilitated the youth's awareness of other points of view and helped situate their judgments in the experiences of youth they learned to trust. Maria said that her judgment towards others changed after participating in the program. As she put it, "I don't think I've been antisocial, but I think I am more social now and not so hard on some people. You never know what people have gone through since you don't know their story and so I guess I just don't judge people as much as I used to." Sue explained the lessons she learned about empathy as changes she saw in herself, as she put it, "I've become more accepting. I am, I guess, more understanding towards others and myself." Others students, like Camila, identified the digital storytelling process and, particularly the story circle, as a pivotal moment,

> "The storytelling, the digital storytelling, but not the digital storytelling itself but whenever we were brain storming for it...when we were in preparation for it and playing around the world in the portable. I really got to see other people's views and see how other people were like and it made me extend my view on some of my opinions."

Similarly for Martha, the digital storytelling process, allowed her to connect her experiences with the experiences of other students,

> "Basically, when I was able to share my story it helped me because I like helping people and stuff. Other people can understand that they are not alone and that they are not the only ones to go through stuff. They have a connection and they have somebody they can lean on."

The opportunities to share their personal stories through the use of digital media contributed to what the youth envisioned as their personal growth. Closely aligned with the literature on digital storytelling and with previous research in this particular area (Gubrium, 2009; Kajder, 2004; Nuñez-Janes, 2009; Robin, 2008; Skouge & Rao, 2002), IamWe facilitated opportunities for youth to use digital media, an important and intimate portion of their daily lives (Robin, 2008), to share their stories and find in their experiences relevant sources of knowledge. In a school environment and outside the boundaries of a set classroom assignment, youth rarely have an opportunity to share their stories. Through the process of creating their digital stories youth learned about commonalities and differences between their lives and the lives of their peers.

7.5.3 Personal Journeys and Praxis

The youth that participated in the IamWe program often described it as a "personal journey." As a deeply personal process, the practice of digital storytelling in the IamWe program involved the combination of several dialogic encounters. That is, conversations involving youth, media, written, and oral stories, images, sound that came together in the digital story itself and that we theorize as the pedagogical praxis of the digital storytelling process. These dialogic encounters relied on media technology and storytelling, involved emotions, and served pedagogical purposes. Indeed, the emotions involved in the process of creating digital stories were hard for the youth to put into words because, as many told us, they were meant to be experienced. Yes, digital stories can be described through the sum of their parts and through the steps involved in making them, but the deep effects of digital storytelling were crystallized in its process and conveyed in its final product. For example, in addition to the emotional content of the story circle youth experienced a multitude of emotions during the weekend long workshop. The emotions varied but included frustration with the technology, exhaustion, and a sense of accomplishment.

The depth of emotions shared during the story circle and permeating the entire process was surprising to many of the youth. Many felt that they were not "prepared" for what they described as the "somber tone" of the circle. One youth described the emotional content of the story circle in the following way, "I mean you are dealing with stuff, like your story is just; your story is about something that brings tears." Yet, despite the difficulties, many youth found the emotional quality to be the most compelling part of the process. The lessons they learned, "never count anybody out," "not to like judge anybody," and "that we could get it all done," had the effect of helping the PALs class "bond" and feel a sense of empathy towards other youth in the group. As one youth told us, "...in the end and stuff it's more easy to care about them [other youth]."

As a personal journey, the dialogic encounters of the digital storytelling process included: 1) conversation, 2) voice and narrative, 3) collective engagement, and 4) media. The conversational aspect of digital storytelling was most evident during the story circle. Several educational scholars and anthropologists discuss dialogue in relation to pedagogy and praxis. According to Freire (2000/1968) open dialogue is creative and liberatory. As a critical element of pedagogical praxis, Freire conceptualized dialogue as exchanges based on respect and cooperation that lead to just actions.

The digital storytelling journey continued by engaging the voices of youth as "counterstories" or "counternarratives," "...a method of recounting the experiences and perspectives of racially and socially marginalized people" (Yosso, 2006, p. 10), to challenge: 1) the use of power to privilege some stories over others, 2) the knowledge produced through stories, and 3) the privilege given to those who are allowed to tell stories (Knight, Norton, & Dixon, 2004; Yosso, 2006). This dialogic encounter with voice is related to the praxis of conscientization that is part of the digital storytelling process. Freire discussed consciousness raising as an important aspect of transforming social reality. In this case the digital stories created by the youth were about raising the consciousness of the group about individual experiences related to absent fathers, drug addiction, alcohol abuse, mothers and grandmothers as mentors and role models, rape, the impact of family, and the love between siblings and friends.

Collective engagement was also an important element of the IamWe digital storytelling process. Feminist scholars have discussed collectivity and community as key elements of praxis. Black feminist anthropologists theorize praxis as situated in collective memories and as a point of departure for theorization, research, and activism (McClaurin, 2001). Chicana/Latina feminist ethnographers also situate praxis in collective experiences (Delgado, Elenes, Godinez, & Villenas, 2006). In digital storytelling, stories are shared and produced in a group setting generating a collective sense of self and giving authority to the ways of knowing of youth. Another dialogic encounter involves transformation. Transformation occurred by involving youth, as the PALs teacher put it, "as a whole person," integrating emotion, voice, and media through the practice of digital storytelling. In the case of IamWe digital storytelling facilitated opportunities for youth to share their individual hardships and triumphs, "Perhaps not in point by point experiences," as the PALs adviser explained, but in the commonality of the struggle of coming to terms with becoming adults and the difficulties of "facing their biggest fears head-on."

7.6 Conclusion and Implications

The digital storytelling process practiced through the IamWe program contributed to facilitate high school youth's personal growth. Through a series of dialogic encounters involving conversations, voice and narrative, collective engagement, and media youth were able to learn about trust and empathy as they participated in trust building exercises, a story circle, and a digital storytelling workshop. These dialogic encounters allowed the youth to venture into emotional spaces, crossing personal boundaries, through a deeply personal journey converging in the digital story.

Yet, for the youth who were part of IamWe one of the most difficult aspects of digital storytelling was the vulnerability that permeated the process and that was most prevalent during the story circle. Youth described the story circle as "awkward" and told us during a group discussion how difficult it was to "open up" and to figure out "how much to tell" during the circle. Sustaining this heightened level of emotion through the whole process was difficult.

Despite the difficulties, most of the youth involved told us that what they liked the most about digital storytelling was also hearing their peers' stories, experiencing their digital stories, and sharing their emotions with each other. Thus, they described the effect of the story circle as helping them "get closer" and build trust. From the process of making a digital story they learned not to "count anybody out" or to "judge." They also felt that getting to know each other and actually finishing the whole process— "getting it done"—helped them feel a sense of accomplishment.

We expanded the lessons gained from youth's personal journeys beyond the PALs classroom into a community film festival. In collaboration with Firme and Felipe Vargas we incorporated the Campecine film festival as an end point to the annual activities that were part of IamWe. This public event drew on the principles of conversation, voice, collective, engagement, and media. It featured some of the youth's digital stories and trust building activities led by the PALs. The emotions of the IamWe process were underscored by the performances of Will Richey and Alejandro Perez, a team of spoken word artists, experts in building emotional literacy with youth. Campecine brought together college students, professors, parents, teachers, and administrators under the leadership of the high school youth. This event was described as "life changing" by the youth and the rest of the participants.

The transformative or life changing impact of the digital storytelling process also had an effect on our own teaching practices and ideas about applying anthropology. First, as educators, we became more attentive to the voices of our own students and we are constantly working on developing strategies to incorporating their experiences as relevant sources of knowledge in our classrooms. Second, in our own collaboration, we became more attentive to our standpoints as well as those of our partners. Wolf (1996) suggests that researchers must accept existing power differentials in the research process. Our commitment to creating more egalitarian research relationships became more realistic. Being more in tune to our own standpoints as professor, graduate student, teacher, or artist allowed us to be more open to our limitations and strengths. Our collaboration deepened and became more efficient as we worked with our differences instead of against them. In this case, the praxis of digital storytelling democratized our own collaborative research process and teaching strategies.

In terms of thinking and doing applied anthropology, the digital storytelling process also led us to reflect about applied research in anthropology. Similar to the experiences of the high school youth, as researchers, it was initially hard to pay attention to the emotions involved in the digital storytelling process as important to our scholarly questions about media and pedagogy. This does not mean that we were unresponsive or dismissive of the youth's emotional responses. However, it was hard to place the youth's emotional reactions at the center of our inquiry and pedagogical practices. Our journey as applied researchers led us to take seriously the mutual and emotional relationships we developed with the youth and place them at the center of our research inquiry and pedagogical practice. The digital storytelling process helped remind us, as Sanjek suggests, of "...other values, brought from the wider social worlds in which we have grown up and in which we live as persons, actors, and citizens" (2015, p. 1). The social effects of digital storytelling drove us to think more deeply about our processes and to seek research opportunities in which we can learn from and work with youth. Because of this we committed almost a decade to IamWe and we strongly believe that long-term engagement in applied research is beneficial and necessary. To this end we continued to incorporate feedback from youth and they continued to inquire and participate in the IamWe activities even after they graduated from high school. Sustaining this kind of engagement is challenging. Justifying and making this kind of collaboration work across educational institutions is difficult. We battled with addressing logistical details related to differences in planning and scheduling. We struggled with having our work recognized as legitimate teaching and scholarship. We personally and professionally experienced the emotional weight that results from this committed praxis and mutuality (Sanjek, 2015). Yet, despite the challenges, these border crossings opened opportunities for anthropological research into new terrains of inquiry where digital media, personal emotional stories, and learning converge through mutual and transformative encounters experienced through the process of digital storytelling.

References

Benmayor, R. (2000). Education: Cyber-teaching in the oral history classroom. *Oral History* 28(1), 83-92.

Bernard, R. H. (2006). *Research methods in anthropology: Qualitative and quantitative approaches.* New York: Altamira Press.

Cammarota, J. (2008). The cultural organizing of youth ethnographers: Formalizing a praxis-based pedagogy. *Anthropology & Education Quarterly* 39(1), 45-58.

Delgado Bernal, D., Elenes, C. A., Godinez, F. E., & Villenas, S. (2006). *Chicana/Latina education in everyday life: Feminista perspectives on pedagogy and epistemology.* Albany: State University of New York Press.

Delgado Gaitan, C. (2005). Family narratives in multiple literacies. *Anthropology & Education Quarterly*, 36(3), 265-272.

Fals Borda, O., & Rahman, M. A. (1991). *Action and knowledge: Breaking the monopoly with participatory action research.* Lanham: Rowman & Littlefield.

Freire, P. (2000). *Pedagogy of the oppressed* (30th anniversary ed.). New York: Continuum. (Original work published 1968)

Glaser, B. G., & Strauss, A. L. (1967). *The Discovery of grounded theory: Strategies for qualitative research.* New York: Transaction Publishers; Reprint 2009.

Gubrium, A. (2009). Digital storytelling as method for engaged scholarship in anthropology. *Practicing Anthropology*, 31(4), 5-9.

Heo, M. (2009). Digital storytelling: An empirical study of the impact of digital storytelling on pre-service teachers' self-efficacy and dispositions towards educational technology. *Journal of Educational Multimedia and Hypermedia*, 18(4), 405-428.

Kajder, S. B. (2004). Enter here: Personal narrative and digital storytelling. *The English Journal*, 93(3), 64-68.

Knight, M. G., Norton, N. E. L., & Dixon, I. R. (2004). The power of black and Latina/o counterstories: Urban families and college-going processes. *Anthropology & Education Quarterly*, 35(1), 99-120.

Lambert, J. (2013). Digital storytelling: Capturing lives, creating community. New York: Routledge.

McClaurin, I. (2001). Introduction: Forging a theory, politics, praxis and poetics of black feminist anthropology. In I. McClaurin (Ed.), *Black feminist anthropology: Theory, politics, praxis and poetics* (pp. 1-23). New Brunswick: Rutgers University Press.

McLellan, H. (2006). Digital storytelling in higher education. *Journal of Computing in Higher Education*, 19(1), 65-79.

Miller, L. C. (2010). *Make me a story: Teaching writing through digital storytelling*. Portland: Stenhouse Publisher.

Moll, L. C. (1992). Bilingual classroom studies and community analysis: Some recent trends. *Educational Researcher*, 21(2), 20-29.

Mukti, N. A., & Hwa, S. P. (2004) Malaysian perspective: Designing interactive multimedia learning environment for moral values education. *Educational Technology & Society*, 7(4), 143-152.

Nuñez-Janes, M. (2009) Historias digitales de estudiantes Latinos como herramienta pedagógica en Texas. In M. F. Montes & W. Müllauer-Seichter (Eds.), *La integración escolar a debate* (pp. 56-79). Madrid: Pearson Educación, S.A.

Nuñez-Janes, M., & Re Cruz, A. (2013). Latino/a students and the power of digital storytelling. *Radical Pedagogy*, 10(2). Retrieved from http://www.radicalpedagogy.org/radicalpedagogy.org/Latino_a_Students_and_the_Power_of_Digital_Storytelling.html

Ochs, E. (2007) Narrative lessons. In L. Monaghan & J. E. Goodman (Eds.), *A cultural approach to interpersonal communication* (pp. 41-49). Malden, Ma: Wiley-Blackwell.

Olmedo, I. M. (1997). Voices of our past: Using oral history to explore funds of knowledge within a Puerto Rican family. *Anthropology & Education Quarterly*, 28(4), 550-574.

Peer Assistance and Leadership (2014, October 31) Retrieved from http://www.statewidetraining.org/pal/

Robin, B. R. (2008). Digital storytelling: A powerful technology tool for the 21st century classroom. *Theory Into Practice*, 47(3), 220-228.

Sadik, A. (2008). Digital storytelling: A meaningful technology-integrated approach for engaged student learning. *Educational Technology Research and Development*, 56(4), 487-506.

Sanjek, R. (2015). Introduction. Deep grooves: Anthropology and mutuality. In R. Sanjek (Ed.), *Mutuality: Anthropology's changing terms of engagement* (pp. 1-10). Philadelphia: University of Pennsylvania Press.

Sheneman, L. (2010) Digital storytelling: How to get the best results. *School Library Monthly*, 27(1), 40-42.

Skouge, J. R., & Rao, K. (2002) Digital storytelling in teacher education: Creating transformations through narrative. *Educational Perspectives*, 42(1), 54-60.

Spindler, G., & Spindler, L. (1997). Cultural process and ethnography: An anthropological perspective. In G. Spindler & L. Spindler (Eds.), *Education and cultural process: Anthropological approaches* (pp. 56-57). Long Grove: Waveland Press, Inc.

Wolf, D. L. (1996). Situating feminist dilemmas in fieldwork. In D. L. Wolf, (Ed.), *Feminist dilemmas in fieldwork* (pp. 1-56). Boulder, CO: Westview Press, Inc.

Yosso, T. (2006). *Critical race counterstories along the Chicana/Chicano educational pipeline*. New York: Routledge.

Darcy Alexandra

8 More Than Words: Co-Creative Visual Ethnography

8.1 Introduction

> The way I write is who I am, or have become, yet this is a case in which I wish I had instead of words and their rhythms a cutting room, equipped with an Avid, a digital editing system on which I could touch a key and collapse the sequence of time, show you simultaneously all the frames of memory that come to me now, let you pick the takes, the marginally different expressions, the variant readings of the same lines. This is a case in which I need more than words to find the meaning. (Didion, 2005, p. 7)

This chapter explores the development of a shared, visual ethnographic practice with newcomer communities in Ireland. Using more than words to find meaning, research practitioners considered the multiple frames of their audio-visual narratives–"the marginally different expressions, the variant readings of the same lines." They edited their audio-visual stories–collapsing and re-opening the sequence of time, selecting images, determining the shot length, the camera movement, and the dialogue and pacing between images. Over time, in this practice of inquiry through media production, participants–the majority of whom had no prior experience critically engaging with photography and video editing–developed diverse approaches to conceptualizing and representing their experiences as newcomers to Ireland. By considering the audio-visual worlds of lived experiences participants developed multi-layered representations of Ireland–immigrant representations of Ireland. Some participants developed their approach to photography through a realist paradigm–seeking visual evidence, interrogating asylum and migrant labor regimes, and forensically documenting their case while other participants developed more poetically interpretative approaches to their visual voice. John Berger (1984) writes that storytelling serves to accompany the storyteller. Given the precarious legal status of the people who participated in the research discussed in this chapter, and the fact that half of participants (as individuals seeking international protection in Ireland) were living in conditions of prolonged confinement and social and economic exclusion,[20] Berger's notion of storytelling as accompaniment is particularly

---

[20] In many western countries, individuals (and their children) who seek international protection are housed in accommodation centers as they await a response on their claim for refugee status. In Ireland, a system of "Direct Provision" was introduced as an emergency measure in 1999. With the implementation of Direct Provision adult asylum seekers lost the right to work, study, and travel freely outside the country while awaiting a decision on their application for refugee status.

instructive. The research findings presented here suggest that the co-creative action of producing documentary media within a "community of practice" (Lave & Wenger, 1991; Wenger, 1999) can serve to accompany the storyteller by facilitating inquiry, learning, and advocacy. To develop a shared anthropological practice (Pink, 2011; Rouch, 1974; Rouch & Taylor, 2003; Stoller, 1992), certain research adaptations to the StoryCenter[21] model (Lambert, 2013) proved to be necessary and productive. This chapter presents an overview of the documentary essays[22] produced with migrant communities in Ireland, an outline of four key research adaptations, and an exploration of the subsequent development of a shared, visual ethnographic practice through the creative labor of two practitioners–Vukasin and Edwina[23].

8.2 Research Overview

Research occurred from July 2007 to April 2010, with follow-up interviews and public screenings between 2011 and 2012.[24] The methodology combined social documentary and arts practice (photography, creative writing, audio-visual editing) with critical pedagogy.[25] During a period of approximately five months for each workshop, participants engaged with their life stories through the development of short, first person documentary essays. In this way, participants had time to inquire into current circumstances and memories, and to develop their craft as emergent photographers, media producers, theorists and ethnographers in and out of the workshop site.

Under the new regime, individuals and families seeking protection are placed in privately run "accommodation centres," or "hostels" most often in isolated rural areas. The Direct Provision scheme renders these individuals and families dependent upon the state's provision of food, accommodation and weekly allowance of €19.10 per adult, and €9.60 per child per week. The system is critiqued as discriminatory, and detrimental to the mental health and wellbeing of people who are lawfully present in Ireland (Fanning, 2001; Free Legal Advice Centre, 2009; Irish Refugee Council, 2013; Loyal 2011).

21 Formerly the Center for Digital Storytelling: www.storycenter.org.

22 I consider "digital storytelling" as practiced within this project to be a genre of documentary filmmaking. Within this context, the audiovisual compositions created by research participants can best be described as documentary essays, but are also referred to as "digital stories," "audiovisual narratives" and "audiovisual compositions."

23 Pseudonyms are used to protect participant researchers' identities when necessary and requested. In the case of Vukasin Nedelhkovic, the legal name is used and granted with permission.

24 Research was supported by an ABBEST post-doctoral fellowship, and a *Fiosraigh* research scholarship. Many thanks to research practitioners for their participation, and to the following institutions and organizations: the Dublin Institute of Technology (DIT), the DIT School of Media, the Forum on Migration and Communication (FOMACS), the Centre for Transcultural Research and Media Practice, Integrating Ireland, the Migrant Rights Centre Ireland, and Refugee Information Services.

25 Pedagogical considerations for this research project are indebted to the work of Cammarota, 2008; Cochran-Smith, 2004; Darder, Baltodano & Torres, 2008; Fine, Weis, Centrie & Roberts, 2000; Greene, 1988; Guajardo, Guajardo & Del Carmen Casaperalta, 2008; and Moll, 1992.

Participants created over 250 photographs and drawings, and developed thirteen self-narrated, audio-visual stories. Upon completing their multimedia narratives, participants had the opportunity to screen the stories publicly in diverse venues, or "opt out" of public dissemination beyond the workshop site. The co-creative production of these stories constituted a means of inquiry in and of itself in which research participants learned fundamental elements of audio-visual production, and critically considered the embodied impact of migration policy through photography, creative writing, and audio-visual editing. In the process, research participants–seven women and six men from African (Democratic Republic of the Congo, Liberia, Morocco, Nigeria, Zimbabwe), Asian (Bangladesh), Eastern European (Serbia, Ukraine), and Middle Eastern (Iran, Iraq) countries–documented their experiences as newcomers to Ireland. They interrogated the structural violence of asylum and migrant labor regimes, and created their own images and audio to document their lives as workers, parents, cultural citizens (Coll, 2010; Rosaldo, 1994), activists, and artists simultaneously adapting to and transforming a new environment. The following table provides an overview of the documentary essays with excerpts from each author and a short description of the videos created during the two workshop series.

Table 8.1: Documentary Essay Overview

Author/Title	Excerpt from documentary essay	Description
Abazu *One Day I Will Not Forget*	"Sometimes we don't speak out because we feel inadequate, or because we think it won't make any difference, or because we are told we shouldn't. In my case, I had heard of racism before, but never imagined I would be a victim."	Abazu, a respected elder in his home country, speaks to an interaction on a city bus that left him feeling "like a nobody," and wonders how to effectively speak up against prejudice and discrimination as an asylum seeker.
Abdel *Abdel's Story*	"The day I came to Ireland I thought my dream was coming true, but life is not always as good as you imagine. I was always looking for a better life. I wanted to do something for the people and the community."	Abdel is originally from Morocco where he holds degrees in law and economics. He came to Ireland with a permit to work in the IT industry. Despite Abdel's job performance, his employer failed to renew his employment permit and Abdel became undocumented.
Edwina *Edwina's Story*	"I brought my son all the way from his home country so he could have a better education and a better future. I am not asking for handouts. I am willing and able to work, to contribute to this society and my family–something I have done all my life."	Edwina discusses the workplace discrimination that led to the loss of legal status, and suggests policy recommendations that would make a difference in migrant workers' lives.

Author/Title	Excerpt from documentary essay	Description
Evelyn *Crossing Over*	"I woke up this morning with a bit of 'hot head' and shivers, even though the room was heated. It is one of those days in Ireland when the sky empties her icy grains."	Evelyn focuses on one day of life in an accommodation center to explore the psychological impact of living in the asylum system.
Farrokh *New Ways*	"What's going on? What's happening to me? I'm riding in an ambulance. My hand is broken. I'm wondering about the Farrokh I was, and the Farrokh I am now. I never expected myself to do something like this."	Farrokh briefly narrates the reasons why he fled his home country of Iran, and details how the social and economic exclusion of life in the asylum system has negatively impacted on his life, his well-being and his sense of self.
Lyubov *Lyubov's Story*	"We have a tradition in Ukraine. If someone is leaving home for a long period of time, the mother gives you an *oberikh*, which is a symbol of happiness, goodness, health, and safe homecoming. It's been four years since I had to leave my family, relatives, extended family, friends, work, and my home country."	Lyubov was recruited from the Ukraine to work in the agro food industry in Ireland. Due to severe workplace exploitation she was forced to leave her job, and subsequently became undocumented. In her story she outlines the workplace exploitation that lead to her loss of legal status, the legal advice and support she found with the Dublin-based Migrant Rights Centre Ireland, and the hope she maintains that she will receive a work permit and be able to travel freely again and see her family.
Marie *Ray*	"It all happened so fast. We would have all been killed if we had not left. Your daddy escaped with you, and I was left with your brother and sister. I hoped and prayed that you were alive and safe. You were only two. You were just a baby."	Marie speaks to her young son who stayed behind in Nigeria, and longs for family reunification after a traumatic separation.
Mona *I Have People I Have Left Behind*	"I left my family four years ago. I don't like to remember the day I left home and the way I left. It is too painful. What I do remember every day are my kids. I always speak to them on the phone, but the communication back home is very bad."	Mona hopes to receive humanitarian leave to remain, but worries she may never reunite with her children who remain in Liberia unless family reunification laws change.

Author/Title	Excerpt from documentary essay	Description
Pierre *An Ireland Called Ireland*	"We settled on an island, an island called Ireland. I love how it sounds. However, we are experiencing how integration on this island is a long way away."	Despite having received refugee status, Pierre wonders how he and his wife will create a future for their family if they cannot exercise their professions.
Rebecca *Aduro Life*	"Aduro life! What a life! *Aduro* is a Nigerian word for asylum seeker meaning 'stand still.' How true! I arrived in Ireland with mixed feelings. Happy I was safe yet sad about the separation from my family. I was enthused about building a new life. My excitement died down as I noticed the stigma attached to the word 'asylum seeker.' It's even worse for female applicants of African origin."	Rebecca interrogates the ways in which female asylum seekers from African countries are particularly stigmatized within the asylum system and society at large.
Susan *Caged Escape*	"It takes courage to leave one's home, family and everything on a good day, how much more when one has to leave in a hurry, afraid for one's life and loved ones? I never expected to have things handed to me on a platter but then, I didn't expect the high level of disbelief that follows one around, especially when you come from my country, Nigeria."	Susan outlines the social and economic isolation of the asylum system and takes comfort in her children and her memories from home.
Vukasin *69/851/07*	"During the 90s some of my exhibitions were banned. As an artist I realized there was no freedom of speech. I got involved in the peaceful student movement against the Milosevic regime. I was abducted and detained several times and had to spend time in prison."	Vukasin narrates the circumstances that lead him to flee his home country of Serbia, and the inadequate and debilitating conditions in the asylum center where he awaits an official response to his application for refugee status.
Zaman *Zaman's Story*	"When I was a kid, my father used to tell me about lots of things. He told me about my future, how to be a good man like him, and so many things. Sometimes I felt bored. But my father worried about me."	Zaman paid several thousand euros to come to Ireland on a valid visa to work for an IT company. Upon arrival in Dublin from Dhaka, Bangladesh, he discovered the IT company did not exist. In debt and without employment, he became undocumented. Zaman narrates a story about his love for his father, and what he thought he might gain through migration and would he found instead.

8.3 Centering the Challenge of Rendering Visible and Audible: Inquiry Adaptations to the Digital Storytelling Method

To serve the needs of research participants, and to develop digital storytelling as a research method–a relatively new project within the social sciences[26]–the following adaptations proved to be necessary.

8.3.1 A Longitudinal Workshop Format

Instead of the standard Center for Digital Storytelling/StoryCenter 1–3 day workshop timeframe, participants met weekly at a Dublin college over a half-year period. During the workshop, participants shared, discussed and developed their images, visual concepts, scripts and documentary essays. The inter-disciplinary seminar curricula drew from critical pedagogy, visual anthropology, and social documentary practice, and focused on scriptwriting, photography, and audio-visual editing. This approach combining practice and theory organically provided opportunities for visits outside the research site during which participants tested out ideas, documented the asylum centres, and developed their narrative and visual ethnographic practice.

A longitudinal approach facilitated greater opportunity to develop ethnographic relationships of trust and reciprocity and explore the possibilities of digital storytelling as a means of inquiry through media practice. Additionally, meeting once a week allowed time for greater integration of media arts learning, as well as emotional and intellectual breathing space. Outside the workshop setting participants had time to reflect on their stories, integrate workshop sessions, develop scripts, collect visual elements from family archives, and produce new images. On-going documentation of the process was conducted–in and out of the workshop site–through ethnographic field notes and photographs.

8.3.2 Valuing Practice and Artefact

In digital storytelling production there has been a tendency to place greater value on the workshop process than the finished artefact (Sanchez-Laws 2010). Due to time constraints, limited resources, and other challenges, school and community-based digital storytelling projects have most often produced artefacts with low production

---

26 See for example, Alexandra, 2008, 2015a, 2015b; Brushwood Rose, 2009; Couldry, 2008; Fletcher & Cambre, 2009; Gubrium, 2009a, 2009b, 2010; Hartley & McWilliam, 2009; Hull & Katz, 2006; Lundby, 2008; Meadows, 2003; Otañez, 2015; Pleasants & Salter, 2014; Poitras Pratt, 2011; Spurgeon et al., 2009.

values (poor sound recording, and limited attention to visual storytelling). Because asylum experiences are often rendered inaudible (Threadgold, 2006; Moreo, 2012) and increasingly disbelieved (Fassin, 2011), and because research participants expressed interest in impacting asylum and migrant labor policies through their digital stories, the finished artefact became as important as the process. To get voices heard beyond the workshop site, access to professional-level media production tools and instruction; collaboration with artists and media professionals; and broadcast-quality production values for the finished artefacts were considered ethical, and strategic aspects of the research design. This design element informed weekly curricula and practice, in and out of workshop site, as participants determined what they would, and would not, reveal and/or conceal, and made on-going dialogue about visibility, "veracity," "evidence," and ethics necessary.[27] Upon completion of the stories, participants had the opportunity to screen them publicly in diverse venues, or opt out of public dissemination. Currently, ten stories are available for viewing on line.

8.3.3 Valuing Sound

Digital stories most often depend on the filmmaker's voice to orient the viewer, and organize the video, and an expressive musical sound track most often accompanies the voice. In the standard workshop setting, there is little time to consider the musical selection, and not always enough time and/or skill to effectively execute the mix. This can result in the music competing with the recorded voice-over, or not being in conversation with the spoken narrative. This project focused on the primacy of the research participant's spoken words, images and voice. Therefore, no music was added to the audio tracks. Instead, the listener is invited to hear the in-breaths and the pauses between the words. Ambient sounds were added during post-production. These sounds were not synchronous, but had an indexical link to the image in the video–for example, the sound of a heavy, institutional-sounding door closing in Evelyn's video, *Crossing Over*. For future projects, there is much to explore in relation to ambient sound gathered on site by research practitioners, and rich possibilities for sonic ethnography.

8.3.4 Thinking With and Through Images: Visual Ethnography

Among media and education scholars who analyze or conduct research involving digital storytelling there appears to be a significant and persistent oversight regarding the incorporation of social documentary and arts practices, specifically the role of audio-

---

27 For discussion on ethics in digital storytelling, see Hill (2014).

visual practices in facilitating inquiry. Meanwhile, until very recently, digital storytelling has largely been absent from the visual anthropology literature. To some degree, this is reflected in the way digital storytelling is most often practiced. The dominant paradigm in digital storytelling production has been for storytellers to present their story first in the "story circle," and subsequently begin the production process with the written script. Starting with the written script can run the risk of developing a primarily illustrative engagement with the visual. For example, when I first began facilitating digital storytelling workshops the curriculum that guided our work did not include careful consideration of photography, nor sufficient time for making images within the workshop schedule. Participants therefore drew almost exclusively from on-line stock image banks and archival family photos. To my mind, this approach limited the interpretive possibilities of the story, and often resulted in visual storytelling that was primarily illustrative, or evidential. During the story circle, people who were new to audio-visual storytelling shared emotionally evocative, thoughtful, humorous and insightful stories. Because there was little consideration of the visual, the stories created in the workshops privileged the oral statement of the story more than the visual statement. For me, as a viewer/listener, this approach often resulted in an unsatisfying trace of the original storytelling performance. What might practitioners encounter, or learn from their stories if they had more time to explore the visual worlds of their oral and written narratives? Might some storytellers want to begin the inquiry and production process with their images? How might a dialogical engagement with the visual be encouraged?

These questions fostered a commitment to facilitating a process in which participants would critically engage with documentary methods by creating their own visual content to explore and depict their stories. Rather than use stock images from image banks, participants would think through and with images to make meaning of their stories and to document their experiences of migration. Instead of understanding images solely as tools for eliciting information, or data and evidence of "what really happened," images were conceptualised as meditational objects (Edwards, 1997; Edwards & Hart, 2004) that facilitate inquiry (MacDougall, 2006: 224) and allow for analytical and poetic engagements with experience (Edwards, 1997). In order to develop this aspect of the practice, more workshop time was dedicated to thinking about the role of images, to making images individually and collectively, and to discussing and critiquing those images. To this purpose, participants played mentorship roles by sharing their photographs with the group, and professional photographers visited the workshop site to discuss their approach to documentary photography. In this way, participants were supported as emergent photographers ethnographically documenting their everyday lives. When invited, I also visited participants in their homes and at the direct provision[28] centres where they lived in

---

28 At the time of the research, seven participants were living in the "Direct Provision" accommodation hostels and centers located throughout Ireland.

order to develop a participatory, visual ethnographic practice. These considerations supported research participants in creating their own images, actively considering the visual worlds of their stories, and employing photography as a form of inquiry. In the following section we will consider these themes through the work of two research practitioners – Vukasin Nedelhkovic and Edwina.

Figure 8.1: "Now I live in the Ballyhaunis Hostel where I am waiting for refugee status." Screen shot from *69/851/07* (2009) written and directed by Vukasin Nedelhkovic. Vukasin photographed a surveillance camera inside his asylum center.

8.4 69/851/07

During the period that research was conducted, Ireland had one of the lowest acceptance rates for asylum applications in the European Union.[29] At the time of the second workshop, only two research participants had been granted refugee status. All other participants were waiting for a decision on their application for refugee status, or their appeals for subsidiary protection or humanitarian leave to remain. Vukasin was among the participants awaiting a decision. He is a Serbian artist born and raised

---

29 Based on Eurostat online data, between 2008 and 2012 Ireland had one of the lowest acceptance rates of asylum claims for international protection in the European Union. During the third quarter of 2010, for example, 1.3% of asylum applicants received refugee status (Albertinelli, 2011).

in Belgrade who fled to Ireland in the spring of 2006. Following is a portion of the script that he developed during the seminar:

> During the 90s some of my exhibitions were banned. As an artist I realized there was no freedom of speech. I got involved in the peaceful student movement against the Milosevic regime. I was abducted and detained several times and had to spend time in prison. After the revolutionary changes in 2000 the new government came. With time I realized that the so-called democratic government didn't change what we were fighting for all those years. They weren't even able to expel Serbian war criminals to The Hague. I recorded a speech against the government on Belgrade B92 radio. I said that our political leaders belonged in the Natural History Museum instead of being part of the EU Parliament. The reactions to my speech were really strong and it was the subject of Serbian parliament and headlines in all the daily papers. One of the political leaders said that I should go to prison for five hundred years. Very soon after that the soldiers came to my house to recruit me for military service. It wasn't safe for me to stay in Belgrade anymore. I had to leave. I fled Serbia and came to Ireland seeking political asylum in April 2006. After a few months in Ireland I began to feel very afraid to go outside. Even to buy food. I felt really lost and lonely.

To develop his visual narrative, Vukasin employed twelve colour images from an accommodation centre in County Mayo, one family photo of his mother from his personal archive, and a get-well card he received while in hospital in Ireland. During a workshop to discuss his photographic practice, Vukasin shared these images with fellow practitioners. Sharing his documentary images from the accommodation centre Vukasin described a "200-year-old building that is cold, drafty, mould-infested and leaks constantly" (field notes November 24, 2008). Vukasin made all but two of the images from inside the hostel, in the present tense, and yet these images narrate the past–Vukasin's story of activism in Serbia, and his exile to Ireland. The opening sequence for his documentary essay is based on a photograph of running shoes smudged with blood (Figure 8.2). Vukasin explained that one of the people in his "accommodation centre" had been in a car accident, and Vukasin documented the moment by taking a photo of the man's running shoes. In re-positioning the photograph within his audio-visual composition, ***69/851/07,*** Vukasin re-purposed the photograph, connecting it to his past as an activist. He explained that the photograph came to represent "the peaceful protests, the endless walks and the beatings we received" (field notes November 24, 2008).

The sole present tense sentence of Vukasin's script is the very last, which reads, "Now I live in Ballyhaunis Hostel where I am waiting for refugee status." In his audio-visual composition, Vukasin couples this last statement with the image of a surveillance camera (Figure 8.1). As he explained, "There are 16 cameras at the hostel. They represent the loss of freedom and privacy and the system of control and surveillance in operation at the hostel" (field notes November 24, 2008). Vukasin's photographs and the discussion of his practice served as a model that encouraged other practitioners to document and interrogate the asylum system through the lens of the camera. The majority of the photographs from *Living in Direct Provision: 9*

Stories workshop series were taken from within the walls of the asylum centers where asylum seeking women and men, and their children, live while awaiting a verdict on their petition for refugee status. These photographs document the detention centers–a bunk bed, mold in the corners of the ceiling, surveillance cameras–the details of institutionalization, disrepair, boredom, socio-economic exclusion and poverty. By finding and making these images, participants explored their daily lives photographically. The resulting photographs served as a means to critically consider and document the material and emotional realities of living in the asylum system. This practice provided an opportunity to ethnographically examine the physical contours of the detention centers, as well as the invisible, internal landscapes of experience.

Figure 8.2: Runners. Screen shot from *69/851/07* (2009) written and directed by Vukasin. "In the '90s some of my exhibitions were banned."

In 2009, Vukasin received subsidiary protection to remain in Ireland and later, Irish citizenship. He continues to photographically document the asylum system in Ireland and is currently a Ph.D. student developing practice-based research into the asylum system. About his research Vukasin writes, the "Asylum Archive originally started as a coping mechanism while I was in the process of seeking asylum in Ireland. It's directly concerned with the realities and traumatic lives of asylum seekers. Its main objective is to collaborate with asylum seekers, artists, academics, and civil society activists, amongst others, with a view to create an interactive documentary cross-platform online resource, which critically brings forward accounts of exile, displacement, trauma, and memory," (http://www.asylumarchive.com).

8.5 Sensing Stories to Find Images

When participants struggled with making images, having a community of practitioners with whom to discuss their developing craft was essential. Boiling ideas/feelings/ moments down to an essence assisted the inquiry process. Questions like, what color is the idea/feeling/moment? What does it sound like? What does it taste like? Which objects and places evidence or evoke that moment/feeling/idea? Where can the image be found? These questions supported participants in developing a sensorial space for stories, and within that space photographs could be made. Participants considered how to visually represent different themes in their stories–the courage of leaving home and family; comforting memories of loved ones; feelings of isolation, loss and grief; expectations, longings, and hopes for new beginnings; stigma, prejudice and race-based discrimination; uncertainty and boredom; love and concern for family; a governmental policy that restricts asylum seekers from working, studying, or living autonomously; and the fear and sense of helplessness of living without legal documentation. These themes presented a series of new questions. For example, how to tell a story that is located in the past or any other place one cannot physically return to? How is a memory visually evoked? How can the storytellers protect and maintain their anonymity in an auto-ethnographic, audio-visual story? These are precisely the questions that research participants faced as they shaped their narratives. The questions provided participants with opportunities to move beyond the evidential and to explore diverse ways of depicting their stories. In the process, photography facilitated a poetic engagement with past and present experiences.

8.6 Edwina's Story[30]

Edwina had travelled to Ireland with hopes of building a better future for herself and her family–professionally and educationally. She left the economic and political turmoil of her home country of Zimbabwe in 2000, and came to Dublin with a valid permit to work. She had learned about Ireland as a young girl attending missionary school, and proudly identified Irish ancestry in her family lineage. Her older sister had immigrated to the United Kingdom, and when Edwina's country was "going through some tough times and getting worse," the opportunity to work in Ireland seemed a viable option for her, and her son. Edwina writes:

---

30 The context and background of *Edwina's Story* is also discussed in my forthcoming book chapter, Re-conceptualizing Digital Storytelling: Thinking Through Audiovisual Inquiry (Alexandra, Forthcoming), which explores the connective tissue between digital storytelling and documentary filmmaking.

As a single parent, I wanted a better life for my son and myself. We came to Ireland leaving family, friends, and venturing into the unknown. Scared but excited, and not knowing what lay ahead for us.

In her documentary essay, Edwina details the workplace abuse, intimidation, and unjustified dismissal that lead to the loss of her work permit, and the beginning of her experiences as an undocumented migrant. She writes,

I had been in Ireland for about 3 years and worked first as a cleaner then as a Manager but I was being verbally abused by member of staff and unfairly treated at work. I worked 6 days a week, 12 hours a day even when I was sick with no break and just a sandwich, which I ate while working. The boss said they could not afford another person. When I complained to the Employer I would always be told that my work permit would be up for renewal. This was to silence me. All things came to a head when I joined the Union. They assisted me when I was told to resign or be fired. I then became undocumented and this was the beginning of a runaway roller coaster nightmare.

Edwina discusses the impact of living without legal documentation, and suggests policy changes that would improve circumstances for migrant laborers. She writes,

Living on the edge, stressed out, looking over my shoulder and feeling like a criminal. Any knock on the door, any Gardaí[31] sirens and I would cringe nervously waiting for the axe to fall.

The Bridging Visa, and more action against employers who abuse their work permit power could be the answer to this roller coaster nightmare.

Being undocumented means losing a part of your life. My dad just turned 80 and I couldn't go to his surprise birthday party. Having raised my 7 siblings and me when my mom died, he has been the most important person in my life.

I brought my son all the way from his home country so he could have a better education and a better future. I am not asking for handouts. I am willing and able to work, to contribute to this society and my family–something I have done all my life. Being documented will mean getting my life back on track, like a bright light at the end of a dark and scary tunnel.

Edwina's audio-visual composition does not visually illustrate the workplace discrimination and abuse discussed in her narrative. But, rather, she visually evokes a story located in the past, in an office she can no longer return to, in the present. To evoke this past, she documented her everyday life in Dublin. When we first began discussing her visual script, Edwina focused on evidential images. The first images for "My country was going through some tough times and getting worse," depicted a nearly empty cupboard (Figure 8.3), economic graphs, and collages she constructed from official documents and other objects (Figure 8.4). Graphs and photographs

---

31 *An Garda Síochána*, commonly referred to as the *Guardaí*, is the Irish police force.

of official documents performed the role of providing evidence of Edwina's lived experiences as she spoke to a public that disbelieves the legitimacy of migrant experiences (Valentine & Knudsen, 1995).

Figure 8.3: One of the first images Edwina took to visually represent "my country was going through some tough times and getting worse."

Figure 8.4: Edwina created a collage to represent the challenges she faced as a migrant employee dependent upon her employer –a government work permit application, a carrot, and her written text.

During the seminar, Edwina shared the first visual approaches to her story, and participant/practitioners considered her images. Some participants found these initial photographs confusing and un-dynamic. These first images played an important role in documenting the story, but when coupled with the poignancy of

Edwina's voiceover, they detracted from the narrative. Based on this feedback from the group, Edwina decided to continue her photographic investigation and develop more options. She began taking photographs daily, and looking for images from her present-day life that might provide the evidential "proof" she was seeking (Field notes 6 October 2007). Through this visual exploration of her story, she began to develop more evocative, and at times, metaphorical and ambiguous images.

Figure 8.5: "I then became undocumented and this was the beginning of a runaway rollercoaster nightmare –living on the edge, stressed out, looking over my shoulder and feeling like a criminal. Any knock on the door, any Gardaí sirens and I would cringe nervously waiting for the axe to fall." Screen shot from *Edwina's Story* (2007).

Edwina started by creating a series of images that navigated the physical interiors and emotional landscapes of her story. Instead of presenting images from her home country to visually express the factors that influenced her decision to migrate, the opening sequence of Edwina's digital story reveals two point of view shots from her apartment building in North Dublin. These two photographs in sequence situate the viewer in the physical space where Edwina spent much of her time after becoming undocumented–afraid to venture out of her apartment and into the city where she feared she might be apprehended and deported. Edwina combined these interior shots with more impressionistic, and associative images–birds in flight (Figure 8.6) and rolling clouds–to create tension between the underlying themes of injustice, and self-determination in her story. She staged visual re-enactments of her story on the body–an open palm, a worried gaze (Figure 8.5), and hands in prayer position bound with rope, which is the most literal image in her series of self-portraits. To evoke her feelings of imprisonment, and her desire for social justice, she juxtaposed these self-portraits with everyday objects–a laundry basket that serves as an impenetrable barrier (Figure 8.6) and a cardboard kitchen roll and tea light that figure in her image of the "light at the end of the tunnel." Edwina's images provoked a resonant response from other workshop participants. Perhaps most importantly, the images establish an intimate connection to Edwina and the story she crafted, while maintaining a degree of anonymity that felt comfortable to Edwina (Interview, 20 January 2009). Echoing Joan Didion's idea of needing more than words for inquiry and expression, Edwina observed that the process of producing her own photographs, and of editing her story gave her "more power" in expressing her experiences and arguments "than words alone." She stated, "I felt empowered by the photographs, by making them. It gave me more power in expressing my feelings than the words alone." (Interview, 20 January 2009). In 2015, Edwina received Irish citizenship.

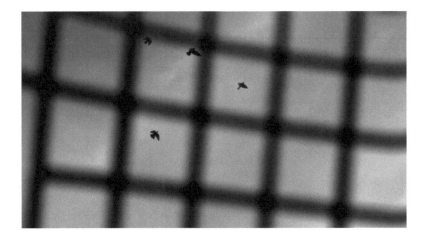

Figure 8.6: "The bridging visa and more action against employers who abuse their work permit power could be the answer to this roller coaster nightmare." Screen shot from *Edwina's Story* (2007).

8.7 Conclusion

This co-creative documentary practice–making images, audio-visual authoring and editing–not only served purposes of creative expression, but also of analysis and advocacy. This approach to digital storytelling served as a means to accompany migrant participants as they navigated institutional barriers to personal and public participation, belonging and well-being. Overall, the collaboration resulted in two series of broadcast quality digital stories–*Undocumented in Ireland: Our Stories* and *Living in Direct Provision: 9 Stories*. These documentary essays have played a role in migrant rights discourse and public policy. For example, the Migrant Rights Centre Ireland (MRCI) used the stories from the *Undocumented in Ireland: Our Stories* series as part of their Bridging Visa Campaign, a successful labor rights initiative for migrant workers. The series have also been screened before diverse audience members (including former President Mary Robinson), at community forums on asylum policy and migrant rights, at the Irish Film Institute (IFI), and the *Guth Gafa* Documentary Film Festival, and at universities and public policy presentations locally and internationally. Ten of the digital stories are currently available for viewing on-line at www.darcyalexandra.com. The longitudinal and inquiry-based approach to digital storytelling offered a dynamic opportunity to develop a shared ethnographic practice building from the audio-visual. As discussed through select images, and in particular the work of Edwina and Vukasin, practitioners originated and edited their own source material as they documented and constructed life stories within a collective. The method served both as a means of engaged inquiry through media practice, and a process for facilitating voice and listening about issues that research participants determined through the stories they selected, the artifacts they created, and the exploratory and contextualizing dialogue that developed over the course of the seminar. It also raised complex questions about the limits of listening and key considerations regarding the politics of voice (Alexandra, 2015b). Given that every research site is distinct, and research participants have diverse needs, goals and circumstances, I am not advocating this particular approach as *the* model to be replicated. Rather, I am suggesting that as we continue to develop shared practices of inquiry through audiovisual media, we value the aesthetic affordances and challenges of engaging with audio-visual platforms and tools and that we conceptualize research participants not solely as "storytellers" but more fundamentally as emergent media producers and ethnographic documentarians of their lives. In this way, we value and honor research practitioners, and the embodied objects they create.

References

Albertinelli, A. (2011). Asylum applicants and first instance decisions on asylum applications in third quarter 2010. *Eurostat: Data in Focus*, January 19, Retrieved on July 20, 2016, from http://ec.europa.eu/eurostat/en/web/products-data-in-focus/-/KS-QA-11-001.

Alexandra, D. (2008). Digital storytelling as transformative practice: Critical analysis and creative expression in the representation of migration in Ireland. *Journal of Media Practice*, 9(2), 101-112.

Alexandra, D. (2015a). *Visualising migrant voices: Co-creative documentary and the politics of listening* (Doctoral Dissertation). Dublin Institute of Technology, Dublin, Ireland.

Alexandra, D. (2015b). Are we listening yet? Participatory knowledge production through media practice. In A. Gubrium, K. Harper, & M. Otañez (Eds.), *Participatory visual and digital research in action* (pp. 41-55). Walnut Creek: Left Coast Press.

Alexandra, D. (Forthcoming). Re-conceptualizing digital storytelling: Thinking through audiovisual inquiry. In M. Dunford & T. Jenkins (Eds.), *Digital storytelling: Story, form and content*.

Berger, J. (1984). *And our faces, my heart, brief as photos*. New York: Pantheon Books.

Brushwood Rose, C. (2009). The (im)possibilities of self representation: Exploring the limits of storytelling in the digital stories of women and girls. *Changing English*, 16(2), 211-220.

Cammarota, J. (2008). The cultural organizing of youth ethnographers: Formalizing a praxis-based pedagogy. *Anthropology & Education Quarterly*, 39(1), 45-58.

Cochran-Smith, M. (2004). Teaching for social justice: Six principles of pedagogy. In M. Cochran-Smith, *Walking the road: Race, diversity and social justice in teacher education* (pp. 64-82). New York and London: Teachers College Press.

Coll, K. M. (2010). *Remaking citizenship: Latina immigrants & new American politics*. Stanford: Stanford University Press.

Darder, A., Baltodano, M., & Torres, R. D. (Eds.). (2008). *The critical pedagogy reader*. New York and London: Routledge.

Didion, J. (2005). *The year of magical thinking*. New York: Alfred A. Knopf.

Edwards, E. (1997). Beyond the boundary: A consideration of the expressive in photography and anthropology. In M. Banks & H. Morphy (Eds.), *Rethinking visual anthropology* (pp. 53-80). New Haven and London: Yale University Press.

Edwards, E., & Hart, J. (2004). Photographs as objects [Introduction]. In E. Edwards & J. Hart (Eds.), *Photographs objects histories: On the materiality of images*. London and New York: Routledge.

Fanning, B. (2001). *Beyond the pale: Asylum seeking children and social exclusion in Ireland*. Dublin: Irish Refugee Council.

Fassin, D. (2011). Policing borders, producing boundaries: The governmentality of immigration in dark times. *Annual Review of Anthropology*, 40, 213-226.

Fine, M., Weis, L., Centrie, C., & Roberts, R. (2000). Educating beyond the borders of schooling. *Anthropology & Education Quarterly*, 31(2), 131-151.

FLAC (2009). *One size doesn't fit all: A legal analysis of the Direct Provision and Dispersal System in Ireland, 10 years on*. Dublin: Free Legal Advice Centres. Retrieved on September 15, 2014, from www.flac.ie/download/pdf/one_size_doesnt_fit_all_full_report_final.pdf.

Fletcher, F., & Cambre, C. (2009). Digital storytelling and implicated scholarship in the classroom. *Journal of Canadian Studies*, 43(1), 109-130.

Greene, M. (1988). *The dialectic of freedom*. New York and London: Teachers College Press.

Guajardo, M., Guajardo, F., & Del Carmen Casaperalta, E. (2008). Transformative education: Chronicling a pedagogy for social change. *Anthropology & Education Quarterly*, 39(1), 3-22.

Gubrium, A. (2009a). Digital storytelling as a method for engaged scholarship in anthropology. *Practicing Anthropology*, 31(4), 5-9.

Gubrium, A. (2009b). Visualizing change: Participatory technologies in research and action. *Practicing Anthropology* 31(4), 2-4.

Gubrium, A., & Turner, K. C. N. (2010). Digital storytelling as an emergent method for social research and practice. In S. N. Hesse Biber (Ed.), *Handbook of emergent technologies in social science research* (pp. 469-491). Oxford: Oxford University Press.

Hartley, J., & McWilliam, K. (2009). *Story circle: Digital storytelling around the world*. Oxford: Wiley Blackwell.

Hill, A. (2014). Digital storytelling and the politics of doing good. In H. M. Pleasants & D. E. Salter (Eds.), *Community-based multiliteracies and digital media projects: Questioning assumptions and exploring realities* (pp. 21-44). New York: Peter Lang.

Hull, G. A., & Katz, M. L. (2006). Crafting an agentive self: Case studies of digital storytelling. *Research in the Teaching of English*, 41(1), 43-81.

Irish Refugee Council. (2013). *Direct Provision: Framing an alternative reception system for people seeking international protection*. Dublin: Irish Refugee Council. Retrieved July 20, 2016, from www.irishrefugeecouncil.ie/wp-content/uploads/2013/12/DP_Report_Final.pdf.

Lambert, J. (2013). *Digital storytelling: Capturing lives, creating community* (fourth edition). New York and London: Routledge.

Lave, J., & Wenger, E. (1991). *Situated learning: Legitimate peripheral participation*. Cambridge, UK: Cambridge University Press.

Loyal, S. (2011). *Understanding immigration in Ireland: State, capital and labour in a global age*. Manchester and New York: Manchester University Press.

Lundby, K. (2008). *Digital storytelling, mediatized stories: Self-representations in new media*. New York: Peter Lang.

MacDougall, D. (2006). *The corporeal image: Film, ethnography, and the senses*. Princeton: Princeton University Press.

Meadows, D. (2003). Digital storytelling: Research-based practice in new media. *Visual Communication*, 2(2), 189-193.

Moll, L. C. (1992). Funds of Knowledge for Teaching: Using a Qualitative Approach to Connect Homes and Classrooms. *Theory Into Practice*, 31 (1), 132-141.

Moreo, E. (2012). On visibility and invisibility: Migrant practices between regimes of representations and self-determination. In R. Lentin & E. Moreo (Eds.), *Migration, diasporas and citizenship* (pp. 72-94). London: Palgrave MacMillan.

Otañez, M., & Guerrerro, A. (2015). Digital Storytelling and the Hepatitis C Virus Project. In A. Gubrium, K. Harper, & M. Otañez (Eds.), *Participatory visual and digital research in action* (pp. 57-73). Walnut Creek, CA: Left Coast Press.

Pink, S. (2011). Images, senses and applications: Engaging visual anthropology. *Visual Anthropology*, 24(5), 437-454.

Pleasants, H. M., & Salter, D. E. (2014). *Community-based multiliteracies and digital media projects: Questioning assumptions and exploring realities*. New York: Peter Lang.

Poitras Pratt, Y. (2011). *Meaningful media: An ethnography of a digital strategy within a Métis Community* (Doctoral dissertation). University of Calgary, Calgary, Canada.

Rosaldo, R. (1994). Cultural citizenship in San Jose, California. PoLAR, 17(2), 57-64.

Rouch, J. (1974). The camera and the man. *Studies in the Anthropology of Visual Communication* 1(1), 37-44.

Rouch, J., & Taylor, L. (2003). A life on the edge of film and anthropology. In S. Feld (Ed.), *Ciné-Ethnography: Jean Rouch* (pp. 129-146). Minneapolis: University of Minnesota Press.

Ruby, J. (1991). Speaking for, speaking about, speaking with, or speaking alongside—An anthropological and documentary dilemma. *Visual Anthropology Review*, 7(2), 50-67.

Sanchez-Laws, A. L. (2010). Digital storytelling as an emerging documentary form. *Seminar.net*, 6(3), 359-366.

Spurgeon, C. L., Burgess, J. E., Klaebe, H. G., Tacchi, J. A., McWilliam, K., & Tsai, M. (2009). Co-creative media: Theorising digital storytelling as a platform for researching and developing participatory culture. In *Australian and New Zealand Communication Association Conference*, 8-10 July 2009, Queensland University of Technology, Brisbane, Queensland.

Stoller, P. (1992). *The cinematic griot: The ethnography of Jean Rouch*. Chicago and London: University of Chicago Press.

Threadgold, T. (2006). Dialogism, voice and global contexts: Asylum, dangerous men and invisible women. *Australian Feminist Studies*, 21(50), 223-244.

Valentine, D. E., & Knudsen, J. C. (1995). *Mistrusting refugees*. Berkeley, Los Angeles, and London: University of California Press.

Wenger, E. (1999). *Communities of practice: Learning, meaning and identity*. Cambridge, UK: Cambridge University Press.

Jason E. Miller

9 This is What I Want for My Children: A Case Study of Digital Storytelling with Latino Im/migrant Parents in Central Florida

"For us Latin parents, the main objective is to adapt ourselves to American culture, while conserving our Latin roots, by whatever means possible. My greatest ambition and wish is to ensure that my children receive higher education and pursue a professional career, since they too are the future of this country." —Isabella

9.1 Introduction

Between 2010 and 2011, I worked with a group of 15 Latino im/migrant[32] parents to help them tell their own stories about what it means to be a Latino im/migrant parent. Over the course of a year, we worked together to create short films—called *digital stories*—about their experiences as im/migrant parents. The stories are powerful and uniquely personal, and they give voice to the struggles endured by these parents to realize their dreams for their children.

It is rare to see positive, humanizing stories of Latino im/migrant parents when we turn on our televisions to watch the news. Rather than an uplifting story of a im/migrant parent learning to read, much of what a U.S. TV news consumer sees when they tune in is anything but uplifting. Instead, stories about im/migrant families are juxtaposed against images of faceless men climbing over fences, wielding knives and guns, and destroying white families through violent crime.

These images contribute to an atmosphere of fear and perceived threat among majority viewers, but are also internalized by minoritized communities. A 2004 study by the Pew Hispanic Center found that 44% of Latinos are "broadly concerned that the English-language media contribute to a negative image of Latinos among English-speaking Americans" (Suro, 2004). It is against this backdrop that the parents' stories play out.

---

32 There is a robust debate in scholarly and activist circles as to how best to collectively describe individuals who migrate and immigrate. *Migrant* is generally used to describe people who participate in temporary, often circular migratory patterns (often for economic reasons) and who plan on returning to their home country. *Immigrant* is often used to describe people who move to a new place with the intention of staying in the receiving country. Throughout this chapter, I use the more inclusive term im/migrants to describe the population in my study. I do this for two reasons: first, the term is more inclusive. Second, both migrant and immigrant parents participated in the creating digital stories.

The perception of a negative image regarding Latino im/migrant parents in the news media was certainly shared by the parents who attended a thrice-a-week evening English literacy academy in urban central Florida. These parents, their teachers, and the program director were keenly aware that the Latino im/migrant parent portrayed on TV did not look at all similar to the individuals diligently studying in their classrooms. Working closely with the program director, Yolanda Ochoa[33], I attended classes, interviewed the parents about their experiences as im/migrant parents, and helped them each create digital stories to document their own voice.

This chapter details one facet of my larger dissertation research, namely, the process and experience of producing digital stories with the im/migrant parents. Beyond this primary purpose, this chapter has three additional foci: first, I explore unique ethical and practical considerations for undertaking digital storytelling with a vulnerable population. This is complicated by the potential of sharing their digital stories with a broader audience. I propose strategies to ameliorate those challenges. Second, I show how digital stories can be used as a tool for research focusing on the themes the parents present in their stories. Finally, I note outcomes for parents, for myself as a researcher and for other (potential) audiences.

9.2 Methodology

Digital stories are a short-format (generally non-fiction) form of media lasting between two and five minutes. They are almost always told in first person and generally feature a narrative structure. The process of creating a digital story relies on simple tools and, ergo, digital stories allow regular people with little experience in creating digital media to quickly create a story. These short "films" rely on simple techniques such as incorporating still photography, short clips of video, music, and simple animation. Digital stories almost always feature the voice of the storyteller narrating the story. The software used to make digital stories also tends to be simple and lacking complex features that could confuse new filmmakers. Importantly, it is also, thus maximizing the number of people who can quickly master the technique and produce a story.

Perhaps surprisingly, many digital storytelling practitioners of this type owe their formatting style to Ken Burns, who pioneered the use of first-person accounts narrated over still images during his 1990 documentary series *The Civil War* (Sylvester & Greenidge, 2009). To this day, the camera panning technique he developed (where the camera slowly pans or zooms in on a particular aspect of a still photograph) is still called the "Ken Burns Effect" in most film editing software

---

[33] All names are pseudonyms to protect the identity of participants.

programs. This editing effect combined with first-person narration heightens the emotion content of the story and brings the photographs to life.

Anthropologist Julie Woletz has documented the rise of this form of digital story and credits storyteller and playwright Dana Atchley at the American Film Institute in 1993 with being the first to use the phrase digital storytelling to describe a short form, narrative film in this style (Woeltz, 2008). Joe Lambert (2006, 2013), a friend and collaborator of Atchley's, is seen as one of the definitive voices of this format, having adapted and refined Atchley's procedure for creating digital stories. Lambert founded the Center for Digital Storytelling in 1993 in Berkeley, California. The Center for Digital Storytelling (CDS), now known simply as StoryCenter, hosts digital storytelling workshops and conferences and publishes extensively about the work of the center.

Lambert and the team from CDS have worked to refine their approach to digital storytelling over the last 30 years. I refer to their approach as the "Traditional CDS Model." In the traditional model, an intensive workshop is held over three days in which eight to twelve participants spend eight hours a day scripting and recording their story. Workshop participants work through several stages. First, they are introduced to the "Seven Elements of Digital Storytelling." These include point of view, dramatic question, emotional content, the gift of voice, the power of soundtrack, economy, and pacing (Lambert, 2006, pp. 9-19). In 2013, Lambert and CDS released a revised and reframed version of the seven elements restyled into the "Seven Steps of Digital Storytelling." These seven *steps* are similar to the seven *elements*: owning your insight, owning your emotions, finding the moment, seeing your story, hearing your story, assembling your story and sharing your story (Lambert, 2013, pp. 54-69). However, they are organized into a process and focus the participant on their own voice as powerful and insightful. Second, a story circle is held where workshop participants gather and share their stories aloud. After each storyteller shares, other workshop participants offer feedback about the story. This can take the form of emotional support (many of the stories are particularly poignant and visibly difficult for the storyteller to tell) but also takes the form of suggestions for improving the mechanics or flow of the story. Subsequently, workshop participants spend time writing a script, gathering and digitizing materials such as still photographs and music, and recording their narration. Participants ultimately edit their films together and share their completed digital stories in a group screening. The process requires a rather intensive time commitment, but otherwise is designed for those who have little technological expertise to be able to complete a story rapidly. Workshop participants do not necessarily have anything in common and can range in age, ethnicity, gender, sexuality, etc. The CDS also hosts custom workshops for specific groups or with specific populations.

Other models have developed in different geographic and historical contexts. For example, Appalshop began training local, Appalachian filmmakers in 1969 to tell their own place-based stories about rural Appalachia in traditional documentary length formats. In 1998 the Australian Centre for the Moving Image began developing digital storytelling projects informed by the CDS model (Simondson, 2009) and in 2000, the BBC began a digital storytelling project in Wales it largely modeled off of the CDS traditional model (Meadows & Kidd, 2009).

The CDS model (or similar models) has been widely used in many different settings for different aims. Several edited volumes have been assembled with examples of digital stories of this type and different applications (Hartley & McWilliam, 2009; Lundby, 2008; this volume). Digital Storytelling has been shown to be particularly useful in public health projects (Gubrium, 2009), in working with youth (Goodman & Greene, 2003), in corporate and organizational contexts (Boje, 2008; Brown, et al., 2005), and in community arts practice (Howley, 2005). In each of these projects, the specific populations and aims are different. However, at its core, digital storytelling is about helping regular people to be able to amplify their voices through the use of emergent media—to share their voices in more profound ways to reach larger audiences or to just reach their own families.

Given this history and context, I set about creating a digital storytelling project with Latino im/migrant parents in urban central Florida who attended classes at a non-profit focused on English literacy. As we began creating a process of creating the digital stories I knew that I had to address several challenges.

First, all of the parents were native Spanish speakers, but were largely illiterate in Spanish. While all of the parents attended English languages classes, most had never written a story in English (or Spanish) before and their English skills were new. Second, most of the parents who participated had little experience using a computer. While all but two of the parents owned and used a cell phone, none of the parents had a computer at home and limited access to computers outside of the literacy academy. By contrast, their children had significant experience using computers in school, which several of the parents identified as intimidating in the process of creating their own digital story. In order to address this, one of the teachers at the Academy spent three Wednesday evenings before we began the digital storytelling process leading classes in how to use computers, how to use Microsoft Word, and about photos and music on computers. The Academy met three nights a week; Tuesday and Thursday evenings were devoted to learning English and Wednesday evenings were spent doing parental involvement activities with the parents' children. Given the multiple demands on each parent's time, attendance was occasionally sporadic, with many parents missing several evenings per month. This was a challenge because it meant that parents often progressed slowly in producing their stories, and the progress they did make on their digital stories between the sessions they did attend required them to "start over" to a certain extent.

In light of these challenges, I adapted the digital story creation process outlined by the StoryCenter in Berkeley, California. (Lambert, 2013; Lambert, 2006). In the traditional StoryCenter model, an intensive workshop is held over three days in which eight to twelve participants spend eight hours a day scripting and recording their story. Since none of our participants had three full, consecutive days to devote to the process of story creation, we broke the process of creating the digital story into eight separate workshops: 1) What is a Digital Story?; 2) Story Circle; 3) What are the Seven Elements?; 4) Script Writing; 5) Storyboarding; 6) Digitizing Photos and Music; and 7) Polishing and finishing stories. These workshops came after the three-week series of workshops on how to use a computer. Workshops were held over the course of 8 Wednesday evenings. We also planned to have three more Wednesday evenings to spend working more one-on-one with particular parents to help them finish their stories.

The first of the seven workshops was completed as planned. On the first evening, I presented the idea of the workshops to the parents and showed several examples of digital stories. I also presented the "story circle" tool (StoryCenter step 2) and told the parents that, if they would like to participate in the project, they should come the following week with an idea for a story or a story to share. We spent the remainder of the time together brainstorming what kinds of stories the parents wanted to tell. Most parents seemed excited at the possibility of creating their own story. The other parents had questions and a few were concerned because they had never used a computer before but were eager to learn how.

During the second workshop, we held the story circle. We sat in a circle and each person took a turn telling his or her story or idea for a story. The first storyteller chose to share her own story of crossing into the United States from Mexico. When she finished, several of the other parents were quietly weeping. One of the women stood and walked across the room to retrieve a box of tissues. After a few moments, I asked if anyone had feedback. Slowly, parents offered their own thoughts by asking follow up questions or offering their own solidarity. Then, each subsequent parent took their turn in telling their own story or story idea. Some were quite long and detailed while others were only general story ideas. Some parents appeared to feel very safe in the circle and shared deeply personal and moving stories about their lives—particularly their border crossing experiences. Other parents were much more guarded sharing only very surface-level occurrences from their lives. Many of the stories directly or indirectly referenced violence, sexual violence, and the extreme poverty many of the parents found themselves in both before and after coming to the United States. Some of the stories were "complete" stories in the Western notion of a story containing a beginning, middle, and end while other storytellers told stories that were more non-linear focusing more on a feeling or a piece of a memory.

During week three, I briefly presented the "Seven Elements of Digital Storytelling" (StoryCenter step 3). We also spent a significant amount of time discussing the ethical ramifications of their stories, which I will discuss later in this chapter. During week four, we discussed the process of script writing and then began drafting story scripts on index cards, later transferring those script outlines to the computer.

It was at this point that the process began to break down. The majority of the parents had missed at least one of the previous sessions. Several of the parents had missed two or three. On the fourth evening, no parent was ready to progress to the storyboarding workshop, as many were still drafting their stories. Ochoa and I met while the parents worked and decided to adapt the format again. Rather than continuing to progress as a group, we decided that each parent would work independently to continue developing their story. Because time was limited, I was not able to work with each of the parents each of the nights. To ameliorate this, I recruited two Spanish-speaking undergraduate anthropology students to assist the parents. The students were trained in Digital Storytelling and, because they were bilingual in English and Spanish, they were able to sit with one or two parents for the entire evening each session and work with them directly on their story. It was this one-on-one approach that allowed the stories to be completed. Between the two student assistants and myself, we were able to ensure that all of the parents involved were supported in the creation of their stories.

9.3 Ethics and Digital Storytelling

One of the major goals of this project was to host a formal screening of the parents' films to share the work they were doing with a broader community and to host the stories on the website of the NGO who hosted the academy. This was important to the NGO and to myself as an applied anthropologist. Before beginning the digital storytelling project, Ochoa and I discussed at length, along with the parents, the idea of a film screening and website hosting. Because this was part of my own dissertation research, I also submitted the entire project through my university's own Institutional Review Board (IRB) and received approval. The parents who participated in this project and my larger dissertation research had a variety of immigration statuses.

As part of the approval from the IRB, I sought informed consent from each parent to participate. However, I also successfully applied for a Waiver of Documentation of Informed Consent from the IRB. This meant that, while I still used an informed consent document with each parent and made sure they understood what they were consenting to, I did not seek their signature on the informed consent document. I also did not collect any personally identifiable data from them. Thus, each parent is effectively anonymous, with no direct link between their identity and my dissertation research. However, one cannot easily be anonymous in a digital story!

Due to the deeply personal nature of digital stories, each parent chose to use their own voice in the creation of the story both figuratively (i.e., their creative voice as author of the script and director) and literally (i.e., the stories are narrated using their own voice). So, too, the stories were composed of photographs and images the storyteller created, and almost all featured the storyteller along with his or her family members. It became impossible to obscure the identity of the participant—a significant challenge because of the real threat of deportation faced by many Latino im/migrant families in the United States. During the third workshop, we spent half of the session discussing the ramifications of a parent being personally identified as a participant in a story. We discussed several scenarios which parents may face because of their participation and then discussed strategies to cope with those scenarios. For example, we discussed using creative angles when taking photographs for the project that would hide the identity of the participant; as in Figure 9.1, a photograph taken by one of the parents whose story concerned her work as a restaurant cleaner after hours.

Figure 9.1: Image taken by Isabella framed in such a way as to conceal her identity. Used with Isabella's permission.

The storyteller is in most of the photos, but we never see her face—she always appears from behind or is partially hidden by a piece of industrial cooking hardware. Thus, her identity is hidden and protected. After this session, several of the parents who wanted to tell stories of their crossing into the United States decided to change their story topics entirely. Two parents decided to withdraw altogether.

By the end of the process, several more parents decided to tell the story they originally wanted to tell, but decided that their stories were too personal to share with others outside of the group. While they had felt very safe telling their story in the intimacy of the story circle, the prospect of sharing their digital story more broadly with an unknown and potentially unsafe broader audience was reason enough to decide to withhold their story. Other participants decided that there was simply too much risk in sharing their stories on a website or in public. Only one parent ultimately was willing to share her story publically. However, her story contained images of the other parents and their children as the topic was about the literacy academy itself. Even though she had given consent for her story to be shared with a broader audience, the other parents who are seen in her video did not consent. Ultimately, I must respect their wishes as a researcher and as the "keeper" of these stories.

Obviously, this was disappointing to the NGO and to myself. After almost a year of work we only had one story to publicly share. The film screening was cancelled and I needed to change the direction of my dissertation to account for the now missing element. However, as anthropologists and filmmakers it is our duty to respect the wishes of our participants and their desire to not publically share their work. It is important to note that while only one of the parents (Isabella) was willing to let her film be screened or images used, they all consented to have their stories used in my research so long as I protected their identities.

9.4 The Digital Stories

One evening in early May, the program director called me into her office when I arrived. She told me that the local church that leased its classroom space to the literacy academy had decided rather abruptly to cease this agreement. The church did not reveal why it made the decision. It was her perception that the church had become aware that "migrants" were receiving free classes on their property and that they were made to feel uncomfortable. While the Academy had enough funds to continue paying rent at a new location, they had yet to find a suitable space. Ochoa informed me that the academy would close in two weeks and asked if I thought any of the parents' stories could be finished by then. We redoubled our efforts and set to work.

In total, five out of fifteen parents completed finalized digital stories. The remaining parents' stories were in a variety of forms of completion, with two additional stories being very close to completion. Of the seven stories that were completed (or were close to completion), each presented a unique approach to the process. A summary of each of the stories is presented below; the following section then analyzes the stories, drawing out three common themes.

Table 9.1: Summary of digital stories, themes and barriers.

Author and Story	Themes	Barriers
Isabella's Story: *Latin Mothers*	• Cultural perseverance • Value of education • Learning English / English as survival • Future and children	• Missed many classes due to work and family commitments
Gabriela's Story: *Querer es Poder (Want is Power)*	• Transnational families • Learning English / English as survival • Future and children • Coping with loss	• Little experience with technology
Eva's Story: *I Want to Learn English*	• Learning English / English as survival • Value of education • Cultural perseverance • Future and children	• Little experience with technology • Lacked confidence in English
Sofia's Story: *La Historia* *(The Story)*	• Cultural perseverance • Transnational families • Coping with loss • Future and children	• Little experience with technology
Ximena's Story: *La Vida (Life)*	• Cultural perseverance • Transnational families • Future and children	• Lacked confidence in English
Francisco's Story: *La Experiencia de un Viajero sin Boleto (The Experience of a Traveler Without a Ticket)*	• Journey to the United States • Transnational families • Future and children • Coping with loss	• Limited Spanish literacy • Little experience with technology
Verónica's Story: *-untitled-*	• Leaving daughters behind • Transnational families • Domestic violence • Future and children • Coping with loss	• Missed many classes
Alicia's Story: *-untitled-*	• Journey to the United States • Transnational families • Future and children	• Limited Spanish literacy • Missed many classes

9.4.1 Isabella's Story: Latin Mothers

Isabella had the strongest English language skills of any parent in the group, but also missed a significant number of classes due to work and parental commitments. In working to complete her story, Isabella felt strongly that she wanted to communicate to viewers that she was proud of her accomplishments and felt dignity even in the face of constant dehumanization as a migrant mother at work, at stores, or at her child's school. Isabella saw learning English as a way to empower herself. "We find that in arriving here, the primary barrier is a language, which is not ours, but if we do not speak or learn, we find ourselves lost, like a goldfish out of its bowl," she says in her story. "Despite these adverse obstacles we continue to struggle without surrendering, despite the hard work we do." Isabella was the only parent who decided that she would be willing to share her digital story with others.

9.4.2 Gabriela's Story: Querer es Poder (Want is Power)

Gabriela came to the United States when she was 16 excited to be able to learn English. However, she found herself unable to act on that hope and instead took a job at a dry cleaner cleaning clothes. Soon, she found herself married with three children but that marriage quickly ended and her former husband, also a migrant, immigrated back to Mexico. She speaks of the difficulty in raising her son without a father, particularly in the face of school-celebrated holidays that often encourage parents to participate. "When it is Father's Day, my son does not want to go school. It makes me feel sad, because he sees all of the children with their fathers. It is moments like this that are very hard to be a single parent." But here she pivots in her story and rather than continue to feel like she has no control, she returns to her dream of learning English and following her aspirations. She concludes her story by moving forward in time three years and celebrating the newfound skills she has acquired after participating in the literacy academy. She, too, concludes by stating that she sees herself as an example for her children of someone who works hard to achieve her dream, and that she wants to pass this on to her children as well. While Gabriela originally was willing to share her story publically, upon screening it in front of two of her teachers she began weeping, and finally declared that the story was much too personal to share with an audience.

9.4.3 Eva's Story: I Want to Learn English

Eva was the quietest participant and the most self-conscious when it came to using her writing and speaking skills. Like the other parents, Eva's story was deeply rooted in her experience of learning English and the struggles she faced as a Latina woman.

She spoke with shame about her inability to communicate with others when she first arrived and how she was unable to order from restaurant menus. Like Isabella, she focused on the literacy academy as a way of improving her life and that of her child. In her story, she writes that: "Thanks to God, I found this literacy academy where they offer help and they teach English. They help us become better parents. They teach me how to read to my child. We do activities together like planting trees, chili, and tomato plants, and flowers. These activities are important to teach them to conserve the environment and we do them together as a family." Eva concludes by identifying her goal: to be able to help her child with his homework and for them all to have a better future. Eva also felt that her digital story was too personal to share with an audience.

9.4.4 Sofia's Story: La Historia (The Story)

Sofia and her husband, Javier[34], both participated in the digital storytelling workshop; one pair of only two husband and wife couples who participated in the project. Sofia and Javier were also the only parents who did not come from Mexico but were both from Honduras. Moreover, Sofia was very clear to point out to me on several occasions that they were in the United States legally. Sofia's story was different from the others in several ways. First, each of the other stories was at least partially about coming to the United States. Sofia's story describes bringing her children to Honduras for Christmas vacation in 2010 to meet both parents' Honduran families. The story chronicles the first time Sofia had returned to Honduras in 13 years. Unlike the other stories, she does not narrate the story in English, but rather in Spanish. She does not include any reference to learning to speak English and presents the story in the form of a digital scrapbook of their trip. She particularly delights in describing dressing her pre-teen son in Honduran clothing for the first time and capturing his reaction on film. "He was so happy and proud to be dressed in clothing that represented a part of his culture." Sofia did not wish to share her story with an audience, though she did not provide a reason for this decision.

---

34 Javier missed many classes. He did not attend the story circle and subsequently never settled on a story topic. He is mentioned here because he often interacted with his wife, Sofia, during class and she often asked him to "look over" her work. However, Javier did not seem to have any editorial impact on Sofia's final digital story.

9.4.5 Ximena's Story: La Vida (Life)

Ximena was the youngest of the parents who participated in the workshop and the most experienced using technology. Ximena used her cell phone extensively for a variety of purposes and used a computer in her job as a secretary. Her written Spanish skills were excellent but she struggled to use English. For Ximena's story, she chose to write about her grandmother who raised her and who died of diabetes when she was 10 years old. Ximena's digital story uses the memory of learning to cook eggs with her grandmother as entrée to discussing her mother's death and Ximena's desire to live each day to the fullest. Ximena did not respond as to whether or not her digital story could be shared. In light of this, we have not shared her story.

In addition to the five stories that were completed, three additional parents completed scripts and storyboards and were gathering photographs and music at the time the Academy closed. I include brief descriptions of these three stories below, even though the films were left uncompleted.

9.4.6 Francisco's Story: La Experiencia de un Viajero sin Boleto (The Experience of a Traveler Without a Ticket)

Francisco and his girlfriend, Verónica, were the other couple that participated in the workshops. Francisco has been in the United States for six years and worked at a local restaurant as a line cook. Francisco had not attended school in Mexico and was largely illiterate in Spanish. This made it very difficult to learn English and he was unable to complete his story. However, he was dedicated and wanted others to hear of his experience. In four months, he did not miss a single class at the academy and worked diligently to improve his English. His story was of crossing the border and the challenges he faced walking without food or water for many days. He also writes of the fear of being discovered by immigration. Once in the United States, he began to work immediately and has not stopped since. "We arrived on a Saturday afternoon and Sunday started working. The start was not easy but after six years I feel I am living the American dream and still fulfilling the promise to help mine." Francisco also owned a cell-phone and often called his mother in Mexico before classes.

9.4.7 Verónica's Story: -untitled-

Verónica missed many classes and her story was never completed. Her story script describes the pain of leaving two young daughters behind in Mexico when she immigrated to the United States. She attempted to bring them with her, but their father prevented it. She saved money to bring them but found herself pregnant and in an abusive relationship making it impossible to save the money needed. "It made me sad and I felt that if I were pregnant I would not be able to achieve the same things and bring my daughters with me. After I had another child, I was alone with my son for days in the hospital. So now I had four children and ten days after giving birth I had to get myself up and go to work," she wrote. In the end, her abusive boyfriend was deported. Even though Verónica's story was never completed, she often commented on the cathartic nature of being able to tell her story to someone who cared enough to listen.

9.4.8 Alicia's Story: -untitled-

Alicia also had limited Spanish literacy skills and had been taking classes at the academy for only 2 years. She had come to the United States at 15 and now some years later was hoping to improve her life by learning English. Alicia's unfinished story was very short and she often was absent from classes for work related reasons meaning that she had little time to devote to the completion of her story.

9.5 Discussion

While all of the stories are unique and speak to the many different circumstances faced by these parents, some common themes did emerge.

9.5.1 Journey to the United States and Coping with Loss

Most of the stories included at least passing reference to the act of migration itself and the impact the border has on their families and their lives. In each case, the storyteller highlighted the challenges they faced and, more specifically, how they coped with loss. Gabriela, Ximena, Francisco, and Verónica's stories in particular speak to the challenges of separating families across international borders and the sadness that comes from the inability to easily move back and forth. This is perhaps most pronounced in Verónica's story and her being forced to chose between leaving her two young children behind and bringing them with her. So, too, the stories speak to the complex interpersonal relationships that must endure, often because of children, across transnational borders when a personal relationship comes to an end. Divorce, separation, and death are additional themes that are prominently featured in several of the stories and are hinted at in others. For example, Sofia speaks of her sadness at not seeing her family for 13 years and writes of her joy at the pride her son takes in his Honduran ethnic identity as he reconnects with his roots. As the viewer, we are left feeling that it may be a long time before Sofia's children are able to see that home again.

Another important aspect of learning to cope with loss as an im/migrant parent was also helping to ensure that your children do not lose their "culture"—not forgetting who they are and where they came from. Isabella, Sofia, Eva, and Ximena each spoke of wanting to provide their children with a deep cultural appreciation of their Mexican or Honduran heritage in a variety of ways—through travel in the case of Sofia, through food in the case of Ximena, and, for Isabella and Eva, through immersing their children in the day-to-day cultural lives of Mexican Americans.

Stories about the journey to the United States were particularly popular during the story circle. Yet, not a single finished story was explicitly about the journey itself. One story, that of Francisco (which never progressed past the storyboarding phase), was about the journey to the United States. Francisco had a very clear recollection of what the journey to the United States was like, but he lacked photographs of the journey. We discussed several possible alternatives to using pictures from the actual event, such as staging photos, taking photos in the present that somehow related to what was being said, or using more abstract photos to evoke the mood or feeling he sought to express. However, none of these proved acceptable to him. Ultimately, Francisco never finished his story. Other parents who proposed telling stories specifically about their own journey to the United States also noted difficulties they saw as insurmountable. For some, stories of the crossing were too difficult to relive. After originally sharing their stories during the story circle, the parents quickly changed to a different topic. Others, like Francisco, struggled with how they would visually construct a story with no images. Regardless, traces of those original stories were left in each of the stories, completed or in progress, simply because the storytellers were implicitly asked to frame their story as a "migrant parent," and that framing influenced the stories they chose to create.

9.5.2 Learning English and the Value of Education

Three of the stories specifically make reference to learning English as a key element of the story (Isabella, Gabriella, and Eva). Moreover, six of the eight stories refer to the importance of English as a coping strategy for im/migrant parents. In each of these stories, English language skills and English language acquisition are prioritized as important tasks for an im/migrant. Perhaps the best example of this is Eva, whose story is aptly titled: *I Want to Learn English*. In the process of creating her story, Eva reflected on the shame she felt at being unable to order food at a local restaurant and being unable to read an English storybook her son's elementary school teacher had sent home. She lamented that even as a second grader, her son could read the storybook better than she. These frustrations are similar to what other parents expressed, both in their stories and in the story circle, where many commented on the challenges of not speaking English whilst simultaneously trying to be a good parent and partner with their children's schools. For Eva, part of the story she wanted to tell was to communicate the importance of learning English and excelling in school to her son. She took great pride and satisfaction in being able to read the first book to him in English. As she made her digital story, she carefully chose images of herself volunteering with her children's school that communicate a discourse of parental involvement and reiterate her desire to show her children the value of education.

Several parents shared the notion that one of the goals of this project was to show their children the value of education. In particular, Isabella very pointedly crafted a story that would show her daughter that she was an empowered Latina mother who took pride in both her Spanish and English language abilities. As she created her digital story, she specifically chose images of herself as a student in class juxtaposed with images of her daughter and son also in class to draw a direct correlation to the journey they were on together. As we discussed how she would sequence the images in her film, she commented that she wanted to keep the images rotating back and forth between herself and her children so that when they watched her film, they could see the importance she placed on education and that their struggles were the same; both were struggling for a better life.

Sofia authored the only story to eschew English. Her story does not reference English or education in any way and the story is told exclusively using Spanish, not English. Sofia also chose to write her story entirely in Spanish and did not translate her story into English. While working with Sofia on her story I attempted on several occasions to ask her why she preferred to work in Spanish instead of English. This was surprising (although not unacceptable) because a major goal of the project was to help the storytellers improve their English language skills and become more confident in speaking English. Each time I enquired, Sofia brushed off my question. However, I think a viewing of her final story may provide the reason. Sofia framed her story, about a recent family trip to Honduras for the first time since she had immigrated to the United States, to communicate to her audience the importance she placed on her Honduran cultural heritage and her deep desire for her children to celebrate Honduran culture, food, clothing, and language. In this way, the use of Spanish became a way for her to aurally communicate to her audience the importance of language for her children. When we reflected on her final film, Sofia confided that she was scared that her children, both of whom had been born and raised in Florida, were highly lacking in their Spanish speaking skills and knew less about their Honduran culture than she would have liked. Viewed in this light, Sofia's story becomes not just about the value of education, but also about reframing notions of formal and informal education and enculturation for transnational families.

9.5.3 Future and Children

The stories the parents told often highlighted the importance of education for both the children and the parent. They also told of the importance of having a career and "making something out of yourself," so the child would not have to live and work as difficult a life as his or her parents. Francisco's story begins:

> "Muchos dicen que no es legal. Muchos dicen que es el sueño Americano. Yo deje a mi madre y a mis hermanos para darles un futuro mejor pero el dejarlos no fue tan facil." [Many say that it is not legal. Many say that it is the American dream. I told my mother and my brothers I was going to leave to give them a better future, but it was not as easy to leave as I thought.]

For Francisco and the other parents, the journey to the United States was framed solely in the context of improving their lives and, in turn, those of their families. For Eva and Gabriela the goal was, unambiguously, to learn English. Perhaps Isabella states it best in her story when she says:

> "We arrived here for various reasons, but the primary reason is that the majority of us are searching for liberty and the opportunity for growth, both economical as much as intellectual, which we may not have in our native countries given that we come from Third World or underdeveloped countries."

Isabella unequivocally declares her journey to the United States is not only for her own economic betterment but also her own intellectual growth and increased quality of life.

Gabriela also spends a significant portion of her story talking about her hopes and dreams for the future three years after her painful divorce. She describes the challenges of being a single parent, but then goes on to describe the pride she felt when her son was selected as student of the month at his elementary school. She speaks of this new dual role she now performs—acting as both mother and father to her children. She ends on an upbeat tone, celebrating the positive things in her life and how much she and her children have grown. She says, "I want the best for my kids, and when they grow up for them to know what I have accomplished." Gabriela ends her story with a collection of whimsical candid photos of herself and her children in stylish clothing and hairdos, smiling and posing for the camera. It's as if she's telling the world: "look at all I've accomplished!"

9.6 Conclusion

Each of the parents who participated felt that the process of creating a story was personally rewarding and the parents took great pride in what they were able to accomplish. None of the parents had ever attempted to tell a story (digital or otherwise) before, and they all found the experience to be gratifying. Participants were able to practice their English language skills by writing their stories in Spanish and then translating them into English. During the translation process the parents had to carefully choose words that retained their intended meaning but also flowed well in English prose. This allowed them to think critically about how they were using English and go beyond the exercises they typically completed in the classroom. Additionally, all but one parent recorded their story in English and thus participants were able to practice their spoken English. Because sections were rarely recorded in one "take," parents got to say each phrase numerous times as they worked on polishing their pronunciation and gaining confidence.

Participants also gained tangible skills in using a computer, word processing software, and photo and video editing software. Each of the seven parents who completed the project, or were close to completion, reported that they felt more confident using a computer. However, this confidence was not distributed equally. Those parents who had some existing familiarity with computers reported higher levels of self-efficacy while those who had little previous experience stated they were more comfortable, but still not very confident in their ability to achieve something like this on their own in the future. Indeed, some of the parents relied very heavily on myself or one of the undergraduate research assistants to troubleshoot for them whenever they encountered an obstacle, rather than trying to find their own solution first.

After each parent completed and viewed their final story (which occurred asynchronously) the parent, Yolanda, and I sat and reflected together on the process. All five parents spoke of their pride at creating their story and commented on how cathartic the process had been. Several of the participants were moved to tears when they heard their own voice and saw their photos on the screen. Yolanda and I hugged and congratulated each parent, and Yolanda would remind the parent that this is what they worked so hard for. Each parent commented that they never thought they could accomplish something as complicated and satisfying as their project.

Originally, Yolanda and I planned to have an open house at the center and invite local community leaders, allies, and others to come and watch the stories and speak with the parents. Four out of five parents ultimately decided to not share their digital stories with others. Unfortunately, the parent's decision to keep their stories private beyond our small group meant that this event could not proceed. While this was challenging from a policy perspective and obviously limited the external impact of the stories, it is imperative that the control of digital stories remains in the hands of the story's authors from an ethical standpoint. I am not sure what might have made the parents more comfortable sharing their stories. To a certain extent, I believe participants may have ultimately been uncomfortable sharing their stories with others because they were created and framed by Yolanda and I as *im/migrant* parent stories. Even if parents were careful to tell stories that did not contain any personally identifiable information or images, it was impossible to wholly conceal who the parents were. As a result, most parents felt a certain level of risk at being promoted as a im/migrant parent that was not justified by any gains they would experience from sharing their stories. Moreover, the unpredictable nature of who would see the stories in a public setting and what would happen to them after they were viewed caused parents to pause and reflect. I do not believe this is a limitation of the method in regards to policy or research but does have implications for those who endeavor to undertake these sorts of projects. Namely, that facilitators need to be mindful of the risks to participants and help them think through the ramifications of sharing their stories. From this perspective, the project was successful in that I was able to help each of the parents assess the level of risk they were comfortable with and make an informed decision.

As this chapter has hopefully illustrated, I believe digital storytelling can be a powerful methodological tool for participants, for research, and for anthropology. It is so powerful specifically because it taps into the emotional core of the storyteller and allows their voice to rise above that of the researcher. I believe this is advantageous over, for example, a more traditional interview, because it allows the researcher and participant to work together in an iterative way to draw out the story. Moreover, the process of creating a digital story allows the storyteller to be in control. Storytellers are responsible for framing the story, setting the mood, setting areas of focus and thus the process shifts power to the storyteller rather than the researcher. In this way, the researcher is a guide helping to facilitate the use of technology and style of storytelling while the storyteller themselves is able to take the lead. Additionally, a benefit of this approach in my specific example is that storytellers worked with each other as a cohort. They provided emotional and informational support to each other (in the form of encouragement, solidarity, feedback, and suggestions) and instrumental support (in the form of sharing photos and songs) to each other across the process. This is similar to a process that can develop during focus groups where members can sometimes seek to gain consensus, but instead, the digital storytelling process worked to build solidarity among the parents who participated.

Lambert (2009) points to the relative dearth of ways that the field of digital storytelling is able to assess their work. He states that a fundamental struggle of the practitioners is how to define success given that success is often frames in terms of the process and not the content of the work storytellers produce (87). Lambert goes on to argue that the arts community often critique the lack of artistic sophistication of the storytellers while service providers critique the lack of professional distance between storyteller and trainer. Here, Lambert (2009, p. 88) cites a potential framework for assessing digital storytelling projects developed by Arlene Goldbard (2006). The framework has 6 criteria:

1. The collaboration was mutually meaningful between communities and reciprocal between participant/community and facilitator.
2. Participants are full co-directors in the process with the facilitator.
3. Participants experience broad cultural knowledge (such as a greater mastery of the arts media used in the project.
4. Participants feel they have successfully expressed themselves through the project.

5. Participants feel their local aims have been addressed as well as their desires to bring their work to a larger audience.
6. Participants feel confident about taking on social and cultural projects and action in the future.

I believe this digital storytelling project met most, but not all of the criteria. The project represented a mutual and meaningful collaboration between participants and me in the role of community facilitator. Participants chose to partake because of their own interests and reported that the found the topics meaningful and important. Moreover, participants were in control at each step of the process being supported but not hindered or controlled by the facilitator. Participants gained not only an increased understanding of how to use software and computers in producing media, but gained additional language skills in terms of writing and speaking in English. All participants who completed films reported that they were proud and felt successful that they had completed their film and shared their story with the group. However, it is unclear if most of the participants' desires to not share their stories in more public ways meant that they felt their own aims were met. In fact, I would argue that most of the parents prioritized personal concrete aims such as learning to use a computer, learning to use the software program *PhotoStory*, writing a story in English, etc. and saw sharing their story to be completely secondary. Moreover, sharing stories was an aim of the non-profit (and myself as the researcher) not the participants themselves. In that way, the aim of the non-profit and facilitator was not met. Additionally, I do not have a clear sense if participants felt any self-efficacy about undertaking further social or cultural projects and actions in the future. Again, the participants' focus was on attaining a different skill set (language and technology related) rather than develop specific skills for social action.

While this specific project was unable to add to the literature on the impact of digital storytelling and social action or policy, I still believe there remains a strong potential for its usefulness and application in that arena. Regardless, the project was able to produce a collection of stories that could be analyzed and viewed within the larger media landscape related to Latino im/migrant parents. As I discuss more fully elsewhere, the stories the parents produced constructed images of parenthood that provided a counternarrative to many mainstream U.S. news media portrayals and transcended these more stereotypical portrayals (Miller, 2016). The parent's digital stories provide rich, ethnographic perspectives that are often lost in wider media portrayals of Latino im/migrants. In her book, The Audience in Every Day Life, Bird (2003) argues that it is challenging to study media's audience directly because of the ubiquitous nature of audiences—media is everywhere; we are all audiences (3). Bird describes the rather problematic nature of attempting to study audiences directly. To that end, Bird advocates for starting with the audience instead of with the media artifact. She does not suggest one particular scope of inquiry or method (in fact, her book is filled with different approaches and forms of media). Instead, Bird encourages media researchers to examine their choices and the questions we ask (9) as part of the "ethnographic encounter" (11). I believe digital storytelling is just such an approach to understanding media ethnographically. Because I was embedded in the process of creating the digital stories along with the parents, I am able to question them, in the moment, about their experiences and their choices when producing media. This, in addition to the yearlong participant observation allows for an ethnographic embeddedness to the digital storytelling approach and makes it a power tool for anthropologists.

References

Bird, E. (2003). *The audience in everyday life: Living in a media world*. New York: Routledge.

Boje, D. M. (2008). *Storytelling organizations*. Thousand Oaks, CA: Sage.

Brown, J. S., Denning, S., Groh, K., & Prusak, L. (2005). *Storytelling in organizations: Why storytelling is transforming 21st Century organizations and management*. Boston: Butterworth-Heinemann.

Goldbard, A. (2006). *New creative community*. Oakland, CA: New Village Press.

Goodman, S., & Greene, M. (2003). *Teaching youth media: A critical guide to literacy, video production, and social change*. New York: Teachers College Press.

Gubrium, A. (2009). Digital storytelling: An emergent method for health promotion research and practice. *Health Promotion Practice*, 10(2), 186-191.

Hartley, J., & McWilliam, K. (2009). *Story circle: Digital storytelling around the world*. Malden, MA: Wiley Blackwell.

Howley, K. (2005). *Community media: People, places, and communication technologies*. Cambridge, UK: Cambridge University Press.

Lambert, J. (2006). *Digital storytelling cookbook*. Berkeley, CA: Digital Diner Press.

Lambert, J. (2013). *Digital storytelling: Capturing lives, creating community*. New York: Routledge.

Lundby, K. (2008). *Digital storytelling, mediatized stories: Self-representations in new media*. New York: Peter Lang Publishers.

Meadows, D., & Kidd, J. (2009) "Capturing Wales" the BBC digital storytelling project. In J. Hartley & K. McWilliam (Eds.), *Story circle: Digital storytelling around the world* (pp. 91-117). Malden, MA: Wiley Blackwell.

Miller, J. (2016). *The construction of latino im/migrant families in U.S. news media: parents' responses and self-representations* (Doctoral Dissertation). Anthropology Department, University of South Florida, Tampa, Florida.

Simondson, H. (2009). Digital storytelling at the Australian Centre for the Moving Image. In J. Hartley & K. McWilliam (Eds.) *Story circle: Digital storytelling around the world* (pp. 118-123). Malden, MA: Wiley Blackwell.

Suro, R. (2004). *Changing channels and crisscrossing cultures: A survey of Latinos on the news media*. Washington DC: Pew Hispanic Center.

Sylvester, R., & Greenidge, W. (2009). Digital storytelling: Extending the potential for struggling writers. *The Reading Teacher*, 63(4), 284-295.

Woletz, J. (2008). Digital storytelling from artificial intelligence to YouTube. In S. Kelsey & K. St Amant (Eds.), *Handbook of research on computer mediated communication* (pp. 587-601). Hershey, PA: Information Science Reference.

Edward González-Tennant

10 Digital Storytelling in the Classroom: New Media Techniques for an Engaged Anthropological Pedagogy

"There is a certain embarrassment about being a storyteller in these times when stories are considered not quite as satisfying as statements and statements not quite as satisfying as statistics; but in the long run, a people is known, not by its statements or its statistics, but by the stories it tells."— Flannery O'Connor

10.1 Introduction

Digital storytelling represents an emerging praxis within the broader pedagogical toolkit. This is especially true for educators who embrace digital technologies, not as a panacea for some supposed 'crises' in the humanities and related disciplines, but as part of the "exceptional promise for the renewal of humanistic scholarship" (Burdick, Drucker, Lunenfeld, Presner, & Schapp, 2012, p. 7) made possible by these technologies. The successful integration of content, pedagogy, and technology requires a thoughtful approach to teaching and learning from both educator and student. This partnering aspect is crucial to developing engaged pedagogical approaches, which requires that we do more than simply insert computers into the space of the classroom. Such an approach is unsophisticated and accomplishes little to improve the overall quality of a student's experience. Achieving the true benefits of digital technologies for teaching and learning requires educators adopt a reflexive stance. Such a position acknowledges that we do not intuitively understand how to adapt new technologies to teaching, and vice versa (Robin, 2008). The creation of an engaged pedagogy incorporating digital storytelling is an experimental process, and the resulting freedom should be a source of joy, not anxiety.

This chapter describes my experimentation with digital storytelling as a research method and pedagogical tool. My approach views digital technologies as relating to both technique (e.g., scripting, video editing) and methodology (e.g., critical media literacy). This later aspect involves moving beyond the technical requirements for making digital videos and engaging with higher levels of thought, and helping students develop critical media literacy. While providing technical instruction is important, finding ways to critically engage with subject matter is often lacking in digital storytelling assignments (Hicks, 2006; Robin, 2008). My approach to these aspects has changed since I first utilized digital storytelling as a pedagogical device in 2010. In the intervening years I routinely included digital storytelling assignments as part of my courses. This engagement has benefited from my scholarly use of digital storytelling and I situate digital storytelling alongside other forms of digital scholarship as part of a mixed methods approach to studying the past (González-Tennant, 2013). My experiments with these technologies are producing an ever-evolving approach to incorporating digital technologies into my teaching, research, and public outreach.

Digital storytelling offers a scalable approach for addressing some of the central concerns of engaged pedagogy. Digital storytelling assignments can be created for large survey classes (100+ students) or smaller seminar-style courses. While the nature of assessing assignments will change depending on the size and level of each course, the successful creation of an engaged pedagogy incorporating digital storytelling necessitates a thoughtful combination of method and theory. This is a fundamental tenet of engaged pedagogy and the following section outlines several approaches. I then describe my use of digital storytelling for research and teaching. The incorporation of digital technologies in my research supports digital storytelling in my courses. This speaks to a primary aspect of an engaged pedagogical approach; the honest, personalized, and politicized investigations of complex issues as a part of the classroom experience (hooks, 1994). I also discuss various approaches to assessing digital storytelling assignments.

10.2 Thoughts on Engaged Pedagogy and Anthropology

My exploration of digital storytelling is part of a conscious decision to explore new teaching strategies. This includes igniting student interest and connecting with them as intelligent actors. Engaged pedagogy supports these and other goals by addressing specific responsibilities of the educator and providing guidance related to critical thinking as a form of emancipatory practice. The works of critical and feminist education scholars such as Freire (1970, 2002) and hooks (1994, 2003, 2010) continue to inspire educators who seek ways to create an engaged classroom. Engaged pedagogy begins with the understanding that the traditional educational experience often produces a stifling environment inhibiting fruitful and enjoyable engagement with the material at hand. This "banking system of education" treats students as passive receivers of knowledge (Freire, 1970, p. 72; hooks, 1994, p.5). Such a view not only denies student agency, it is also deeply disrespectful of difference. Recognizing and altering the hierarchical classroom to engage with students as whole-persons faces considerable obstacles. The most powerful of which are the entrenched attitudes and expressions of power held by educators and university administrators. Unfortunately, many educators seem less interested in engaging their students and more "enthralled by the exercise of power and authority within their mini-kingdom, the classroom" (hooks, 1994, p. 17).

Engaged pedagogy is an exercise in liberation and I associate this as part of a broader movement in the social sciences to decolonize the scholarly mind and toolkit (Harrison, 1997; Smith, 1999). The emancipatory potential of engaged pedagogy centers on the willingness of the educator to embrace new teaching strategies which celebrate diversity. This includes the diversity of an increasingly multicultural classroom as well as individual difference. It also requires educators experiment with new assignments and assessment strategies. Understanding that teaching is a performative act represents a necessary step in realizing the goals of an engaged pedagogy (hooks, 1994, p. 11). This realization motivates me to maintain a playful and open classroom, even as I talk about shameful aspects of US history such as race riots and lynching, a focus of much of my research (González-Tennant 2017). An open classroom requires active participation from both educator and student, and this develops only when unnecessary hierarchical posturing is actively addressed and eliminated. I attempt to accomplish this with an open discussion of the nature of higher education and challenge my students to recognize how the structure— not to mention spatial arrangement—of education seeks to reduce them to passive recipients. Challenging the status quo of the classroom is inherently a counter-hegemonic practice. While certainly a struggle, such emancipatory work need not be a negative enterprise. Recent works by hooks (2003, 2010) and Freire (2002) discuss the emotionally uplifting aspects at the heart of an engaged pedagogy. They agree that the delight educators feel from a successful teaching experience is something to cultivate. This can be accomplished by the educator leading the way in deconstructing the hierarchical classroom. A candid and open discussion of the modern classroom represents a powerful and reflexive strategy for accomplishing these goals. In my experience, having such a conversation at the beginning of the semester supports more active student involvement. Addressing and honestly attempting to dismantle hierarchies of race, class, gender, sexuality, and so forth supports a classroom environment where students feel empowered and are challenged to realize their full potential. In turn, this empowering perspective often (re)ignites student interest in both the course subject and the educational process.

Another central tenet of engaged pedagogy is the creation of personal connections between educator and student. In the modern classroom—flooded with paternalistic notions of *in loco parentis*—the ability to connect with students is overshadowed by the pressure to produce a politically neutral classroom. This naïve attempt at objectivity actually privileges certain perspectives (white/male/upper-class) and is essentially dishonest (hooks, 1994, pp. 35-41). Addressing this imbalance requires educators and students to listen to one another. This is a fundamentally different experience from the banking method of teaching described above. Other factors may limit our ability to connect with students, including the growth of classroom sizes and the expansion of general education requirements, which many students feel push them to unnecessarily enroll in courses outside of their chosen major. Instead of viewing these as challenges to overcome, an engaged pedagogy might view them as opportunities waiting to be realized. Creating an engaged classroom does not require assignments critiquing the status quo or addressing large political and social issues. Assignments supporting an engaged pedagogy can be relatively innocuous. For instance, finding ways of connecting students from different majors with the disciplines of their general education courses supports this goal. The current system of higher education in the United States, often framed in terms of *disciplinary silos*, detracts from the holistic pursuit of knowledge and the development of student skills oriented towards the collection and evaluation of evidence. Digital storytelling assignments which focus on asking students to identify and examine their choice of major supports a serious exploration of the possibilities inherent to interdisciplinary approaches.

Unfortunately, the emotional component of an engaged pedagogy makes many educators uncomfortable. This discomfort has many possible causes; they include self-indulgence in networks of power and privilege, an unwillingness to challenge ourselves (as educators), a fear of appearing soft or not rigorous to our peers, or simply a lack of knowledge regarding possible alternatives. As educators, we must recognize the emotional aspects of teaching and embrace them as part of an engaged pedagogy. These same emotional strains are felt by our students, particularly in a social climate where acknowledging the politics of difference (e.g., race, class, gender, sexuality) are discouraged through creeping notions of a post-racial present. Honestly engaging with the emotional aspects of teaching is the first step in understanding how the same issues affect our students. This requires a mix of "rage and love, without which there is no hope," engaged pedagogy is "meant as a defense of tolerance—not to be confused with connivance" (Freire, 2002, p. 4). In the modern, depoliticized classroom which many educators find themselves, the creation of an engaged pedagogy can feel like a radical position.

While I think many of the above comments will ring true with readers of this collection, I would be remiss if I failed to mention the potential difficulties relating to the creation of an engaged pedagogy. Educators who embrace imagination and passion and seek ways of confronting prejudice and various axes of inequality do so at some risk. The decision to creatively explore alternative strategies can be a risky one, particularly for younger academics like myself (Emihovich, 2005). The politicization of complex issues, increasingly seen as an ethical obligation for anthropologists (Angel-Ajani & Sanford, 2006) requires specific classroom approaches to ignite student interest. Overcoming the detachment many students feel towards social issues is difficult to accomplish. The use of digital storytelling, and particularly its focus on engaging individual perspectives and creativity, represents a powerful addition to an engaged pedagogical toolkit for anthropology.

Digital storytelling cogently addresses many of the central concerns of an engaged pedagogy. Igniting student interest in a subject is crucial, and digital storytelling is an important tool for accomplishing this goal. Digital storytelling also provides unique avenues supporting the thoughtful and honest connection between educator and student, something increasingly difficult in the 21st century classroom. The new media nature of digital storytelling represents a post-industrial logic, a point I return to later. This aspect supports an emancipatory practice by supporting critical media literacy; students are able to explore on their own terms the decisions and practices involved in creating media. In my experience, accomplishing the various goals of an engaged pedagogy in regards to digital storytelling assignments also requires educators themselves to experiment with new methods of disseminating scholarship. This process of experimentation has become a key component of my research, a point I turn to after a brief introduction to digital storytelling.

10.3 An Introduction to Digital Storytelling

While an overview of digital storytelling is covered elsewhere in this volume, I think it is valuable to understand how each author conceptualizes this emerging practice. The following paragraphs present my own views on the development and importance of digital storytelling. This is followed by a brief overview of the ways I utilize digital storytelling as part of a mixed methods practice investigating the tragic history of Rosewood, Florida. I then reflect on the use of digital storytelling in the anthropology classroom.

Digital storytelling traces its roots to a series of workshops in Los Angeles during the early 1990s. These workshops proved so successful that a StoryCenter was created shortly thereafter and remains the national center for working with digital media to tell personal stories (Lambert, 2009, pp. 1-10). Indeed, the impulse to share personal lives continues to characterize digital storytelling and Lambert's (2009) book by the StoryCenter captures this spirit as well as outlining the components, themes, and methods for creating digital stories.

Lambert outlines nine types of stories conducive to digital representation (Lambert, 2009, pp. 24-27). The first group is character stories relating the experiences between people. Memorial stories share personal views on why certain events, people, and places are important to us. Adventure stories document travel experiences and personal exploration. Accomplishment stories relate the experiences of achieving a personal or communal goal. Place stories explore those spaces and landscapes that are particularly important to individuals and/or communities. Job stories discuss professions. Recovery stories reveal the struggles of overcoming a great challenge. Love stories explore romantic relationships between people. Discovery stories reveal personal realizations and their effects on people. A broader grouping of digital stories is offered by University of Houston's Educational Uses of Digital Storytelling Web site (http://digitalstorytelling.coe.uh.edu/). This site groups digital stories into three major categories: personal stories, stories that inform, and stories that re-tell historical events (Robin, 2008, pp. 224-225).

In addition to discussing the varieties of stories people tell, Lambert goes on to discuss the specific methods storytellers employ when crafting digital stories. As the majority of digital storytelling projects center on one or a handful of individuals, and focus on bringing out the emotional aspect of personal experiences. Digital storytellers are encouraged to own their insights, find their voice, and use it to speak. As digital stories are often personal stories, the importance of confessing one's true feelings and opinions is paramount. Lambert stresses the importance of emotional content because it creates a more interesting story and reflects reality in more genuine ways.

In addition to the personal content, planning the actual structure of the story is highlighted. This includes clarifying the story's meaning by the use of storyboards and other traditional aspects of filmmaking. Lambert encourages the use of music, but warns against using copyrighted material; instead, he encourages digital storytellers to utilize copyright-free music and to always provide attributions for content created by others. The importance of mapping out a digital storytelling project's general timeline and script is encouraged, even for short pieces. As most digital stories range between five and twenty minutes, many neglect the importance of planning out a story from start to finish. The final consideration for digital storytellers is their method of delivering digital content. Will the video be presented online, at a public location, distributed via DVD?

My goal for adopting a digital storytelling approach as an emerging method to share historical research was motivated by numerous concerns. First, the major benefit digital storytelling has over traditional film/documentary making is cost. Digital stories can be created with little investment of time and resources. The primary equipment required can be broken down into three parts. The first consists of a laptop or desktop computer – the hardware component. The second involves an image and/ or audio capture device. These typically take the form of camcorders and digital voice recorders. The final component is the software, programs for editing both video and audio content. Just a decade ago these three components could easily cost thousands, even tens-of-thousands of dollars. In the intervening years equipment and programs have dramatically dropped in price. Low-cost computers and video capture devices are increasingly available to people around the world. Indeed, modern mobile phones often have the required hardware and sharing capacities to quickly create and effectively share digital stories.

My second concern views the internet as a primary delivery method for sharing research. Using the internet to freely deliver content makes research immediately accessible to a broader audience. Also, using the internet eliminates the necessity of hard media such as DVDs, further reducing the cost of sharing research. A third goal for exploring digital storytelling grew out of a commitment to social justice education, and specifically the ways emerging digital technologies such as virtual world environments and digital storytelling can assist in the creation of a critical view of minority disenfranchisement in regards to American history (Gonzalez-Tennant 2013).

10.3.1 Digital Storytelling in Rosewood, Florida

The former site of Rosewood is located approximately nine miles from the Gulf of Mexico in Levy County, Florida (Figure 10.1). The town was settled during the late 1850s (Hawks, 1871, p. 57), and its name and initial economic vitality derived from the large stores of red cedar in the area (Dye, 1997, p. 29). By 1900 the majority of residents were African American and by 1920 the town had three churches, a black masonic hall, a black school, and a mix of house sizes (Jones, Rivers, Colburn, Dye, & Rogers, 1993, p. 23). The economic fortunes of Rosewood declined after the Cummer and Sons Lumber Company built a large sawmill in nearby Sumner around 1915. This was followed by the relocation of most businesses to Sumner by 1918. Although these developments challenged Rosewood's residents, the town continued to survive and grow (Jones, 1997, p. 194). This came to an abrupt end the first week of 1923.

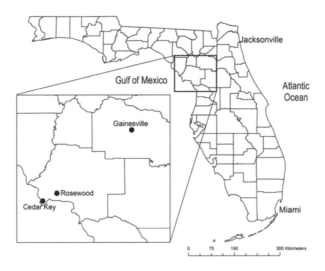

Figure 10.1: Location of Rosewood, Florida

What has become known as the Rosewood Race Riot was in fact a weeklong series of events. According to oral testimonies collected in the 1990s, the violence began following the accusation by Fannie Taylor, a white woman in Sumner, that a black man had attacked her. The general consensus today is that Taylor fabricated this assailant to hide the injuries she received during an altercation with her white lover. While Sumner residents believed her story, black witnesses stated the assailant was a white man with whom Taylor was having an affair (Jones et al., 1993, pp. 25-27).

Following the accusation, the sheriff was notified and a posse organized to track the assailant. Hounds led the group to nearby Rosewood, most likely following the scents of residents whose daily walks between the two towns provided an easy trail to follow. The posse rapidly grew beyond the men initially deputized by the sheriff. The mob speculated on the assailant's identity. The consensus identified Jesse Hunter, a black man who had recently escaped from a local labor camp, as the possible assailant. Rumors suggested that Hunter had been in the company of Sam Carter, a longtime resident of the area and Rosewood's blacksmith (Jones et al., 1993, p. 30). While under considerable pressure, Carter admitted to giving Walker a ride in his wagon to the nearby town of Gulf Hammock. When the bloodhounds were unable to pick up the scent, and after Carter was unable to satisfy the mob's inquiries, his body was riddled with bullets and left on the road between Sumner and Rosewood. After Carter's murder, the posse approached other homes in Rosewood seeking more information. In the growing frenzy the posse nearly hanged several other residents. Hostilities then ceased for several days.

On January 4th a "party of citizens" went to investigate unconfirmed reports that a group of blacks had taken refuge in Rosewood (Jones et al., 1993, p. 38). What spurned these reports is unknown, but it is likely that some residents simply sought additional confrontation after the relatively anti-climactic events of Monday. The group targeted the Carrier household and two members of the mob attempted to break into the home (Jones et al., 1993, p. 40). The Carrier's opened fire and a pitched gun battle commenced.

The battle continued into the early hours of Friday, January 5th. Reports of wounded white men in Rosewood roused local whites, including members of the KKK from Gainesville, Florida. When whites left Friday morning to replenish ammunition, African Americans fled into the surrounding swamps. The white mob returned to Rosewood later that day and burned several homes and at least one church. They also reportedly found the bodies of Sylvester and Sarah Carrier in their home, victims of the previous night's gun battle (Jones et al., 1993, pp. 43-44). The mob also killed Lexie Gordon, an African American widow of approximately fifty, by shooting her in the back as she fled her burning home (Jones et al., 1993, pp. 44-45). The death toll now included four African Americans and two Euro-Americans (who died from injuries received during the previous night's fight). The seventh death occurred later that day when whites shot Mingo Williams in the head as they drove through nearby Bronson on their way to Rosewood.

A train run by two brothers came through Rosewood at 4am on Saturday, January 6th. It stopped at several towns along the way including Rosewood, Wylly, and Otter Creek to rescue frightened African Americans. Only women and children where allowed on the train, which took survivors to Archer and Gainesville where descendants remain to this day (Jones et al., 1993, p. 61). That Saturday, James Carrier briefly returned and was apprehended by whites. He became the eighth death when the mob lynched him near the fresh graves of his mother and brother (Jones et al., 1993, pp. 50-51). On Sunday, the mob returned to Rosewood and burned every remaining African American building (Figure 10.2).

Figure 10.2: Ruins of House near Rosewood, from January 20 1923 Literary Digest

My scholarly use of digital storytelling concentrates on several interrelated goals. I addressed these goals with the construction of a 26-minute digital story exploring the history of Rosewood's community (available online at www.virtualrosewood. com). This digital video is titled *Remembering Rosewood* and provides a transparent overview of my research questions and methods. I describe my mixed methods approach integrating oral history, documentary evidence, geographic information systems (GIS), historical archaeology, and heritage visualization to represent Rosewood as a dynamic community instead of a single event[35]. Approximately half of the digital story shares the life stories of two survivors, Robie Mortin and Mary Hall Daniels. These two women were both present in Rosewood during the events of 1923, Mortin was eight and Daniels was three. A particularly touching moment in the digital story occurs when Mortin describes meeting her father for the first time following the riot. She describes how her father quickly recognized how the accusation of rape and subsequent attacks on Rosewood might turn into large scale violence. He sent Robie to nearby Williston with her sister. After hearing about the destruction of Rosewood several days later, and not being able to meet up with their father, the two girls assumed he had been killed. They worked as migrant laborers in Florida citrus fields and over several months made their way to Riviera Beach, north of Miami. Mortin (Figure 10.3) shares what happened one morning when she went to a newly constructed church several months after moving to Riviera Beach:

> There was a ditch that separated Riviera Beach from the black neighborhood. There was a bridge across it, and there was a Hearst Chapel AME Church there. They had built that church right on our side of the ditch. So, we, my sister and I, went to church, and would you believe our daddy was there, and we didn't know where he was, hadn't seen him in months. We didn't even know he was still alive, and there he was in the front of that church (Interview with Robie Mortin and Author, 2009).

---

[35] In addition to the 26-minute digital documentary, visitors to www.virtualrosewod.com can also explore a virtual reconstruction of Rosewood as it existed in late 1922.

Figure 10.3: Still of Robie Mortin from *Remembering Rosewood*, interviewed by author in 2009

The ability of digital storytelling to share touching moments like these with my students represents an important intersection for engaged pedagogy. Students immediately realize how scholars can engage with complex and emotional histories in sensitive ways. This avoids the depoliticization which so often haunts the modern classroom. Mortin's words, delivered in her soft, ninety-four-year-old voice, touches viewers in an unmistakable way. The emotional impact of her brief story demonstrates the trials, and in this one example happy surprises, which make a life scared by trauma bearable.

10.4 Assigning and Assessing Digital Storytelling for the Anthropological Classroom

My exploration of digital storytelling in the classroom began with a *General Anthropology* course I taught at the University of Florida in the autumn semester of 2010. This was a large survey course with 120 students. I approached this assignment by dedicating an entire class to discussing digital storytelling. This included a presentation and student handout describing various types of digital stories, a summary of Lambert's seven steps of digital storytelling, a brief discussion of technology, and useful online resources for copyright-free images, music, and sounds. The presentation included brief introductions to platform specific video and sound editing software. The presentation ended with a showing of my *Remembering Rosewood* video as an example of digital storytelling.

I gave students the choice of working alone or in groups of three or less. The assignment stipulated that each video be between five and ten minutes in length. The videos had to address one of two questions: what is your favorite aspect of anthropology, or how do you see anthropology intersecting other disciplines? As a general education course at the University of Florida, typically 50% or less of the students are anthropology majors and minors. I designed these questions to better understand how my students responded to the course content. Initially, my goals for digital storytelling focused on the creation of a creative assignment allowing me to gauge my course content and what aspects of an introductory, four-field anthropology course ignited student interest. Given the relative freedom of designing their own message in regards to anthropology, what would students choose to represent as key ideas and sentiments of the discipline? I also shared my hopes with students regarding the assignment and its ability to invert the usual hierarchy of learning in a lecture-based class.

The assignment was discussed at various points throughout the semester, and specific deliverables required at regular intervals. This included a one-page outline and a time-table. The relatively small number of related assignments in my early explorations of digital storytelling reflects the large size of my classes (100+ students per course each semester). I emphasized the importance of the story above the technology and regularly reminded students that their grades were not based on technical proficiency. Creating a digital storytelling assignment for a large lecture course required a flexible approach to grading. Initially, I scored assignments as essays. I assessed them on clarity of purpose and point of view, pacing and voice, appropriate use of media, economy of composition, and appropriate use of grammar and language.

My initial exploration of digital storytelling resulted in 94 separate videos, available online at www.youtube.com/AnthroDigitalStories. Many of the videos show students in private settings – their homes and dormitories – speaking to the camera in a confessional manner. I was drawn into their videos by their posture and quiet speaking style. I wondered if this was simply reproducing the style of a video diary common to reality TV programs, or if this pointed to a deeper pedagogical possibility. For some, this represented the path of least resistance as it required less effort and planning than other approaches. For others, this provided me with an opportunity to learn more about my students and their opinions on my class, their chosen majors, and how these things integrate into the larger experiences associated with college life today. Determining which confessional style videos were of the former type is easy. It is immediately clear when students failed to plan their videos. For instance, some of the longest videos submitted by students conform to this confessional style, but are recorded in one sitting and without any editing. These students typically failed to address the other parts of the assignment, which was also reflected in the supporting deliverables (e.g., time table) as well as the overall quality of the videos.

I interpret the unexpected confessional nature of many of the videos as speaking directly to the goals of an engaged pedagogy. Students revealed personal perspectives rarely shared in a traditional classroom environment. This is particularly the case in large survey and introductory courses where classroom discussion is difficult to initiate and sustain due to the number of students. These videos demonstrate the ability of digital storytelling to bridge the chasm which typically separates educators and students. Digital storytelling also inverted the usual hierarchy of learning by giving students the opportunity to expand the scope of the course, to reflect critically on the assigned readings and lectures, and to teach the instructor and other students about students' first-hand experiences of complex issues such as discrimination and non-(hetero)normative lifestyles.

These videos often revealed hidden aspects of student lives, their hopes and desires, their personal connections with anthropology, and their hidden assumptions. The videos ranged between thoughtful and revealing treatments of anthropology to half-hearted attempts to hastily produce a video satisfying some students' uncritical belief about what I wanted from them. I interpret the thoughtful treatments as partially reflecting my own commitment to teaching a four-field anthropology and demonstrating its increasing importance in today's world. I see these responses as supporting the idea that anthropology's perspectives and methods can speak to a generation disillusioned with traditional forms of scholarship and education. I view the half-hearted attempts in one of two ways. The first set corresponds to the subset of students who simply fail to take adequate time or care to complete their assignments. The second set corresponds to those students who remained uncomfortable with visually expressing their opinion in the format of a digital video. In recent years, I have attempted to address this by expanding these kinds of assignments to include the creation of graphic novels/comics, photography essays, and even abstract paintings. Regardless of the assignment, there is always a subset of students who fail to take the assignment seriously, but my experiences remain positive and the majority of students appreciate the extra freedom in expressing themselves.

Formal methods of assessing digital storytelling assignments have been created by other educators. They all agree on the necessity of a rubric. One well-known example is the University of Houston's sample rubric (http://digitalstorytelling. coe.uh.edu/page.cfm?id=24). I believe this ten-point rubric is particularly useful for educators who are not personally involved in digital storytelling as part of their research. This rubric helps students understand how the digital storytelling project differs from a conventional term paper and gives them a framework for considering the possibilities. I initially took a highly subjective approach to grading digital storytelling, often delighting in my students' work as much as they clearly did while creating it.

I continue to utilize digital storytelling assignments in my courses, and have adapted my approach to smaller classroom sizes. This includes integrating digital storytelling as part of a semester project alongside other deliverables such as timetables, scripts, and formal papers describing the project and stating how the video satisfies the assignment. These additional assignments allow me to better track a student or group's progress through a semester. The paper supports a more traditional form of assessment. I have found this necessary as mainstream "education currently doesn't encourage, and rarely requires, students to produce schoolwork in 'new media' formats such as digital stories" (Ohler, 2008, p. 62). I agree with Ohler that this stems from the fact that most educators are not comfortable creating or assessing new media artifacts. I would add that the maintenance of a hierarchical learning environment also plays a role in the resistance many educators have for this type of work, even as they celebrate interdisciplinary scholarship in their classrooms. I have found Ohler's approach (2008, pp. 65-67) to assessing digital storytelling particularly helpful. Instead of a standard rubric, he proposes nine considerations that provide a rough guide as well as specific deliverables/artifacts that can be assessed by educators.

The first involves setting clear goals. This step is familiar to educators and we would not assign papers or other work without clear goals (e.g., page length, reference style, number of citations). The same holds true for digital storytelling assignments. The second point focuses on the story and the student's ability to present an orderly narrative. This involves students creating videos that draw on additional sources to support their assertions. I discuss various ways students can bring traditional forms of scholarship into their digital storytelling projects, including the referencing of texts and incorporation of other media objects. Ohler (2008) stresses the importance of assessing all artifacts created as part of a digital storytelling project. This allows educators to understand the general process of content creation and understanding. Assessing student planning also supports the need to assign and assess multiple artifacts. The next two considerations assess grammar and the presentation of content. Educators should discuss with their students appropriate ways of using media to support their assertions. Asking students to critically engage with content in their assignments represents an aspect of digital storytelling that is similar to traditional artifacts such as essays.

Since many digital storytelling assignments involve group work, determining methods for assessing shared responsibilities and effective use of resources is a vital component. I accomplish this by having a mix of group and individual assignments. The timetable and script are good group artifacts. Individual essays discussing the project and assessing the overall quality of the video allows me to identify which students invested greater effort and thought. I typically accord the individual paper a large percentage of the overall project's grade, 50% percent or more. I have also found that including "a performance or publication venue at the outset" improves the overall quality of student work (Ohler, 2008, p. 66). Setting time aside in class to show the videos addresses this aspect of assessment and supports peer review of the videos. This addresses Ohler's final point of including some form of self-assessment at the conclusion of the project.

Incorporating these considerations into my own digital storytelling assignments supports an expanded experimental engagement with alternative assignments. In addition to regularly assigning digital storytelling projects, I have experimented with other forms of self-expression. In a recent *Anthropology of Religion* course I allowed students to draw on any form of expressive culture as part of a final research project. Students enthusiastically responded with artifacts that further challenged my ability to assess their work. This included the production of abstract paintings by one student as part of her project on vampire folklore from Eastern Europe as well as photo essays examining the role religion plays in addressing personal loss. These assignments further pushed me as an educator and I sought out colleagues in the fine arts programs to get advice on assessing these new (to me) forms of expressive culture. I have also replaced digital storytelling assignments with graphic novels in my freshman seminar on zombies. My previous experiences with digital storytelling—requiring multiple deliverables—proved equally useful for these types of student project.

10.5 Discussion

Lev Manovich, in his seminal work *The Language of New Media*, not only provides us with the most concise definition of the term new media, but also presents five characteristics useful in conceptualizing the use of digital storytelling for engaged pedagogy. New media is the "translation of all existing media into numerical data accessible through computers" (Manovich, 2001, p. 20). This includes the translation of analog materials (e.g., photographs, movies, records) into digital formats as well as the creation of fully digital artifacts like digital images and 3D models. New media is what happens when media and computer technologies meet.

"All new media objects... are composed of digital code" (Manovich, 2001, p. 27) represents the first characteristic, and while modern media such as film follow an industrial logic (large scale production studies, expensive equipment costs, necessity of labors), new media provides us with a post-industrial method, one not regulated by mass standardization. This aspect of new media means its potential as an emancipatory form is literally hardwired into its very structure. The technical and equipment aspects of digital storytelling, made widely available through modern manufacturing, should not be confused with the logic underlying their use. Traditional media (e.g., film) is organized like a factory and the physical objects associated with these technologies require standardization to function. Standardization has resulted in a restricted set of values and expressive modes in Hollywood, and the entertainment industry in general. These modes are driven by both mass standardization and corporate funding streams. In contrast, new media expresses a post-industrial logic by highlighting "individual customization, rather than mass standardization" (Manovich, 2001, p. 29). Although the individual components may be produced in factory, the wider potentials of self-expression which exist with digital technologies allows for a wider range of expressive modes not available/accepted by mass media.

Secondly, new media is modular; parts can be deleted, re-arranged, and added without destroying the original. This invites experimentation and exploration. This feature is easily coupled with pedagogical interests related to teaching media literacy.

A third aspect involves automation, and this is particularly important for sharing digital storytelling artifacts via websites like YouTube and Vimeo. The most common form of automation is the creation of programs to access information, and while Manovich focuses on the proliferation of access agents (e.g., Google) for sorting through the bewildering amounts of information now available online, without automated access, our ability to share digital stories would be limited to hard media such as DVDs.

The fourth characteristic centers on the variability of new media objects. This flexibility is useful for digital storytelling and allows users to present alternative and even contrasting perspectives side by side. This addresses the hierarchical classroom and its desire to produce one authoritative view of a subject. Engaged pedagogy recognizes the value of different perspectives and respects how standpoint influences multiple engagements with a topic, all potentially as true and valid as one another. This aspect also supports the creation of a variety of interfaces with the same content. The same content can now be delivered via traditional formats like television or via interactive websites.

The final characteristic of new media is cultural transcoding. This involves the interaction between cultural ideas and new computer methods. At present, this is dominated through analogy with traditional media: the printed page becomes a webpage, cinema becomes online video (edited and navigated based on analog concepts like fast forward), the human computer interaction of fingers on keyboard become fully immersive virtual reality. In regards to digital storytelling, this satisfies the engaged pedagogical impulse to respect difference. Students are less constrained than in traditional assignments and their unique, culturally-informed experiences can be positioned side-by-side and equally valued. As with the birth of any new technology, we can only begin to hypothesize about the range of potential applications. The term "transcode" means to translate, and how educators and students translate traditional assignments into these new formats, and the reciprocal effect on our practice as educators is only beginning.

The unnecessary hierarchical posturing associated with traditional education is one of the first things jettisoned by thinkers exploring an engaged pedagogical practice. The traditional classroom setting, disciplined through centuries of tradition represents a socializing spatial arrangement subjugating student knowledge and experience to that of the educator. A critical approach to engaged pedagogy simultaneously recognizes the professor's unique knowledge while respecting the ability of students to contribute important insights. This perspective also acknowledges the unique value offered by the lived experiences of students from underrepresented groups; particularly in regards to race, nationality, sexuality, age, and so forth.

My ongoing exploration of digital storytelling intentionally intersects many of engaged pedagogy's central tenets. This begins with a sincere engagement on my part with the technologies and techniques of digital storytelling as part of my research. The alternative format of digital storytelling, coupled with traditional assignments (e.g., individual essays), helps to ignite student interest and invert the traditional hierarchy of the classroom. These types of assignments invite students to become active producers of content and responsible viewers of work produced by their peers. The emancipatory potential of new media supports these goals as well. The creative exploration of new media invites students to participate in the educational experience in more active ways. This also provides a bridge allowing educators and students to connect in ways that are increasingly difficult in today's classroom.

Digital storytelling also addresses other aspects of 21st century education. The exploration and creation of digital media artifacts represents a crucial aspect of developing critical media literacy. This form of literacy seeks to expand "the notion of literacy to include different forms of mass communication and popular culture as well as deepen the potential of education to critically analyze relationships between media and audiences" (Kellner & Share, 2007, p. 4). Specific methods for accomplishing these goals include understanding how media is generated and engaging with the work of others in critical ways. Digital storytelling can support these goals by exposing students to the intentional choices that are made while fashioning a news report, documentary, or popular television show. Dedicating portions of class to viewing the results of digital storytelling assignments allows students to question these decisions and recognize how their own biases influence their representational decisions in unforeseen ways.

I see digital storytelling as a core pedagogical component regarding the recent rush to embrace digital humanities among many scholars, academic institutions, and funding agencies. Unfortunately, what is often less clear in this exploration is the reciprocal relationship between the digital humanities and pedagogy (Brier, 2012, pp. 390-391). Digital storytelling offers a powerful suite of methods for engaged pedagogy in the college classroom. The preceding pages offer one possibility for addressing the pedagogical deficit within the digital humanities. I believe the sincere impulse to make new media meaningful for current and future generations is centrally important to education, particularly in the present moment. It is "highly irresponsible in the face of saturation by the Internet and media culture to ignore these forms of socialization and education" (Kellner & Share, 2007, p. 4). Digital storytelling represents a powerful form of self-expression addressing the central concerns of an engaged pedagogy while simultaneously teaching students to create and critically evaluate new media artifacts in their daily lives.

10.6 Conclusion

My experimentation with digital storytelling began as an outgrowth of my interest in engaged pedagogy. The scalable nature of digital storytelling allows me to tailor assignments to different class sizes, student levels, and course content. I have found digital storytelling to be a powerful form of engaged pedagogy allowing me to invert the traditional hierarchical nature of the college classroom and connect with my students as active and intelligent participants. The ability of my students to share personal experiences that are unavailable to me represents a core methodology for bridging the divide between educator and student. This divide is the result of centuries of tradition and overcoming it requires specific and dedicated effort. Digital storytelling represents a powerful bridge allowing me to access student perspectives and knowledge(s) in sensitive and active ways. This also supports active learning and provides students with the skills and peer feedback necessary for understanding the constructed aspect of media. The 21st century's reliance on distributed networks of communication technologies is neither malignant nor benign. It poses the same problems and possibilities of traditional media, and I believe teaching digital storytelling represents a central methodology for supporting a critical engagement with new media.

In many ways, new media offers a new set of tools, ones not found in the master's house (Lourde, 1984, pp. 110-113) and therefore potentially very liberating, a constellation of approaches and technologies not regulated by gatekeepers and tradition—although certainly in dialogue with them. Obvious and sizable obstacles to full participation in new media include the manifestation of a digital divide as well as the (re)inscription of negative identity politics within virtual spaces (Nakamura, 2008). Just as the printing press was utilized in the past to democratize knowledge, so too can we teach ourselves to draw on new media methodologies for a similar purpose. Only time will tell if this optimistic viewpoint will produce transformative fruit or if mass standardization will reassert itself. I choose to remain hopeful, because the alternative deprives our students of potentially liberating educational possibilities.

References

Angel-Asani, A., & Sanford, V. (Eds.). (2006). *Engaged observer: Anthropology, advocacy, and activism*. New Brunswick, NJ: Rutgers University Press.

Brier, S. (2012). Where's the pedagogy? The role of teaching and learning in the digital Humanities. In M. K. Gold (Ed.), *Debates in the digital humanities* (pp. 390-401). Minneapolis: University of Minnesota Press.

Burdick, A., Drucker, J., Lunenfeld, P., Presner, T., & Schapp, J. (Eds.). (2012). *Digital_Humanities*. Cambridge, MA: MIT Press.

Dye, R. T. (1997). The Rosewood Massacre: History and the making of public policy. *The Public Historian, 19*(3), 25-39.

Emihovich, C. (2005). Fire and ice: Activist ethnography in the culture of power. *Anthropology & Education Quarterly, 36,* 305-314.

Freire, P. (1970). *Pedagogy of the oppressed.* New York, NY: Continuum.

Freire, P. (2002). *Pedagogy of hope: Reliving pedagogy of the oppressed.* New York, NY: Continuum.

González-Tennant, E. (2013). New heritage and dark tourism: A mixed methods approach to social justice in Rosewood, Florida. *Heritage & Society, 6,* 62-88.

González-Tennant, E. (2017). *The Rosewood Massacre: An Archaeology and History and Intersectional Violence.* Gainesville, FL: University Press of Florida.

Hawks, J. M. (1871). *The Florida Gazetteer.* New Orleans, LA: Bronze Pen Publishing Company.

Harrison, F. V. (Ed.). (1997). *Decolonizing anthropology: Moving further toward an anthropology for liberation.* Washington, DC: American Anthropological Association.

Hicks, T. (2006). Expanding the conversation: A commentary toward revision of Swenson, Rozema, Young, McGrail, and Whitin. *Contemporary Issues in Technology and Teacher Education, 6*(1), 46–55.

hooks, b. (1994). *Teaching to transgress: Education as the practice of freedom.* New York, NY: Routledge.

hooks, b. (2003). *Teaching community: A pedagogy of hope.* New York, NY: Routledge.

hooks, b. (2010). *Teaching critical thinking: Practical wisdom.* New York, NY: Routledge.

Jones, M. D. (1997). The Rosewood Massacre and the women who survived it. *The Florida Historical Quarterly, 76,* 193-208.

Jones, M. D., Rivers, L. E., Colburn, D. R., Dye, R. T., & Rogers, W. R. (1993). *A documented history of the incident which occurred at Rosewood, Florida, in January 1923: Submitted to the Florida Board of Regents 22 December 1993.* Tallahassee, FL: Board of Regents.

Kellner, D., & Share, J. (2007). Critical media literacy, democracy, and the reconstruction of education. In D. Macedo & S. R. Steinberg (Eds.), *Media literacy: A reader* (pp. 3-23). New York, NY: Peter Lang.

Lambert, J. (2009). *Digital storytelling: Capturing lives, creating community* (3rd ed.). Berkeley, CA: Digital Diner.

Lourde, A. (1984). *Sister outsider: Essays and speeches.* Freedom, CA: Crossing Press.

Manovich, L. (2001). *The language of new media.* Cambridge, MA: MIT Press.

Nakamura, L. (2008). *Digitizing race: Visual cultures of the internet.* Electronic Mediations. Minneapolis: University of Minnesota Press.

Ohler, J. (2008). *Digital storytelling in the classroom: New media pathways to literacy, learning, and creativity.* Thousand Oaks, CA: Corwin Press.

Robin, B. R. (2008). Digital storytelling: A powerful technology tool for the 21st Century classroom. *Theory Into Practice, 47,* 220-228.

Smith, L. T. (1999). *Decolonizing methodologies: Research and indigenous peoples.* London, UK: Zed Books.

Nina Shapiro-Perl

11 The Digital Story: Giving Voice to *Unheard* Washington

11.1 Introduction

In the introduction to his path-breaking book *Digital Storytelling: Capturing Lives, Creating Community,* Joe Lambert (2009) contextualizes the art of storytelling:

> All of the contemporary movements of change—from slow and local food movement... to yoga and meditation... to community arts and storywork in a million permutations... *are all responses to globalization* [italics added].... The more we share the stress and strain of a corporate monoculture based on greed and accumulation, the more we want a gentle authenticity of experience. The more we search for authenticity, the more we turn our attention away from the siren call of bland uniformity, and we search for something individuated. And the way to hear those stories is not to change channels, or surf the machine-made media, but to listen to our own stories, our own hearts, and the stories of our rich local communities. (p. xv)

This same impulse—for authenticity and individuation—has driven me as an anthropologist and filmmaker over the past 30 years to seek out the "small" stories of people within the larger fabric of history (Lerman, 2002, p. 60).

This has meant exploring larger social issues from an anthropological perspective and then particularizing the process through individual stories, both complex and nuanced. As a filmmaker, it has meant, for example, capturing the healthcare crisis and the routinization of care from the point of view of an ICU nurse—stretched to the point of exhaustion after a 12-hour shift, working short-handed. Or understanding the story of immigration reform through the eyes of a janitor—separated from her children for 16 years, living through photographs, and messages on her answering machine. It has meant seeking out and telling stories that document the lived experience of people who are marginalized and dismissed, suffering and fighting back against the coarse rule of capitalism. Telling stories, as Arlene Goldbard (2005) says, that support resistance, connection, and possibility.

Most of my work has followed the method of the traditional documentary filmmaker: researching a topic, finding subjects, recording in-depth interviews, capturing their daily lives on film, constructing a storyline, writing the treatment or script, editing and pacing the film, selecting the music, and telling the story, wherever possible, *in the subject's own words*.

Then, 12 years ago, I saw a digital story.

11.2 Digital Stories and Documentary Filmmaking

A digital story is a five-minute video narrative, written and directed by a first-time filmmaker, that combines one's recorded voice, still and moving images, music, and other art into a short digital film. I quickly saw the transformational potential of this new method of filmmaking—*participatory* filmmaking—where the *subject* of the film is actually the *lead participant* in the production. Where the power dynamic shifts from the traditional documentary model and, with the help of a trained practitioner, the subject tells his or her own story and learns digital storytelling skills in the process (Hill, 2008, p. 49).

Traditional documentary filmmaking serves to privilege the role of the director to shape the story. Here the director—either alone or collaborating with others—writes the treatment, conducts the interviews, forms the story arc, selects the locations to shoot, supervises the shooting, selects photographs or other archival materials, selects the interview segments to be used, oversees the editing, and oversees the music. Overall, the director shapes the look and feel of the film and, at its root, decides on the film's intention and meaning. Most importantly, the director decides whose words or voices will be used to tell the story.[36] The whole process can take several months to several years, depending on a host of factors and choices.

The digital story is a form of documentary filmmaking. But in the digital story, the *storyteller* shapes and tells the story. In place of high-tech cameras and months-long production, the subjects of the digital story craft their own deeply felt five-minute stories with simple photographs and images in a digital format that is highly flexible. These stories can be created in the space of an intense three-day workshop as developed by StoryCenter (formerly the Center for Digital Storytelling.) Or, as in my course, students create their own digital stories over a four-week period and then assist community storytellers in creating their stories over the next nine weeks. But the method is the same for both students and community storytellers. Through a facilitated story circle, the participant is helped to "find" his or her story. With support, they then write, visualize and edit the 250-word story, a process that enables the subject to get to know their own story better. Through this, one comes to understand oneself better, while creating a tool that can be used with family, friends, community, and the wider social world to tell a story from one's life in one's own, authentic voice. The digital story is also a creative tool for public knowledge and action. It is a way for an audience to see and hear—in a short, powerful form *and in their own words*--from members of a community who are too often unseen and unheard.

---

36 This list focuses on the creative elements that go into filmmaking. It is not exhaustive nor does it include the all-important fund-raising, publicizing and marketing the film through social media, which often begins even before the film is started.

As I discuss below, digital storytelling at its best is a two-way process of connection and transformation for both the community storyteller and the student/witness/collaborator. As a form of participatory filmmaking, it provides the opportunity for both parties to cross the social divides of class, race, ethnicity, neighborhood, age, gender and sexual orientation and meet each other as people.

The constraints of a five-minute story encourage the storyteller to go deep, *quickly,* adding to the story's power. As Jean Burgess (2006), a researcher of cultural participation in new media contexts says:

> Economy is a core principle of this aesthetic. The philosophy behind this economy is that formal constraints create the ideal condition for the production of elegant, high-impact stories by people with little or no experience, with minimal intervention by the workshop facilitators. Digital stories are in general marked by sincerity, warmth and humanity.... And cultural studies researchers often don't know what to say about them. *This is because for too long we have been interrupting the ordinary voice, speaking instead of listening* [italics added] (pp. 207-209).

As a documentary filmmaker who has followed the traditional model in most all my productions, I have profound respect for the way documentaries can shed light onto people in the shadows or onto a problem that goes unnamed or unnoticed. But a participatory approach to documentary storytelling does something the traditional documentary does not: That is, *it enables the subject to get to know his or her own story better, and tell it more succinctly.* Through the process of digital storytelling, one's story can become a source of empowerment and self-knowledge to share with a wider public, while the storyteller develops skills in the process. From my perspective, it is a powerful tool to hear the stories of community residents whose voices have been silenced, whose lives have been erased from the mainstream. It is these people—Washingtonians of different neighborhoods, backgrounds, and histories—who tell their stories with the assistance of my students. They have been encouraged to think about their lives and focus on a transformational event that they then sculpt into a digital story. The story circle is that place where the work begins. As I discuss below, the story circle is the site where the process of breaking down the social barriers that divide us starts, transforming the storyteller and the witness/facilitator alike.

After 20 years as a filmmaker for the Service Employees International Union (SEIU), I began teaching documentary storytelling at American University. I started with a class of anthropology and film students who, working in teams, would create short documentary–style films for non-profit organizations in the area.

In my work in the labor movement over two decades, traveling across the country, I met scores of social justice activists working in non-profits, essential to their communities, with little or no media to tell their organization's story—and with no time, money or expertise to produce the work. My intention was to match this need with the film student's perennial search for subject matter and the anthropology student's yearning to have their research find a public audience.

My goal was to take students beyond the comforts of classes in Northwest Washington, D.C. to the "the *other* Washington." That is, to go beyond the ivory towers, beyond the monumental buildings of the nation's capital, and, through filmmaking, explore instead the parallel universe of people struggling with poverty, degraded environments, poor health and poor schools, violence, and homelessness.

According to a report published in September 2012 by the DC Fiscal Policy Institute, using data from the 2010 Census, the District of Columbia has the third-highest level of income inequality in the nation. The average income of the top 20 percent is $259,000. That is 29 times the average income of the bottom 20 percent ($9,100). The District has one of the highest rates of poverty in the nation and this is felt the hardest by Latinos and African-Americans.[37]

My goal was to start a community storytelling project that would illuminate this *other* Washington by telling the stories of people in their own words. It was my hope that these stories would humanize rather than demonize the poor, working class, and immigrant communities in this acutely segregated and unequal city.

By "the other," I reference the construct developed by Edward Said of demonization and dehumanization of one group by another in order to justify domination. Said (1978) noted how the dominant group emphasized the perceived weakness of marginalized groups as a way of stressing the alleged strength of those in positions of power. The cultural "essences" seem immutable, as they have been enhanced and embellished poetically and rhetorically for a long time, even though the truths are illusions.[38]

With the support of American University's School of Communication and the Anthropology Department, and the Surdna Foundation, I began an initiative called the Community Voice Project.[39] This project set out to capture, through filmmaking, stories of *unseen* and *unheard* Washington, and in the process help train a new generation of social documentarians.

Over a period of eight years, my students produced 31 short documentary-style films for non-profit organizations in Greater Washington. The subjects ranged from gentrification, to HIV/AIDS, to immigrant workers' organizing, to homelessness, to veterans suffering from PTSD. Students consulted with the directors of the non-profits to determine the kind of storytelling that the organization needed and to identify

---

37 I am grateful for the insights into class and race in Washington, DC, of Anthropology Professor Brett Williams and Anthropology PhD student Sean Furmage, quoted in a journal entry with his permission.

38 Thanks to my colleague in Anthropology, Professor David Vine, for his insights into the process of treating people as "the other"...from "Southeast Asia to Southeast Washington."

39 For more on the Community Voice Project, now part of American University's Center for Media and Social Impact, and to screen all films and digital stories see http://cmsimpact.org/community-voice-project/ Since the fall of 2008, the Community Voice Project has produced 31 documentary-style films and 44 digital stories by community storytellers for 25 community organizations in Greater Washington.

people served by the organization who could help tell that story. Every effort was made to have students engage in deep interviewing to be able to tell the organization's story through the voices of the people it served.

Part of this initiative included working with the Smithsonian Anacostia Community Museum located in Southeast Washington—a historically marginalized, largely African American community plagued by poverty, unemployment, and violence. As part of the Museum's Community Documentation Initiative, we completed several successful short documentary-style films together. A year into our collaboration, I showed the Museum some digital stories and convinced them to experiment with this method. I then convinced American University to let me develop a digital storytelling class.

In the fall of 2010, 15 students spent the first five weeks of the semester creating their own digital stories, learning first-hand the method and the difficulty of telling one's own story. The process began with the story circle, where students come face to face with their own story... and with each other. It is a time when the facilitator (myself) creates a safe space and an opportunity for each individual to speak for five minutes—uninterrupted—and to be listened to. The storyteller then has five minutes to receive respectful feedback from the facilitator (and other students, if time permits) before the focus moves to the next student. The facilitator asks questions to help the storyteller find a moment of transformation in their narrative, around which they can sculpt their story—enough to start writing a first draft. The stories unfold: a mother's schizophrenia, an emotionally distant father, the death of grandparent, a rape in freshman year, the paralysis of a close friend, coming out to a family member, etc. The stories tumble out among students who barely know each other. Stories that people didn't expect to tell. Stories that people felt empowered to tell when they heard the risks others were taking. With tears and laughter, stories flowed, going beyond social divides of race and ethnicity and gender and age and style that the students started with. The room shifted, and class dynamics changed from then on. Students observed these changes, writing about them in their journals. People started seeing each other in a new light. For the next four weeks, students attended class and worked on their own to finish their stories. In the fifth week, the final digital stories were screened and discussed. It was a watershed for classmates to witness how each story had grown and changed from the story circle barely four weeks before. The students' stories went beyond race, gender, ethnicity, social class, and national origin. Rather, they were nuanced, complex narratives that lived inside wider social constructions.

The storytelling process began anew the following week when small groups of students met in a story circle with community members selected by the Anacostia Community Museum – a plan that I had arranged in advance with the Museum.

In the first digital storytelling effort with the Museum, students assisted 11 public artists from Southeast Washington in creating stories from their lives, using photographs, family documents, community archives, and their own voices to create first-person narratives. These community artists ranged from mixed-media artists and photographers to tattoo artists and spiritual singers.

In one digital story, tattoo artist Charles "Coco" Bayron speaks of growing up in his Bronx neighborhood where apartment buildings went up in flames all the time, and you never knew if your building was next. "We used to carry our family pictures with us *just in case...* Tattoos are like that. They're something nobody can take away. I think a lot of people are getting into tattooing to hold onto something," Coco says in his digital story.

When asked to reflect on the digital project, Coco said: "It was a good experience. It showed me an appreciation for where I've been in my life, where I came from."

The Anacostia Community Museum included Coco's digital story in an exhibition on "Creativity in the Community" and said the digital stories yielded new information about their community. As Sharon Reinckens, Deputy Director of the Anacostia Community Museum put it:

> While the Museum worked with one of the artists particularly closely, Charles "Coco" Bayron, visiting him a number of times and conducting an oral history interview, it was not until he had the opportunity to *author his own story* (my emphasis) that he directly connected his art of tattooing to a critical need to preserve family memory and identity in the face of ongoing loss (personal communication, November 12, 2014).

These stories affected not only the storytellers but the students—as audience, as collaborator, as witness. This was reflected in the journals I required students to keep to record their thoughts and feelings over the course of the semester. After working with a community artist who had suffered much in his life, one student wrote:

> The digital stories we are working on are an act of re-humanization, not only for the storyteller but for the witness. I can say that having been both storyteller and witness, I now have new tools and empowerment at my fingertips to resist de-sensitization to others' suffering, and to the desensitization I have imposed on myself, in regards to my own trauma. In meeting Dante (a pseudonym) for the first time. . . I felt like I was breathing clean air. I was finally able to feel connection to another's suffering. . .a feeling I have not felt since high school. (A.H)

The Museum wanted to do more. In Fall 2011, a new class of students worked with local residents along the Anacostia River on an Urban Waterways project with the Museum called "Reclaiming the Edge." The Anacostia River has notoriously been a site of environmental neglect (Williams, 2001). But, as the digital stories show, it has also has inspired hopes and dreams, culture and community. Again, the Museum included many of these digital stories in their exhibit.

> Members of the Community Voice Project that explored the Anacostia River provided many thoughts on relationships to our local waterways that realized many of the themes presented by the curators in the exhibition "Reclaiming the Edge." The perspectives on the waterways were explored in stories that talked of the river as a mode of transportation, as a muse for an artist, a salvation for an addicted and destructive life style, and as a way for urban kids to find the natural world. (S. Reinckens, personal communication, November 12, 2014).

One story by environmental activist Brenda Richardson documents her experience growing up along the Anacostia River...*but never going into it*. For the first time, she links the anxieties she faced as a young single parent—both financial and social—to her fears about the water. In her digital story she describes her first trip in a canoe:

> I was so frightened of the river, yet found some solace. . .As I listened to the swish of the paddles. . .I felt this amazing healing sensation. . .Through this experience I began to see things through a very different lens. I learned that the Anacostia River, even with all its problems, was a source of healing for a people who have been forsaken and ignored in our nation's capital.

For some, like Brenda Richardson, creating a digital story can be transformative. As Joe Lambert (2013) writes, "When people experience trauma, violence and oppression, what happens is a designification of their lives. The loss of power in being brutalized reflects itself in people feeling invisible." (p. 148) There is a feeling that there is no "sign" of their existence which others in their families, their communities, their social world need to hear. Digital storytelling, Lambert (2013) continues, like all cultural work "is about resignifying people and giving them the tools to declare the value of their existence and insist on being heard" (p. 148).

It was not only the storytellers like Brenda Richardson who were transformed by the experience. As Allison Arlotta, the student who worked with Brenda, wrote in her journal:

> I experienced the transformational power of personal digital storytelling in two ways – once with my own story and once working with a community member to help her create her digital story. Completing my own story was a difficult and emotional process. I chose to share a very personal story and struggled with how to communicate it. . .Going through this process helped me work with my community member, Brenda Richardson. Brenda was a gregarious and lively presence in our story circle and I was thrilled to be paired with her. When we first started working together, she was reticent to talk about herself. I remember her first draft being an eloquent, glowing story—but about a friend of hers. With some gentle prodding and asking the right questions, Brenda came to realize this on her own and ended up creating a beautiful, quiet story about her relationship with the Anacostia River. Through the digital storytelling experience, she was able to discover things about herself that she never knew—like the origins of many of her anxieties and the significance of environmental activism in her life. Seeing Brenda light up when she presented her story to the rest of the audience at our showcase was truly unforgettable.

In another set of digital stories with the Museum, themed around their exhibit "Twelve Years that Shook and Shaped Washington: 1963-1975," students worked with activists in the struggle for civil rights. In one story, social worker Cecilia Johnson recounts not only the segregated city where she grew up, but how her father instilled in his daughter the need for a professional education and the necessity of protesting inequalities when the situation demanded it. As one student who assisted Cecilia with her story wrote in a reflection paper, "Discrimination, oppression and violence of the past are not the whole story. Cecilia's father passed down self-respect and the importance of education, and took concrete steps to insure his daughter's preparation for the world" (Holly Wiencek). In reflecting on her work with Cecilia, Holly wrote that she expected Cecilia's story to be more focused on discrimination she faced growing up. But from their first meeting, Cecilia said, "My tribute to my dad is the greatest thing I can leave." In deeply listening to her, Holly said, "I got to know Cecilia for who she really is and the story she wanted to tell." She said she realized that "a story must be focused inward for it to be honest and to have impact."

11.3 Conclusion

From my storytelling work with students and community members, I have come to understand that digital storytelling at its best is a two-way process of connection and transformation, for both the storyteller and the witness/facilitator. The story circle with the students provides the basis for the storywork students will do four weeks later with the community residents. It prepares them with the skills to "find" and then create a digital story. But it also allows them an opportunity to safely open up and be vulnerable and recognize the weight of what they are doing. It affords them an understanding of the power of telling one's story and the responsibility involved in assisting someone else on that journey. As one student wrote:, "Opening up to the class and making that first digital story was the most therapeutic thing I've ever done...Then, working with my community storyteller, it was amazing to see another woman tell her story of personal struggle and the journey of finding herself" (Delana Listman). Another student wrote, "I think the greatest thing I've learned about is the power of digital storytelling to help facilitate the emotional emancipation of any and all participants" (Tabria Lee-Noonan).

Digital storytelling can take us into the lived experience of communities and people not often heard from, in a way that even the most sensitive traditional documentary filmmaking cannot. Because of their authenticity, these digital stories help break down a sense of "otherness" from both sides of a social divide, changing the storyteller and the witness in the process. In its place are *people,* in all their complexity, with nuanced narratives of life. Life shaped by wider social forces of class inequality, racism, sexism, homophobia, etc., but lives inextricably woven with deeply personal experiences of trauma, pain, and loss, as well as spirituality, hope and beauty.

> These films demonstrate the power of an engaged community anthropology in bringing out the finest aspects of our humanity, even when those aspects are memories filled with pain and suffering that arises from alienation (Prof. of Anthropology Chap Kusimba's introductory remarks at a community screening of digital stories.).

This is the transformative potential of the digital story—its capacity to effect personal and social change in both storyteller and witness. It allows us to listen deeply to each other, across the divides of neighborhood, class, race, and culture, allowing us to connect *as people*.

References

Burgess, J. (2006). Hearing ordinary voices: Cultural studies, vernacular creativity and digital storytelling. *Continuum: Journal of Media and Culture Studies, 20,* 201-214.

Goldbard, A. (2005). The story revolution: How telling our stories transforms the world. Retrieved November 29, 2014, from http://wayback.archiveit.org/2077/20100906202511/http://www.communityarts.net/readingroom/archivefiles/2005/01/the_story_revol.php.

Hill, A. (2008). 'Learn from my story': A participatory media initiative for Ugandan women afflicted by obstetric fistula. *Agenda: Empowering women for gender equality, 77,* 48-60.

Lambert, J. (2009). *Digital storytelling: Capturing lives, creating community* (3rd ed.). Berkeley, CA: Digital Diner Press.

Lambert, J. (2013). *Digital storytelling: Capturing lives, creating community* (4th ed.). New York, NY: Routledge.

Lerman, L. (2002). Art and community: Feeding the artist, feeding the art. In D. Adams & A. Goldbard (Eds.), *Community, culture and globalization*. New York, NY: Rockefeller Foundation.

Said, E. (1978). *Orientalism*. New York, NY: Vintage Books.

Williams, B. (2001). A river runs through us. *American Anthropologist, 103,* 409-431.

Aaron Thornburg

12 Digital Storytelling as Autoethnography in Anthropological Pedagogy and Practice

12.1 Introduction

Digital storytelling is a process of creating narrative, computer-/internet-based video projects that has seen increasing use in teaching and research at colleges and universities in recent years. It is deemed by many to be useful in the teaching and practice of a range of academic disciplines. In this chapter I will address digital storytelling's particular relevance to anthropological teaching and practice. I will first discuss my own introduction to digital storytelling and the way I have utilized it in teaching an anthropology course. An assessment of the range of digital storytelling assignments I have received as part of teaching anthropology classes will help to illustrate digital storytelling's usefulness in teaching anthropology in that all of the digital storytelling projects I have received have been autoethnographic, allowing students an opportunity to apply anthropological concepts to their own lives.

I will then look at advancements in visual media technology and their relation to both digital storytelling and anthropology. Changes in video production technology are reducing producers' need to have access to desktop computers with particular software installed, thus making it easier for anthropologists to utilize digital storytelling and like media production processes in their teaching and research. The overall effect of these innovations is increased access to the means of producing digital media, which has significant implications for both anthropological teaching and research practice.

12.2 My Introduction to and Experience with Digital Storytelling

In the Spring 2010 semester I received approval from the Department of Cultural Anthropology at Duke University, in which I was a PhD Candidate, to teach a Self and Society course. This course was one that had been offered by the department for some time, but the professor who originally developed the course had moved to another university and no one voiced an interest in teaching it. I had long been aware of the course title and thought that a "Media, Self, and Society" course, in which students would explore a range of media studies approaches and apply those to media in their own lives, would be a very productive course that would draw substantial numbers of students. When I was approached by my department to see if I would be interested in teaching a course in the Fall of 2010 they suggested several possibilities; Self and

Society was not among them. I decided to chance my arm and proposed the media-oriented version of Self and Society. They liked the idea and gave me the go ahead to teach the course in the Fall 2010 semester.

I already had broad ideas about the content of the course, but I had hardly begun to think about the assignments that would be included. A fortuitous workshop changed that. At the same time I was given permission to teach my roughly envisioned course, Dr. Hugh Crumley, who was an Instructional Technology Specialist at Duke University's Center for Instructional Technology, offered a three-day session on digital storytelling. In this workshop participants produced their own one-minute digital stories using *iMovie*, *GarageBand*, and other readily available software programs.

It did not take long for me to recognize the potential benefits that digital storytelling assignments had for my proposed course. As stated above, from the earliest stages of developing my course I wanted students in the class to engage with the concepts and theory of academic approaches to media covered in the course in order to analyze the media-saturated environment(s) in which they lived. Digital storytelling seemed to be the perfect vehicle to achieve this goal. I began to develop a "critically autobiographical video" final assignment in which students would be required to apply ideas from the scholarship we would cover in class, or equally rigorous academic approaches to media, in order to critically assess the ways in which their self, or selves, may have been affected or shaped by media.

My experience using digital storytelling assignments in the course far exceeded the expectations I had for them. The students seemed energized by the projects they created, enthusiastically applying academically rigorous theories and concepts in order to look at and describe their own lived experience in ways that I have never seen done in more standard written assignments. A couple of examples will illustrate this.

12.2.1 Digital Stories on Museums and More

One of the more notable digital storytelling final projects I received in the first semester I taught the course was an evaluation of the possible effects of museums as a type of media. Expanding on a topic we touched on in the course of the semester through a discussion surrounding Mark O'Neill's article "Enlightenment Museums: Universal or Merely Global?" (2004), the student who produced this project explored the ways in which the display principles common to museums prefigure the ways audiences approach the items displayed and, perhaps, the world generally.

One of the particularly interesting aspects of the project is that the student details her personal experience of curating an exhibition of Chinese artifacts as part of an internship she completed at the Nasher Museum of Art at Duke University. One of her duties associated with this exhibition was to write the general information labels that were to accompany the display. Analyzing the writing of these labels, the student recognizes a process of interpellation involved in the process.

I was told to write for a broad audience and not to assume that they had prior knowledge. But, I realized as I was writing that I was making assumptions about who would read the text. I couldn't use any of the Chinese names for the objects, thereby assuming the viewer to be someone with a Western background. Yet, I could assume the reader to be educated enough to recognize the geographical locations I was referencing. It was as if the text I was writing set a standard that included one kind of visitor, and excluded another. Though museums today strive to be more global, we must question what these institutions assume about its viewers as subjects.

The student's focus on a media creation process of which she was an integral part brought a personal element to the project that is a common element of digital storytelling as a genre. It was a common aspect of most, if not all, of the final projects submitted in this course as well as those I have received in teaching the course at Duke and elsewhere in subsequent semesters.

I have written about and given presentations in which I have addressed this museum digital story in the past (Thornburg, 2011; Thornburg, 2014). It was produced by a senior Visual and Media Studies major with well-articulated academic interests and a definite vision of a career in museums after graduation. As a result, the project makes productive use of media theories to analyze a topic that has clear bearing to the student's particular interests. It was not the only digital story I received that did this. Another project I received from a senior pre-med student in the first semester that I taught the course addressed medical diagnostic imaging technologies (MRI, ultrasound, x-ray, etc.) as a form of media and their effect on how we perceive the body and ourselves. I have used this example in a presentation of the use of digital storytelling in the anthropology classroom as well (Thornburg, 2012b). I have come to refer to projects like these as "focused" projects. Early on in my use of digital storytelling assignments these seemed the most appropriate examples to use in discussing the advantages of giving digital storytelling assignments.

As I have continued to teach the class and have gotten a wider range of examples of digital story final projects, however, I have begun to notice other types of digital stories. These projects are more often produced by first-year or sophomore students taking the class and they tend to be more general in nature, exploring a range of media in their lives and how it has affected their identity and/or perspective. I have come to refer to digital storytelling projects like this as "general" projects.

A notable example of this general type of project was produced by a first-year student who came to Duke University from Newport Beach, California. In her project, this student examines the way that her move to Duke and her exposure to "a completely new sea of foreign media and stimuli" shaped her personal identity. In one frenetic part of the project the student quickly listed the range of media available to her during her daily life at Duke: books, magazines, newspapers, signs, posters, banners, flyers, e-mail, websites, lectures, events, and much more. The student explored how all these forms of media impinge upon her as she (re)creates her identity in her new surroundings. "Sifting through the storm of media that comprises Duke I am beginning to redefine myself here," the student claims.

Another similar, general, example produced by a student from the Bay Area of California was also turned in at the end of that first semester that I taught the course. I screened this project as part of my presentation at the American Anthropological Association's Annual Meeting in San Francisco that is one of the bases for this chapter and this collection (Thornburg, 2012a).

I now recognize that in the early stages of evaluating the advantages of utilizing digital storytelling assignments in anthropology courses I deemphasized this general type of project in favor of those by senior students with more focused interests and projects. However, I am increasingly considering these general projects in combination with the focused projects in order to determine what an analysis of all of them can tell us about the use of digital storytelling assignments. In this regard, I am struck by what a comparison of general digital story final projects and more focused, topical projects, like the museum piece described above, can tell us about the potential benefits of assigning digital storytelling projects in anthropology courses.

12.3 Digital Stories as Autoethnography

One of the things I noted as I compared the range of final projects that have been submitted as part of my classes is that they are all ethnographic. Each of them explores cultural phenomena, media in particular, with the intent of providing a description of the knowledge and practice of the group of people exposed to it. However, the direct focus is most often on the producer him- or herself. In that sense, these projects can be considered instances of autoethnography.

Autoethnography is particularly hard to define. In the introduction of her 1997 edited collection *Auto/Ethnography,* Deborah E. Reed-Danahay (1997) provides a history of uses of the term autoethnography. She notes two major uses of the term: "whether or not the accent is on autobiography or ethnography" (p. 8). She suggests that the accent is on (native) ethnography in the writings of anthropologists such as John Dorst, David Hayano, Mary Louise Pratt, Marilyn Strathern, and John Van Maanen. Autoethnography is tied to autobiography in the writings of Stanley Brandes, Alice Deck, Norman Denzin, and Phillipe Lejeune. Looking to reconcile these two definitions of autoethnography, Reed-Danahay (1997) states that in her volume autoethnography will be defined as "a form of self-narrative that places the self within a social context" (p. 9). This definition is strikingly appropriate for the digital stories submitted as final projects in my course.

In other venues I have written about what I see as the advantages of assigning digital storytelling assignments in anthropology classes (Thornburg, 2014). In this work I highlighted the writings of social anthropologists Simon Coleman and Bob Simpson (2004). Coleman and Simpson argue that in teaching anthropology it is preferable to move from substantivist pedagogical strategies, in which the emphasis is on imparting a body of disciplinary knowledge, to imaginativist pedagogical strategies that help students learn to apply anthropological knowledge in effective ways. Anthropology, Coleman and Simpson (2004) suggest, is all about "the contextualisation of knowledge, action, belief, meaning and language" (p. 20). And, any teaching strategy that fails to incorporate student experience into the learning process, Coleman and Simpson (2004) go on to say, is missing a crucial pedagogical opportunity (p. 20).

In their chapter, Coleman and Simpson give examples of autoethnographic assignments that they claim have facilitated the application of anthropological knowledge and methods to their students' lived experience. In particular, they describe autobiographical/life history assignments submitted by a student they call Joyce, who provides an ethnographic analysis of her experience growing up in the coal mining district in northern England. These assignments allowed Joyce to apply anthropological concepts to her own experience, resulting in a better understanding of the concepts and approaches taught in her anthropology courses.

"Joyce's example is one of many that could have been identified to illustrate the way students combine perspectives gained from an anthropological 'worldview' with reflections from their own past," Coleman and Simpson claim (2004, p. 28). Through these autoethnographic assignments, students are able to better understand the concepts and ideas they have been exposed to in their anthropology classes. "[W]e are here describing a pedagogical strategy whereby students are encouraged to perceive and write about places that are familiar, but to do so through an anthropological lens that defamiliarises and even, to some extent, objectifies them" (Coleman & Simpson, 2004, p. 29). This is exactly what I contend is the advantage of the digital storytelling assignments given in my own course.

A general survey of the range of digital storytelling projects that have been submitted to me by students in my course shows that in almost all cases students are applying the media studies and anthropological approaches covered in the course, and/or similarly academic approaches from outside the class, to analyze some aspect of their media environment. This process has the effect of defamiliarizing what is very often taken for granted in their lives. This process is very much in line with anthropology's oft cited project of making the familiar strange.

This is the case with all successful autoethnography. Good autoethnography is able to bring anthropological concepts and approaches to bear in order to evaluate and think about things in the life of the autoethnographer that quite often go unanalyzed. It has the effect of notablization: highlighting bits of experience that often go unnoticed in the wash of everyday activity and making it significant. This process is at the very heart of the drive to defamiliarize the familiar that is a longstanding goal of anthropology.

Both the assignments described by Coleman and Simpson and the digital storytelling projects I received as a part of my course are examples of this process. Joyce's assignments gave her new understandings about the social environment in which she grew up. In both the general and focused digital storytelling projects I received, students explored their position as media consumers and producers and developed new insights regarding the significance of themselves and the media with which they interact.

The fact that these assignments are effective in teaching anthropology is precisely because the process of creating them is at the heart of anthropological practice. In sum, these assignments make good anthropological pedagogy because they make good anthropological practice.

12.4 Technology Change and Anthropology

12.4.1 Technology Change's Past Effect on Anthropology

Technical innovation in the field of visual media production has long had significant effects on the practice of anthropology. In particular, those innovations that have made audio-visual technologies lighter and more easily portable have facilitated change in the practice of, at least some, anthropologists.

For example, one significant innovation that had a large impact on the practice of some anthropologists was the transition from larger 35-millimeter cameras to smaller and lighter 16-millimeter format cameras. Jean Rouch (1975) attributes this innovation, which he characterizes as a "breakthrough," to technical developments precipitated by World War II (p. 89). The first portable tape recorders appeared in 1951, and improvements continued on those tools (Rouch, 1975, p. 89). "It was in the attempt to satisfy our demands (lightness, solidity, quality) that excellent portable tape recorders and portable silent cine cameras were perfected around 1960" (Rouch, 1975, pp. 89–90).

The introduction of videotape also facilitated "steadily accelerating activity" among anthropologists (de Brigard, 1975, p. 30). Video recording was increasingly used as a form of note-taking or data recording as well as in the creation of visual ethnographies (de Brigard, 1975, p. 31).

As evidenced by the range of projects presented in this volume, digital storytelling and the technologies associated with it have, likewise, led to changes in practice by some anthropologists. However, as Emilie de Brigard (1975) claimed, "the existence of technology has never been a sufficient condition of scientific advance" (p. 30). Only when these technologies and techniques are appropriately paired with well-thought-out approaches and analyses is anthropology as a field altered.

12.4.2 Continuing Change

Technological change continues with regard to digital storytelling and audio-visual media more generally. These technological changes will continue to have potential implications for the teaching and practice of anthropology. Two innovations that may hold particular promise for anthropologists are the development of remote video editing services and the advancement of mobile digital storytelling.

12.4.2.1 Remote Video Editing Services

One of the potential difficulties involved in utilizing digital storytelling in anthropological teaching and practice concerns the availability of the computer tools needed to produce digital stories. Especially if anthropologists are attempting to facilitate the digital storytelling process for others, be they students or research participants, it is sometimes problematic to provide consistent access to computers with the range of software, video, and audio production programs that are required to construct the video projects installed.

An advance in video production technology that promises to ameliorate these difficulties is the advent of remote, software-as-a-service (SAAS), video editing sites. These services, such as *VideoToolbox*, *WeVideo*, and others, take the burden of maintaining software on the computers used by anthropology students or research participants away from the teacher or research project organizer. Internet-ready computers and Internet access are still necessary, but the software needed to produce digital stories is "housed" at the remote video editing service.

A further advantage of using these types of services is that they arguably help to facilitate collaboration between students or research participants. Often, more than one video producer can be logged into and working on a single project at any given time, allowing people to cooperate in the production of a video without having to be in the same room, sitting around the same computer.

This innovation in video production technology has been met with much enthusiasm by academics in anthropology and other disciplines and by the digital storytelling community. I recently had a conversation with a faculty member in the Communication Studies program at my institution in which he suggested that the use of *WeVideo*, or like services, would greatly benefit classes, like my Media, Self, and Society course, in which digital storytelling and like assignments are given. The development of remote video editing services, this faculty member pointed out, may hold particular benefits for courses taught online. This is because distance-students who have less access to the physical facilities of the college or university, on which instructors teaching courses with "new media" assignments so often rely, will still be able to complete the assignments without having to buy or otherwise acquire the software needed to do so.

There are also indications that the digital storytelling community, more generally, is embracing the development of these SAAS video production sites. For example on November 1, 2013, I received an e-mail from the StoryCenter in Berkeley, California, announcing their first online course/webinar on using *WeVideo* to produce a digital story. The innovation of remote video editing sites has every indication of being a great example of how the movement of functions once confined to a single computer to "the cloud" has the potential to alter teaching and practice in anthropology and a range of fields.

12.4.2.2 Mobile Digital Storytelling

A second technological innovation relating to digital storytelling is the move of video editing processes from laptop and desktop computers to pad and smartphone devices. This is part of a wider trend toward ubiquitous computing (see Dourish & Bell, 2011). Video production apps have now been developed for both mac iOS and Windows based devices, so that people can record video, take pictures, download assets (images, music, etc.) from the Internet, record voiceovers, and combine all of these things into complete video projects, all on a single pad or on their smartphone device.[40] This innovation has the potential to detach students and other video project producers from laptop or desktop computers entirely.

The potential that mobile digital storytelling processes have for teaching and practicing anthropology is notable. In anthropology classes, students will be able to quickly produce anthropology-oriented video projects and upload them using college or university Internet resources. Anthropologists can also bring mobile devices to their research sites where finished media projects can be produced (either by the anthropologist him- or herself, or by research participants) to be uploaded using the resources of a cooperative institution or at researchers' home institutions when they return from the field.

In line with the potential this audio-visual technology innovation has for anthropology, I organized a mobile digital storytelling Innovent[41] at the 2012 Annual Meeting of the American Anthropological Association in San Francisco. Titled "Media in Motion in the Mission: Mobile Digital Storytelling" (Thornburg, 2012c), the stated purpose of the event was to "provide (participants) an opportunity to get acquainted with a media form and process that is rife with potential for anthropological pedagogy and practice" (Society for Visual Anthropology, 2012). Eleven conference attendees participated in the Innovent. We all met at a café in the Mission District of San Francisco with our iOS or Android devices in hand. After the Executive Director of the StoryCenter Joe Lambert, who ran the workshop event, gave a short demonstration

---

40 Remote video production services, like *VideoToolbox* and *WeVideo*, are also developing their own applications that will allow users to, at least, work on a rough cut of a video project on their mobile device and later upload the unfinished project file to their website for finishing and saving. For more info see (WeVideo, n.d.) and (Google Play, n.d.).

41 Innovents were events other than paper-based panels that occurred in association with the American Anthropological Association's annual meeting, though often at a site other than the conference venue. Innovents, along with Salons, have now been subsumed into the category of Installations (American Anthropological Association, n.d.).

of 'best practices' taking photos with our mobile devices and a quick prompt-based, free-writing session, we were set loose on the Mission District to take pictures of the area's beautiful murals and/or other things that caught our attention. We had about an hour of exploring and picture-taking before we met at a restaurant at the other end of the district for a quick tutorial on editing our pictures into a complete digital story project.

Fun was had by all the Innovent participants. More importantly, however, after just two hours most left the event discussing the potential uses these techniques and processes had for their own anthropological teaching and/or practice. The potential that mobile digital storytelling practice has for anthropology teaching and research should not be understated. Or, as put in an e-mail received from Joe Lambert on November 15, 2012, in the run up to the Mobile Digital Storytelling Innovent, "[i]f you are wondering what this has to do with Anthropology. In 20 years, improvised self-documentation in location engaging diverse citizens immediately available to a planetary discourse, ie the mobile digital storytelling workshop, will be anthropology. I don't know what they will call the stuff you folks have been doing."

12.5 Discussion: Democratization, Digital Divides, and Anthropology

The overall effect of the technical innovations just described is the increasing of accessibility of the processes of digital media production, or what has been heralded as the increased "democratization" of media. Media scholar Dan Gillmor, for example, has suggested the media is becoming increasingly democratized and that this process takes two major forms. First, technological innovations make it possible for a growing number of people to produce quality media. In Gillmor's (2008) words, "the tools of creation are increasingly in everyone's hands" (p. 4).

The second aspect of the democratization of media is that, given the presence of the Internet, it is much easier than ever before to share the media content produced. That is, "we can make what we create widely accessible" (Gillmor, 2008, p. 4).

These two changes in the media landscape have had effects on media, media audiences, and the relationship between them. "The democratization (of media) gives people who have been mere consumers the ability to be creators. With few exceptions, we are all becoming the latter as well as the former" (Gillmor, 2008, p. 4). This fact has led Gillmor (2006) in other venues to write of the "former audience," people who have transitioned from being solely consumers of media to being contributors to and producers of media (p. 238; also see Shirky, 2008, p. 7).

In the midst of this technophilic talk about how the technological innovations discussed here may empower the masses it is important that we not ignore the idea that it is the already affluent and privileged that are able to reap the benefits of these changes while those of lower socio-economic classes are unable to do so; that is the idea that there is a "digital divide." In her book on the concept of the digital divide, Pippa Norris (2001) distinguishes several types of divides. The one addressed most directly here is a "social divide," which "concerns the gap between information rich and poor in each nation" (p. 4).[42]

Many, if not most, commentators on the development of digital media will acknowledge that there are disparities between the digital "haves" and "have nots." However, the general discourse and drive is toward putting media production technology and Internet access into the hands of those traditionally excluded from the benefits of technological innovation. Especially in the field of education, there are concerted efforts to provide underserved communities with the Internet and related technologies. As a result of this, some have claimed that the digital divide is continually narrowing.

> Perceived gaps are closing among various ethnic, racial, and geographical groups in access to the Internet. At least two factors account for the rapid diffusion of Internet technology: steadily decreasing costs of use, and steadily increasing ease of use. (Morrisett, 2001, p. ix)

So, while disparities in access to and the knowledge to utilize computer-based media production tools no doubt continue to exist, efforts at increased inclusion are being made.

This discussion about access to the means to create and share media representations is innately related to the discipline of anthropology, many practitioners of which have, since at least the 1980s, striven to "give voice" to those with whom they have done their research. The increasing democratization of the means to create and distribute digital media projects allows anthropologists to more easily help those they work with to produce their own (auto-ethnographic) representations. Those same anthropologists are, in turn, helped by those they work with to bring ethnographic representations to a wider public. The increasing ease in providing the hardware and software required to produce media can aid anthropologists in facilitating the creation of representations of cultural life both for pedagogical purposes and as part of ethnographic research projects.

---

42 Other forms of divides discussed by Norris (2001) include "global divides," which relate to the disparities in Internet access between industrialized and non-industrialized countries, and "democratic divides," which relate to disparities between those who do and do not utilize the Internet and related digital resources "to engage, mobilize, and participate in public life" (p. 4). These forms of digital divides are also related to discussion here.

12.6 Conclusion

Digital storytelling is a process of creating (often) short, narrative video projects addressing a range of topics (often) from a personal point of view. It is a technique that has its origins in the computer-revolution age of the early- to mid-1990s and based on the efforts of those in the arts and other fields. It had early ties to higher education and continues to gain traction in K-12 education as well as multiple academic disciplines in colleges and universities.

As the contributions to this volume demonstrate, digital storytelling practices are contributing greatly to anthropological research and teaching. One of the reasons the processes involved in digital storytelling can be such a great benefit in both the teaching of anthropology and anthropological research is that it facilitates students' and research participants' ability to produce effective autoethnography. Digital storytelling makes good anthropological pedagogy precisely because it makes good anthropological practice.

Advancements in digital video production technology, in the form of software-as-a-service systems and mobile digital storytelling innovations, have the potential to further facilitate the use of digital storytelling and like digital media production methods by teachers of anthropology and ethnographic researchers. Just as innovations in audio and visual media production equipment following World War II proved beneficial to a great number of anthropologists, so the "democratization" of media production brought on by advancements in computer technology can assist today's anthropologists to bring autoethnography, for both teaching and research purposes, to a larger population. This may prove to have the effect of "giving voice" to a larger number of people than ever before.

References

American Anthropological Association. (n.d.). Installations. Retrieved May 15, 2016, from http://www.americananthro.org/AttendEvents/Content.aspx?ItemNumber=2040.

Coleman, S., & Simpson, B. (2004). Knowing, doing and being: Pedagogies and paradigms in the teaching of social anthropology. In D. Dracklé & I. R. Edgar (Eds.), *Current policies and practices in European social anthropology* (pp. 18–33). New York, NY: Berghahn Books.

de Brigard, E. (1975). The history of ethnographic film. In P. Hockings (Ed.), *Principles of visual anthropology* (pp. 13–43). The Hague: Mouton.

Dourish, P., & Bell, G. (2011). *Divining a digital future: Mess and mythology in ubiquitous computing.* Cambridge, MA: MIT Press.

Gillmor, D. (2006). *We the media: Grassroots journalism by the people, for the people.* Sebastopol, CA: O'Reilly.

Gillmor, D. (2008). Principles for a new media literacy. Retrieved July 11, 2014, from https://cyber.law.harvard.edu/sites/cyber.law.harvard.edu/files/Principles%20for%20a%20New%20Media%20Literacy_MR.pdf.

Google play. (n.d.) Video toolbox editor. Retrieved July 11, 2014, from https://play.google.com/store/apps/details?id=org.androidideas.videotoolbox.app.

Morrisett, L. (2001). Forward. In B. M. Compaine (Ed.), *Digital divide: Facing a crisis or creating a myth?* (pp. ix–x). Cambridge, MA: MIT Press.

Norris, P. (2001). *Digital divide: Civic engagement, information poverty, and the Internet worldwide.* Cambridge, UK: Cambridge University Press.

O'Neill, M. (2004). Enlightenment museums: Universal or merely global? *Museum and Society,* 2(3), 190–202.

Reed-Danahay, D. E. (1997). *Auto/Ethnography: Rewriting the self and the social.* Oxford, UK: Berg.

Rouch, J. (1975). The camera and man. In P. Hockings (Ed.), *Principles of visual anthropology* (pp. 83–102). The Hague: Mouton.

Shirky, C. (2008). *Here comes everybody: The power of organizing without organizations.* New York, NY: Penguin Press.

Society for Visual Anthropology. (2012). Media in motion in the mission: Mobile digital storytelling. Retrieved July 11, 2014, from http://societyforvisualanthropology.org/2012/10/media-in-motion-in-the-mission-mobile-digital-storytelling.

Thornburg, A. (2011, March). Stories and/of self: The use of digital stories in teaching anthropology. Paper presented at the annual meeting of the Southern Anthropological Society, Richmond, VA.

Thornburg, A. (2012a, November). Digital stories in the anthropology classroom: Crossing the substantivist/imaginativist divide. Paper presented at the annual meeting of the American Anthropological Association, San Francisco, CA.

Thornburg, A. (2012b, November). Digital storytelling in the anthropology classroom: Potential problems and pedagogical promise. Paper presented at Eastern Oregon University, La Grande, OR.

Thornburg, A. (2012c, November). Media in motion in the mission. Event held at the annual meeting of the American Anthropological Association, San Francisco, CA.

Thornburg, A. (2014). Stories and/of self: Using digital storytelling in the anthropology classroom. *Southern Anthropologist,* 36(1), 33–47.

WeVideo. (n.d.). Mobile video editor. Retrieved July 11, 2014, from https://www.wevideo.com/mobile.

List of Figures

List of Tables

Index

CPSIA information can be obtained
at www.ICGtesting.com
Printed in the USA
BVHW02n0258030918
525132BV00027B/2/P